The Global New Deal

NEW MILLENNIUM BOOKS
IN INTERNATIONAL STUDIES
Deborah J. Gerner, Series Editor

NEW MILLENNIUM BOOKS issue out of the unique position of the global system at the end of the Cold War, the end of the twentieth century, and the beginning of a new millennium in which our understandings about war, peace, identity, sovereignty, security, and sustainability— whether economic, environmental, or ethical—are likely to be challenged. In the new millennium of international relations, new theories, new actors, and new policies and processes are all bound to be engaged. Books in the series are of three types: compact core texts, supplementary texts, and readers.

Editorial Board

Titles in the Series

The Global New Deal: Economic and Social Human Rights in World Politics
William F. Felice

*The New Foreign Policy: U.S. and Comparative Foreign Policy
in the 21st Century*
Laura Neack

Global Backlash: Citizen Initiatives for a Just World Economy
Edited by Robin Broad

*Negotiating a Complex World: An Introduction to
International Negotiation*
Brigid Starkey, Mark A. Boyer, and Jonathan Wilkenfeld

Military–Civilian Interactions: Intervening in Humanitarian Crises
Thomas G. Weiss

Forthcoming in the Series

Introduction to Global Studies
Patricia J. Campbell and Aran S. MacKinnon

Globalization and Belonging: The Politics of Identity in a Changing World
Sheila Croucher

Liberals and Criminals: IPE in the New Millennium
H. Richard Friman

Law in International Politics: Key Issues and Incidents
B. Welling Hall

International Law in the 21st Century
Christopher C. Joyner

*Global Politics as If People Mattered: World Political Economy
from the Ground Up*
Ronnie D. Lipschutz and Mary Ann Tetreault

The Peace Puzzle: Ending Violent Conflict in the 21st Century
George A. Lopez

Political Violence
Philip A. Schrodt

The Global New Deal

Economic and Social Human Rights in World Politics

William F. Felice

ROWMAN & LITTLEFIELD PUBLISHERS, INC.
Lanham • Boulder • New York • Oxford

ROWMAN & LITTLEFIELD PUBLISHERS, INC.

Published in the United States of America
by Rowman & Littlefield Publishers, Inc.
A Member of the Rowman & Littlefield Publishing Group
4720 Boston Way, Lanham, Maryland 20706
www.rowmanlittlefield.com

P.O. Box 317, Oxford, OX2 9RU, United Kingdom

British Library Cataloguing in Publication Information Available

Library of Congress Cataloging-in-Publication Data

Felice, William, 1950–
    The global new deal : economic and social human rights in world
politics / William F. Felice.
        p.   cm.—(New millennium books in international studies)
    Includes bibliographical references and index.
    ISBN 0-7425-1781-0 (cloth : alk. paper)—ISBN 0-7425-1782-9
(pbk. : alk. paper)
        1. Human rights.   2. Social rights.   I. Title.   II. Series.
JC571 .F424   2003
330—dc21   2002008919

Printed in the United States of America

♾™ The paper used in this publication meets the minimum requirements of
American National Standard for Information Sciences—Permanence of Paper
for Printed Library Materials, ANSI/NISO Z39.48-1992.

Contents

Illustrations

Table

Boxes

Acknowledgments

It is a joy to publicly thank some of the many people who have helped me prepare this manuscript. My gratitude to all of them is immeasurable.

Robert L. Sanderson has been instrumental through every stage in the creation of this book. Only a loyal best friend would read and *reread* drafts and revisions of every chapter. Bob's wise counsel and advice provided the critical support needed to push the project to completion. He is a fountain of ideas and his recommendations enhanced and invigorated the manuscript.

Sigrun I. Skogly read each chapter with great thoughtfulness and care. I was the beneficiary of her expertise in international human rights law which informed her exceptional and constructive feedback.

Maurice Williams helped me sharpen my argument and strengthen the manuscript. His insights, drawn from his years of experience at the United Nations and at the U.S. State Department, helped me ground the ideas of the Global New Deal into the reality of real world politics.

My dear friend Nancy Mitchell also read the manuscript with care and provided critical editorial feedback. Nancy's continued interest in my work gives me inspiration and direction.

Michael J. Smith is not only one of the leading scholars in ethics and international affairs, but also selfless in his willingness to help train and teach others in the profession. His critique of the manuscript helped me to clarify some of the central ideas in the Global New Deal and present the thesis in a manner that will (hopefully) be accessible to a wide audience.

The staff of the Office of the High Commissioner for Human Rights in Geneva were extremely helpful to me in researching the UN human rights system. For their time and assistance, I wish to thank Päivikki Aaku, Virginia Dandan, Stefanie Grant, Cecilia Möller, Sylvie Saddier, and Kitty Arambulo Wilson.

It is my good fortune to work at a wonderful liberal arts college committed to its students. Eckerd College's devotion to creative pedagogy is unrivaled. This book was enriched through my interaction with my colleagues and, most importantly, with my students. I, in particular, appreciate the support I received from Dean Lloyd Chapin and my colleagues in political science and international relations and global affairs. I am indebted to Becky Blitch for her outstanding editing of the final draft.

Most of the research for this book was presented at the annual meetings of the International Studies Association (ISA). I am grateful to my ISA colleagues, in particular Mary B. Geske, Catherine V. Scott, and Michael Windfuhr, for providing substantial feedback and direction.

Jennifer Knerr, executive editor at Rowman and Littlefield, was a tremendous source of support from the very beginning of this project. I thank her for her professionalism and skilled editorial supervision. Editorial assistant Renée Legatt was also of enormous assistance in helping to sharpen the draft for publication. I am also indebted to production editor Jehanne Schweitzer for her hard work finalizing the manuscript. I am honored for the inclusion of this book in the distinguished Rowman & Littlefield series "New Millennium Books in International Studies."

I wish to acknowledge with gratitude permission to draw on the following previously published work: "The UN Committee on the Elimination of All Forms of Racial Discrimination: Race, and Economic and Social Human Rights," *Human Rights Quarterly* 24, no 1 (February 2002), "The Viability of the United Nations Approach to Economic and Social Human Rights in a Globalized Economy," *International Affairs* 75, no 3 (July 2000), and "Militarism and Human Rights," *International Affairs* 74, no 1 (January 1998).

It has taken over six years to write this book. My partner, Dale Lappe, has stood by me every step of this journey. I thank him for his patience and support.

A Note to the Reader on Terminology and Acronyms

As with any specialized field of study, International Relations has developed its own language of terms with specific meanings known only to those immersed in the discipline. To most readers, however, these expressions (e.g., rational choice, international regimes, structural constructivism, and so on) are often unintelligible and undecipherable. Compounding these communication difficulties are the dozens of specific acronyms used by scholars of international politics, including IGO, NGO, IFI, TNC, MNC, WTO, IMF, and so on. This problem is particularly acute in studies of the United Nations. Experts on the UN routinely refer to the numerous UN committees and treaties by their acronyms, including UNCTAD, ECOSOC, CESCR, CERD, CEDAW, CRC, CCPR, and so on. These references are clear to those working in the UN system and to experts in the field, but to the rest of the world, they are incomprehensible—or nearly so.

To reach beyond the academy, I have minimized the use of specialized terminology and acronyms. A list of all acronyms used in the book is provided here for easy reference. In addition, I refer to key UN human rights treaties and committees by subject matter and not acronym, as follows:

The Covenant on Economic, Social, and Cultural Rights (CESCR) becomes the Economic Rights Treaty. The CESCR Committee becomes the Economic Rights Committee.

The Covenant on Civil and Political Rights (CCPR) becomes the Political Rights Treaty. Its treaty body is the Human Rights Committee.

The Convention on the Elimination of All Forms of Racial Discrimination (CERD) becomes the Minority Rights Treaty. The CERD Committee becomes the Minority Rights Committee.

The Convention on the Elimination of All Forms of Discrimination against Women (CEDAW) becomes the Women's Rights Treaty. The CEDAW Committee becomes the Women's Rights Committee.

References to the UN's Women's Rights, Minority Rights, and Economic Rights Committees clarify the subjects under discussion. This eliminates confusing references to the CEDAW, CERD, and CESCR Committees.

KEY INTERNATIONAL TREATIES AND UN COMMITTEES

Treaty	Abbreviated Treaty Name	UN Treaty Body	Individual Complaint Mechanism
Covenant on Economic, Social and Cultural Rights (CESCR)	Economic Rights Treaty	Economic Rights Committee	No
Covenant on Civil and Political Rights (CCPR)	Political Rights Treaty	Human Rights Committee	Yes
Convention on the Elimination of All Forms of Racial Discrimination (CERD)	Minority Rights Treaty	Minority Rights Committee	Yes
Convention on the Elimination of All Forms of Discrimination against Women (CEDAW)	Women's Rights Treaty	Women's Rights Committee	Yes

Abbreviations and Acronyms

CCA	Common Country Assessments
CFA	Comprehensive Freshwater Assessment
CITES	Convention on International Trade in Endangered Species
CPM	capability poverty measure
CRS	Congressional Research Service
CSD	Commission on Sustainable Development
CSW	Commission on the Status of Women
CTBT	Comprehensive Test Ban Treaty
CWC	Convention on the Prohibition of the Development, Production, Stockpiling and Use of Chemical Weapons and their Destruction
DAWN	Development Alternatives with Women for a New Era
ECOSOC	Economic and Social Council of the United Nations
ESC	Economic Security Council
FAO	Food and Agriculture Organization
GAD	Gender and Development
GATT	General Agreement on Tariffs and Trade
GDI	Gender Development Index
GDP	gross domestic product
GEF	Global Environment Facility
GEM	Gender Empowerment Measure
GEMS	Global Environmental Monitoring System
GNP	gross national product
HDI	Human Development Index
HPI	Human Poverty Index
HURIST	Human Rights Strengthening Project
ICFTU	International Confederation of Free Trade Unions
IFI	international financial institution
IGO	intergovernmental organization
ILO	International Labor Organization

IMF	International Monetary Fund
IPCC	Intergovernmental Panel on Climate Change
IPE	international political economy
IPF	Intergovernmental Panel on Forests
LDC	less developed country
MNC	multinational corporation
NAFTA	North American Free Trade Agreement
NGO	nongovernmental organization
OHCHR	Office of the High Commissioner for Human Rights
OPCW	Organization for the Prohibition of Chemical Weapons
SAPs	structural adjustment programs
TNC	transnational corporation
UDHR	Universal Declaration of Human Rights
UN	United Nations
UNCTAD	UN Conference on Trade and Development
UNDAF	UN Development Assistance Framework
UNDP	UN Development Program
UNEP	UN Environment Program
UNESCO	UN Educational, Scientific, and Cultural Organization
UNHCH	UN High Commissioner for Refugees
UNHCHR	UN High Commissioner for Human Rights
UNICEF	UN International Children's Emergency Fund
UNIFEM	UN Development Fund for Women
USTR	US Trade Representative
WAD	Women and Development
WCED	World Commission on Environment and Development
WEDO	Women's Environment and Development Organization
WEO	World Environment Organization
WHO	World Health Organization
WID	Women in Development
WTO	World Trade Organization
WWF	World Wide Fund for Nature

1

Global Policy Choices:
There Are Alternatives

I have a privileged life; I am a teacher. It is hard to imagine a more rewarding and fulfilling job. It is a joy to go to work. As a teacher of International Relations, I am able to engage young women and men on the crucial issues confronting the planet. My students are demanding and will not accept shallow explanations or superficial theories. They challenge me to be clear, relevant, and thoughtful. Their contemporary and fresh approaches to life and knowledge continuously force me to reevaluate my thinking and to modify my understandings. This ongoing intellectual and human colloquy with students enriches my life immeasurably.

To my dismay, however, over the last ten years I have also witnessed a very disturbing phenomenon. The vitality and richness of youth that these students bring to the classroom is tempered by an overwhelming cynicism and despair about the possibility of bringing about positive fundamental change. Conservative, liberal, and radical students express again and again the futility of challenging an economic and political system dominated by corporate power. To these students, the corruption of our political system is beyond repair. The students search in vain for a Kantian "moral politician" who is not groveling before the wealthy class; a politician not eager to serve elite interests.

Students recognize the real problems that confront humanity. They are outraged by the callous destruction of our ecosystem. They are shocked by the needless suffering occurring in every country as a result of preventable poverty, preventable malnutrition, and preventable disease. Yet, many of these students believe that nothing can be done to stop this anguish. These students believe that the current economic and political system, responsible for a great deal of human misery, will never really change. They argue that perhaps some small steps can be taken and some examples of gross maleficence can be exposed, but nothing beyond minor reform is possible. Nothing can be done to change the system overall. These students are profoundly cynical and see little hope in working for fundamental structural change. There is too much money involved, and these powerful interests are committed to the status quo. These students, therefore, consider it utopian and foolish to talk about creating policy to end world hunger, create global peace, or maintain ecological balance. There is no room for such dreamy "idealist" and "utopian" thinking in the "realist" minds of many of today's college students.

As a teacher, I am frustrated by this pessimism. It limits the imagination. It prevents one from looking at feasible policy options to create necessary change. It can block true understanding. Let me give an example.

According to the World Bank, almost half of the world's people—2.8 billion—live on less than $2 a day, and 1.2 billion—a fifth—live on less than $1 a day. In poor countries, as many as 50 percent of all children are malnourished.[1] The United Nations Development Program (UNDP) notes with dismay that the deaths of more than 30,000 children every day from mainly preventable causes go largely unnoticed.[2]

Now imagine that 30,000 people died every day from plane crashes or buildings collapsing. The outrage would be palpable! Demands would be made for the government to intervene to stop the slaughter. Public policy would be quickly enacted to make planes and buildings safer. Corporations manufacturing planes and construction companies erecting buildings would be held legally accountable to higher standards. These public policy changes would happen quickly and lives would be saved. These attempts to craft public policy to guarantee the construction of safer planes and buildings would not be labeled "idealist" nor "utopian." Instead, they would be viewed as "realistic" approaches to ending a tragic loss of life and essential to the security of the society.

Yet, the attempts today to craft public policy to end the daily deaths of 30,000 children from preventable causes *is* labeled "idealist" and "utopian." There is no sense of urgency to end the pain and suffering of these innocents. This lethargy stems in part from ingrained, comfortable "common sense" ideology, that is, the poor will always be with us, we are doing all we can, scarcity is a fact, there is nothing that can be done, and so on. But more disturbing, this acceptance of unnecessary human misery comes from an overwhelming sense of the futility of challenging existing structures of economic and political power. This sense of the impotence and uselessness of challenging enduring arrangements of power and wealth infects many young people today.

At the end of his final exam in my International Political Economy course, a student wrote to me the following note:

You have taught me that solving the problems of economic globalization will involve "thinking outside the box." Global priorities have to include ensuring that human rights apply to all (ending all forms of discrimination!), demilitarization of the planet, and the preservation of the environment. But I don't honestly see how we can make the jump from here to there. Economic principles of efficiency and order will never be sacrificed or compromised to achieve common global public goods like human rights and environmental balance. The Bretton Woods system and the great powers would have to restructure their economic and foreign policies to allow for such change. Unfortunately, I don't see that happening. I will try to cling onto the hope your class gave me, but I fear I will lose it very quickly.

This student clearly wanted to believe in humane alternatives, but he feared that these options were probably not viable. But at least he was open to looking at alternatives. Many other students quickly reject such global reforms as utopian nonsense. When I try to show that in fact we can end needless suffering in the world, these students look at me as if I am a relic from the 1960s. The demise of "socialism" in the former Soviet Union reinforced the perception that current economic and political models of development are the only game in town. The daily message from the *New York Times* and the *Wall Street Journal* is that "there is no alternative"[3] to the neoliberal economic model (discussed in chapter 2) dominating the post–Cold War world. Students are bombarded with this message: *There is no alternative to the existing global economic system and model of development. It is fool-hardy and counterproductive to challenge the fundamentals of the current economic development model. Unfortunately, there are some who won't benefit from the "creative destruction" that accompanies economic globalization. But since there are more winners than losers—and particularly since we are among the winners—we should all support this process. The protestors in Seattle against globalization and the World Trade Organization (WTO) should stop fighting history. And besides, no one has come up with anything better. The system may not be perfect, but it's the best that human beings have created.* This is the message that our young people are indoctrinated with over and over. It preaches the wisdom of accepting the status quo and of working for only small, minor reforms. It teaches the folly of conceiving of, let alone promoting, fundamental change.

Students recognize the failures of the current system. They are concerned about economic and social human rights, ecological balance, and peace. They speak out and act for equal rights for women, ethnic minorities, and gays and lesbians. They volunteer by the thousands to help the homeless and feed the needy. Yet beneath these noble actions is a quiet acceptance of the way things are. Since there are no alternatives to existing structures, the most that can be done is individual action to try to protect the vulnerable. Volunteering for Habitat for Humanity or the local soup kitchen is to be applauded. But if we are serious about ending suffering we must go beyond volunteerism and charity.

So let me scream out: There are alternatives! There are policy options. There are ways in which we as a global community can end needless suffering. The goal of this book is to address the quandary of my political economy student who could not see the path from here to there. This book hopefully provides a direction for viable structural reform to protect those left behind by the global economy. There are policy options for states to implement to protect the vulnerable and to end needless suffering. This book attempts to define that global public policy and to articulate the conditions for the fulfillment of economic and social human rights for all.

A poster on campus recently proclaimed: "Imagination is more important than knowledge." Yes, imagination is vital. We do need to expand our imaginations to break out of the limitations of the current era. We need to open our minds and imaginations to the idea that as a human species we can do better. It is unfortunate that the "great debates" of the twentieth century, including the viability and validity of liberation theology, socialist humanism, and moral incentives, seem to have ended with the end of the century. Few people living in developed countries now imagine a world different from the present. A recent exposition at the New York Public Library on visionaries, futurology, and imaginative alternative lifestyles ends in the 1980s. This must change. The creation of a pathway toward global humane governance will require us to rediscover our creativity and break open our imaginations.

Nevertheless, the poster is misleading: Imagination is not more important than knowledge. Rather, imagination and knowledge are equally vital. Knowledge provides the means to achieve our visions and inspirations. Our ability to craft effective public policy depends on our knowledge of the successes and limitations of existing policy and programs. On a global level, this means examining the work of the existing international organizations committed to ending human suffering. The work of the specialized agencies of the UN is a particular focus of this book because of these agencies' stated commitment to the protection and fulfillment of economic and social human rights. The insights gained from a critique of the development experience of the UN will enhance the proposals for global policy reform. Imagination alone can be utopian. Knowledge and imagination combined can produce results.

What are some of the problems in the global economy that public policy must address to protect economic and social human rights? The examples leap out from the daily news:

- Slavery has become a defining characteristic of the new global economy. The organization Anti-Slavery International defines a slave as someone "forced to work under physical or mental threat, and where the owner or employer controls the person completely—where a person is bought or sold." These slaves receive no pay (or very little), their movements are monitored, and they have no say over working hours, holidays, or rest. Using this definition, a UN advisor on forced labor estimates that there are approximately 27 million people enslaved today. In addition, tens of thousands of children are transported from country to country in West Africa to fill a demand for cheap labor. The International Labor Organization (ILO) reports that at least 250 million children, instead of receiving schooling, work in mines, factories, and plantations, often in conditions of slavery.[4]
- Bangladesh offers the global economy some of the world's cheapest labor. The 3,300 garment factories in the country are inadequately regulated and are among "the worst sweatshops ever to haunt the human conscience." It is the "wretched of the earth who do the world's tailoring." Workers toil from twelve to eighteen hours a day with few breaks. Holidays and overtime pay are a myth. Workers are expected to work virtually every day of the year. Most wages range from $25 to $50 a month—or as little as 6 cents an hour, with children earning less. If workers complain, they are locked out of the factories. A fire at one of these garment factories in November 2000 killed 52 workers, as 1,250 people hurried to a stairway to escape the flames. At the bottom of the stairs was a locked folding gate. The fifty-two victims were trapped in the dark stairway amid screaming, pushing, and frantic men, women, and children fleeing the inferno. Bangladesh has reportedly received a $4.3 billion economic boost from its apparel industry. Yet, this "economic boost" has not trickled down to the people of Bangladesh. These sweatshops consolidate poverty and brutalize human beings. This is exploitation, not "development."[5]
- As China enters the global economy and meets the demands of the WTO to liberalize its economy, it is dismantling state-supported social services. As a result, huge numbers of China's 800 million rural residents are in a medical free fall. A side effect of the market-oriented changes is that the free rural clinics have disintegrated, and the famous system of "barefoot doctors" has vanished. According to the UN, health costs in China increased between 400 to 500 percent from 1990 to 1997. Medical care is now so costly rural citizens have stopped seeing doctors altogether, enduring pain, chronic infection, and the risks of childbirth at home. Health statistics are now beginning to reflect this lack of access to basic health care. Infant mortality, which had been declining for almost forty years, is beginning to

creep up. The UN reports that the number of tuberculosis cases has quadrupled in the last fifteen years. A simple hospital stay could cost more than the yearly income of most peasants.[6]

- Under the North American Free Trade Agreement (NAFTA) chapter 11, investors can bring claims against the government of the country where they made their investment. An anonymous three-person tribunal will hear the complaint and issue a verdict. In a recent case, Methanex Corporation of Canada is challenging California's decision to phase out the use of a gasoline additive containing methanol, which Methanex makes. California considers the additive a health hazard when it enters the water supply. The city of Santa Monica, California, had to shut down most of its municipal wells when gasoline containing this additive leaked into its drinking water. Methanex wants the NAFTA tribunal to grant it $970 million in compensation for not being able to do business in California. If this succeeds, other states and cities may hesitate before protecting their drinking water from methanol. Democratic principles are not valid here. The health standards of water in the United States appear to be compromised by the actions of a secret tribunal set up to enforce trade law.[7]

- The ILO reports that 75 percent of the world's estimated 150 million unemployed workers have no jobless benefits. As economic globalization has accelerated, even the most generous countries have been cutting assistance to the unemployed. The ILO notes that these cutbacks represent a significant threat to economic development because they undermine the financial security of employed workers.[8]

- How is one to react to the pharmaceutical companies' attempts to prevent the distribution of life-saving drug therapy to the millions of people with AIDS in developing countries? In December 2000, the UN reported that 25.3 million people in sub-Saharan Africa had AIDS or HIV, the virus that causes AIDS. In 2000, 2.4 million people in the region died of AIDS. Yet, the Agreement on Trade-Related Aspects of Intellectual Property Rights prevents states from distributing cheaper generic AIDS drugs. The big pharmaceutical companies claim that this patent protection, which enables them to charge exorbitantly high prices, is essential to cover start-up costs and pay for innovation. Yet, many drugs are initially developed with government money with no risk to the transnational corporation (TNC). These huge pharmaceutical TNCs, after taking little or no financial risk, are then able to gouge AIDS patients for incredible profits. The sick in poor countries where these drugs are unaffordable are left to die. Only a sustained effort by nongovernmental organizations and AIDS activists forced the pharmaceutical industry to drop its effort to prevent South Africa from importing cheaper anti-AIDS drugs and other medicines.[9] These pharmaceutical TNCs seem more concerned with profits and marketing than research and innovation. Just examine the distribution of revenues of GlaxoSmithKline, the world's largest manufacturer of AIDS medicines: 37.9 percent on marketing and administrative costs, 27.8 percent on profits, 20.4 percent on manufacturing, raw materials, and related production expenses, and 13.9 percent on research.[10]

This list could go on and on. Pick up today's newspaper and add to this list yourself. Chances are you will quickly find another example of the negative impact of economic globalization on the lives of the most vulnerable. You will probably also find numerous examples of the destruction of such global public goods as clean air and clean water accompanying economic development and industrialization on all continents (see chapters 2 and 4). Our leaders seem unwilling either to aid the vulnerable or to protect our fragile ecosystem from the onslaught of destructive global forces.

Perhaps we need to modify the criteria we use to evaluate our public officials. Politicians should be judged on the basis of their actions to protect the most weak and vulnerable. Those politicians who let child poverty and homelessness rise on their watch or who do nothing while controllable diseases devastate poor communities should be voted out of office. Leaders who ignore the negative impacts of globalization on the weak while continuing to subsidize the rich and powerful should be sent packing. Economic and social human rights should apply to all and not just to the winners in the global economy. In addition, our leaders should act to protect global public goods, including environmental sustainability and the preservation of the global commons. It is in the self-interest of all (all classes, all races, and all states) for these global public goods to be realized. It is not an exaggeration to state that the very survival of the human species is linked to the protection of global public goods.

International Economic and Social Human Rights

International human rights law defines economic and social human rights (see chapter 3). Economic rights refer to the right to property, the right to work, and the right to security of income. Social rights, on the other hand, are those necessary for an adequate standard of living, including rights to food, shelter, health, and education.

During the Cold War, many Western countries considered economic and social human rights to be socialist propaganda. Since the end of the Cold War, the category of economic and social human rights is still often criticized by academics and practitioners in the developed world for its supposed "vague" content and "unrealistic" claims. The U.S. government, for example, refuses to ratify the International Covenant on Economic, Social

and Cultural Rights (hereafter Economic Rights Treaty). Many of these critics contend that these economic and social claims are merely aspirational
goals achievable only in some future, utopian world. It is thus misleading,
according to these critics, to argue that these economic and social objectives represent valid human rights claims.

The UN Committee on Economic, Social and Cultural Rights (hereafter
Economic Rights Committee) has spent a great deal of time defining the
core content of the claims articulated in the Economic Rights Treaty.[11] The
Economic Rights Committee attempts to establish a minimum threshold of
compliance that should be achieved by all states regardless of their economic situation. The burden of proof lies with the state. States must prove
to the Economic Rights Committee that they have mobilized their resources
to meet the needs of the most vulnerable, and that any remaining poverty,
destitution, and hunger are due to factors beyond their control. The Economic Rights Committee thus works to establish universal criteria to hold
states accountable for the economic and social rights of their citizens.

Yet problems persist. It is exceedingly difficult to establish minimum
thresholds and standards for economic and social rights at the international level. Are different criteria to be applied to resource-poor as opposed
to resource-rich countries? Should the minimum level be raised in those
countries that have the ability to meet a higher level of demand? And
which actors are responsible to meet these rights obligations? In a globalized economy, the impact of transnational actors—TNCs, international
financial institutions (IFIs), and so on—often has a direct impact on the
well-being and/or destitution of a population.

The Global New Deal focuses on the practical steps that state and nonstate
actors can take to fulfill their duties under the Economic Rights Treaty to
protect the vulnerable and to respect, protect, and fulfill economic and
social human rights. Chapter 2 examines economic and social rights
through the lens of international political economy (IPE) and introduces
three concepts central to the achievement of these rights: global public
goods, economic equality, and the capabilities approach. Chapter 3 reviews
the UN's approach to economic and social human rights, with a particular
focus on the work of the Economic Rights Committee. Chapter 4 discusses
the priority of ecosystem protection and sustainability within all growth
strategies. The debates surrounding a human rights approach to ecological
balance are summarized and the work of the UN Environment Program,
Commission on Sustainable Development, and the Global Environment
Facility are reviewed. Chapter 5 analyzes the degree of racial bias in global
economics and reviews the work of the UN Committee on the Elimination
of All Forms of Racial Discrimination (hereafter Minority Rights Committee). Chapter 6 turns to issues of gender and women's rights and the work
of the UN Committee on the Elimination of All Forms of Discrimination
against Women (hereafter Women's Rights Committee). Feminist theories

of IPE are critiqued in relation to approaches to women's rights in international law. Chapter 7 addresses the impact of military spending on economic growth and the achievement of economic and social human rights. And finally, the public policy proposals of the Global New Deal are presented in chapter 8. The Global New Deal is a set of recommendations for global public policy designed to facilitate the achievement of economic and social human rights.

The Global New Deal identifies the policies that state and nonstate actors (TNCs, IFIs, and so on) can pursue in these six areas—IPE, the UN and international organizations, the environment, race, gender, and military spending—to implement economic and social human rights. Achieving economic and social human rights depends on addressing all six of these areas as progress in one is dependent on progress in the others. There is a symbiotic, interdependent relationship among the six areas. Under international human rights law, governments have a legal duty to take action in all six areas to alleviate suffering and provide for human security. State and nonstate actors have the responsibility to respect, protect, and fulfill their economic and social human rights obligations. The Global New Deal presents a roadmap for action and demonstrates that these rights are more than aspirations: They are a legal and practical framework to guide public policy. The project combines legal and economic approaches to achieve sustainable economic and social public policies. Through a comprehensive evaluation of the successes and failures of both legal and economic avenues to social protection, clear policy directions for rights fulfillment are articulated.

Current international economic structures are unresponsive to the approximately 1.6 billion impoverished people on our planet.[12] These human beings are so poor that they are irrelevant to international markets. Since the 1970s, world food prices have dropped by one-half, yet these millions of people still do not receive an adequate caloric intake in their diet. They are economically invisible. They can neither participate in world commodity markets, nor buy internationally traded food. They cannot compete with the market demand for grain to feed the cattle of the world's wealthy people. Many of the desperately poor have been denied the means to farm their own food. The structures of the global market economy entrench rather than alleviate this suffering. Equal freedom from hunger has not been respected.[13]

I believe that all thoughtful scholars and practitioners want destitution on this extreme level ended and that the disagreements are over the most effective means to achieve this goal. The post–Cold War period should give us an opportunity to innovate. We cannot remain fossilized in limited theories that offer bleak hope to those millions on the bottom. We have the ability to end massive destitution.[14] The means are available. The global community can face this moral imperative and find imaginative methods to guarantee everyone basic economic and social human rights. The Global New Deal takes on this challenge and charts a clear direction for economic and social rights fulfillment.

The Global New Deal

The Global New Deal draws its inspiration from Franklin Delano Roosevelt's New Deal for America. The negative impact of economic globalization has brought forth a number of calls for global reform.[15] As a global community, we can summon strength from Roosevelt's attempt to create a government responsive to the needs of the victims of economic development. We can act for the global public welfare and enact a new global covenant.

Eliminating slavery, combating AIDS in Africa, abolishing sweatshops in Bangladesh, and protecting the quality of the water supply in the United States will require multilateral action through international organization and international law. These examples dramatize the clear links between economic and social rights protection and the global economy. An individual state often has limited ability to counteract the negative consequences of globalization. Global problems require reforms at the global level.

The public policy proposals of the Global New Deal, described in detail in chapter 8, are realistic and doable. In addition to new ideas, I also incorporate into the Global New Deal many specific recommendations for change proposed over the last decade by activists and scholars concerned about global social justice. The Global New Deal is my attempt to bring together a comprehensive program for structural reform to create the conditions for the fulfillment of economic and social human rights.

A great deal of progress has been made in (1) defining economic and social human rights in international law and (2) documenting the impact of economic globalization on the poor. Not enough attention has been paid, however, to the development of public policy to meet basic human needs in this economically interdependent world system. This project is designed to close this gap through an approach that combines theories of economic development with international human rights law.

Scholars have inadequately elaborated the link between IPE and international human rights law. The UN has attempted to relate IPE strategies with human rights through the right to development. In 1986, the UN General Assembly defined the right to development as the right of "every human person and all peoples . . . to participate in, contribute to and enjoy economic, social and cultural and political development, in which all human rights and fundamental freedoms can be fully realized." But the General Assembly did not define what states must do to fulfill this right. What are the human rights obligations of state and nonstate actors under the right to development?[16] In its 1998 publication *Integrating Human Rights with Sustainable Human Development,* the UNDP called for a rights-based approach to economic planning. But again, the responsibilities of state and nonstate actors remained vague. The Global New Deal develops this approach more fully by defining the economic policies that governments and nonstate actors (TNCs and IFIs) have a duty to implement in order to respect, protect, and fulfill economic and social human rights.

Implementing the Global New Deal involves strengthening the UN and its related agencies (see chapters 3, 4, 5, and 6). The well-publicized flaws and weaknesses of the UN have led many to question the viability and utility of the organization. While I recognize the political and structural deficiencies of the UN system, I do not believe that the system is beyond repair. Many of the reforms of the Global New Deal thus focus on making the UN system responsive to the needs of the vulnerable and the weak. The UN system, to a large extent, is the only forum of international cooperation in existence. Rather than start over, the attempt here is to rehabilitate and transform the UN structure to be able to meet the challenges of economic and social rights implementation.

At this point, you may be thinking that given the current conservative political environment, particularly in the United States, there is no chance of implementing a Global New Deal. To many, proposals to strengthen international law and international organizations are unrealistic. They think that these ideas, although appealing to moral and ethical sensibilities, are not based in the realities of power politics and thus have no chance of moving forward. For the last thirty years, for example, the UN has been put in a defensive posture and has struggled to just survive. You may thus be skeptical that new programs to strengthen human rights enforcement and the UN system would be either adopted or implemented.

I urge you to set aside this "realist" logic for a moment (at least while you are reading this book). Our knowledge of the current international system allows us to imagine a more just future—knowledge *and* imagination. Each proposal of the Global New Deal is based on a comprehensive evaluation of the successes and failures of current efforts to address economic and social human rights. The analysis undergirding the proposals of the Global New Deal is presented throughout each chapter of this book. The logic and practicality of these reforms will be clear to all readers, I hope, by the end of the book.

Both empathy and self-interest are central to the human condition and are found within each individual human being and collectively within the community of states. The Global New Deal appeals to both of these human characteristics. On the one hand, the Global New Deal provides a means to show compassion for those who suffer. Its programs are a concrete means for people in all states on all continents to act to protect the vulnerable, end destitution, and save our ecosystem. For millions of people, compassionate action on behalf of the community is central to their sense of self and key to what it means to be a human being. On the other hand, the Global New Deal appeals to individual self-interest and selfishness. It is not a platform of charity, but one of self-interest. The rich and the poor, the strong and the weak, all need clean drinking water, unpolluted air, and a demilitarized planet. All communities and states suffer from the destabilizing consequences of massive economic and environmental refugee flows, deepening global poverty, and diseases that cross borders. Global warming and the loss of the earth's biodiversity will harm not only the weak, but the powerful as well. It is thus in everyone's self-interest to enact the Global New Deal. From a purely selfish perspective, the United States should take the lead and push this reform program forward. The citizens of the United States depend on the protection of global public goods and will benefit from programs focused on economic equality. Each state's national security depends on attention to the issues addressed in the Global New Deal.

History teaches us that profound change can happen quite quickly and often when least expected. Our theories of how the world works have proven unable to predict change. For example, not one theory of International Relations predicted the end of the Cold War. Scholars were unable to decipher the currents at work within the former Soviet Union that undermined the state and brought about its rapid demise. Today, in countries around the world there are forces for change at work within civil society, beneath the level of the state, promoting the normative principles underlining the Global New Deal. Hundreds of thousands of people on every continent are working for environmental preservation, human rights protection, and the provision of basic human needs. There is growing recognition and appreciation in many countries of the importance of international organization and cooperation to resolve global issues. None of us knows where all of these efforts will lead. They may lead to a more relevant and powerful UN or they may go nowhere. Current economic and political structures are strong and resilient and will resist change. Political realists thus have us believe that these reform efforts are doomed. But I believe that more modesty is in order. Those theorists who were so wrong about the former Soviet Union should be a bit hesitant before labeling the Global New Deal "utopian idealism." The currents at work behind these ideas are strong and vibrant. None of us knows how or when change will occur. If history is our guide, change happens quite abruptly.

2

International Political Economy and Economic and Social Human Rights

How do theories of international political economy (IPE) address economic and social human rights? Are there public policies that flow from each theory that would help protect the economic and social human rights of the most vulnerable? What is the impact of economic globalization on the attainment of these rights? What are "global public goods"? Do the ideas of "economic equality" and the "capabilities approach" help provide a direction for economic and social policy formation?

Theories of IPE attempt to articulate comprehensive frameworks for organizing efficient and fair systems of production and consumption on a global basis. Each theory of IPE is based on certain normative values and ethical assumptions. This has unfortunately resulted in advocates of competing theories pushing their perspective as the most moral choice with debates taking on a religious fervor. But economics should not be confused with theology. The idea is not to adopt a new belief system. Rather, through the study of IPE it should be possible to structure public policy to better meet basic human needs and alleviate needless human suffering. Since there are aspects of truth found in all theories, it is groundless to claim that any one theory has a comparative advantage over the others. The utility of IPE lies in its ability to demonstrate how insights from a variety of perspectives can help direct and guide the formation of a just economic system.

The goal of IPE is to articulate policies that work, understand why other policies fail, and predict which policies hold more promise for the future. This work is ongoing. Since the world does not stand still, new factors must be constantly integrated into successful policy analysis. Thus, even relatively effective policies must be modified over time, especially in a period of rapid technological and scientific change. In this era of expanding economic globalization, it is foolish to cling to a single model of IPE as the solution to our deepening social and environmental quandaries.

This chapter examines economic and social human rights through the lens of IPE. Three different concepts from IPE central to the achievement of economic and social human rights are global public goods, economic equality, and the capabilities approach. These ideas are explored in the following sections:

- Economic and social human rights and theories of IPE, with a particular focus on global public goods;
- Economic and social human rights and economic globalization;
- Economic and social human rights and economic equality; and
- Economic and social human rights and the capabilities approach.

Economic and Social Human Rights and Theories of IPE

IPE is the study of the interaction and tension between (1) the market and the state and (2) the market and international economic entities—including transnational corporations (TNCs) and international financial institutions (IFIs), such as the World Trade Organization (WTO), the International Monetary Fund (IMF), and the World Bank. Central principles of IPE include efficiency, autonomy, equity, and order. States try to create economic efficiency, protect their sovereign autonomy, respond to demands for the equitable distribution of goods and services, and follow the rules of IFIs that create a degree of order in international economic relations.

However, in the real world these principles often conflict, and states are forced to make trade-offs between these principles. A state, for example, may act to regulate the market and sacrifice efficiency in order to address issues of equity and autonomy. States' interests in fact frequently collide with market and IFI priorities. State action is often advocated to monitor the market and patrol actions of TNCs and IFIs. However, these policies of state modification of market mechanisms are controversial and often produce unforeseen side effects. This chapter explores these tensions through the lens of human rights. What is the proper balance between the state and the market to guarantee human rights protection for the vulnerable? Are regulations and controls needed on the actions of IFIs to promote economic and social rights fulfillment?

Economic and social human rights are fully defined and articulated in international law (as described in chapter 3). Economic rights include the right to property, the right to work, and the right to social security. Social rights include those rights necessary for an adequate standard of living, including rights to food, health, shelter, and education. The following is a brief review of the major IPE theories, summarizing their strengths and weaknesses in relation to the fulfillment of economic and social human rights.

Conflicting approaches to IPE and economic and social human rights can be roughly summarized as follows:

1. Conservative/realist/libertarian
2. Liberal/globalist/utilitarian
3. Structuralist/dependency/egalitarian.

Conservative/Realist/Libertarian

The combination of the demise of statist Soviet totalitarian economic models with the poor economic performance of "welfare state" social-democratic governments in Europe has resulted in a resurgence of conservative economic theories and practices since the mid-1990s. The logic of conserva-

THEORIES OF INTERNATIONAL POLITICAL ECONOMY: STRENGTHS AND WEAKNESSES IN RELATION TO ECONOMIC AND SOCIAL HUMAN RIGHTS

	Conservative	Liberal	Structuralist
Approach to world politics	Realism	Globalism	Dependency
Ethical framework	Libertarian	Utilitarian	Egalitarian
Strength	Understanding of market efficiency	Understanding of global integration	Understanding of global economic structures
Weakness	Limited protection for the vulnerable	Lack of recognition of structural violence	Lack of a theory of incentives
Attitude toward public goods	Provide through market-based solutions	Provide through state action only when the market fails	Provide through state action and remove from the market altogether

tive economics is well known. Human beings—as aggressive, self-centered, and calculating individuals—need positive (wage raises) and negative (threats of unemployment) material incentives to be productive. A competitive, free enterprise economy allows each individual to achieve maximum personal liberty and material well-being. If individual decision-making units (individuals, households, or firms) are allowed to act freely and rationally through the market, society as a whole will develop and move forward. Open and free competition breeds efficiency by driving the inefficient out of business. Conservatives claim that government interference in this free market process impedes economic growth.[1]

Conservative thinkers thus stress libertarian rights: freedom from the state, individual liberty, and private ownership of material resources and property. Libertarian conservatives oppose taxation and favor a laissez-faire economic system. In general, conservatives call for limited government and a minimalist state. The most important functions of the state are to provide for national security and to maintain social order. Laws for the protection of private property and contracts are necessary for capitalism to operate freely.

Individual effort and competition is at the core of the conservative paradigm. Human rights, according to these thinkers, should focus on individual freedoms and property rights. Wealth is often considered the reward for a person's superior natural abilities. Poverty, on the other hand, is often seen as the result of a person's laziness or inadequacy. The best government from this perspective is one that governs the least. Competition for wealth and power is natural and necessary. Conservative economic thought has been cast as a form of social Darwinism, for example, the "natural" ability of some to succeed, while others "naturally" fail.[2]

There is a strong overlap between conservative economics and realist political theory. Realist theory depicts states acting in a world of anarchy. There is little possibility for cooperative action between states. The view of human nature is similar to that of conservative theory: people are aggressive, competitive, and egotistical. We exist in a world of insecurity and must struggle and compete with others to survive. According to theologian Reinhold Niebuhr, human beings project a "will to power" in an attempt to transcend this insecurity and control their destiny. "Man is insecure and involved in natural contingency; he seeks to overcome his insecurity by a will-to-power which overreaches the limits of human creatureliness."[3] This desperate search for security leads to relations of power and domination among all human beings. As Niebuhr writes, translating this to the political sphere, men and women seek to fulfill this search for security by projecting the drive for power to the collective plane. They thus pledge their loyalty to the nation. For Niebuhr, the politics of nations is a fight for power and security. Altruism and morality are absent. In the jungle that is international relations, each nation must concern itself with its power position vis-à-vis every other nation. The most that can be hoped for is a balance of power between states.[4]

How does this realist conservative framework provide for economic and social human rights?

Advantages: A much discussed advantage of the conservative economic model is that it provides incentives toward efficient production and personal productiveness. The profit motive encourages entrepreneurs to work hard, innovate, and move ahead in a theoretically free market economy. Furthermore, these economic incentives affect those far beyond the level of the owners and managers of firms. Jennifer L. Hochschild documents how the belief that an individual can attain success and virtue through strenuous effort is the essence of the American dream and the very soul of the United States.[5] She shows how the poor of all races hold this dream, even when it remains an unattainable myth. The dream thus provides strong motivational incentives.

Conservatives argue that progress is the result of individual effort and competition. Competition is a natural process to determine who is the most fit, efficient, and best. The result will be the most goods and services for the most numbers of people—Pareto optimum.[6] Governmental economic controls and planning, as well-known British economist Friedrich A. von Hayek argues, disrupt this system. Hayek envisions private property and individual economic freedom as the basis of democratic government.[7] Thus, the human rights focused on by conservatives are libertarian principles of individual freedoms and property rights.

Disadvantages: The economic and social human rights of those who succeed in this competitive environment are protected. However, the major disadvantage of conservative economic theory is that it provides limited protections for those who fail and for the weak who cannot compete. The theory does not recognize the principle of social injustice, that is, that unemployment and suffering may be the result of the economic structures of a market economy. In fact, on a global scale the causes of human suffering can often be traced to the impact of economic structures on states and societies, which override individual effort, hard work, and natural abilities. From a perspective of economic and social human rights, the "safety net" for those who don't end up on the winning side has too many holes. Thus, the major flaw of conservative theory is its lack of recognition of structural injustice and the lack of protection for the most vulnerable.

Liberal/Globalist/Utilitarian

The depression of the 1930s appeared to discredit the conservative laissez-faire approach. In response to the economic catastrophe of the time, John Maynard Keynes argued that the capitalist economic system was not self-correcting and would not generate a high enough level of investment to maintain full employment. He felt strongly that the government had the responsibility to borrow and spend money to prevent economic depressions. The economy in general, however, should be left free to respond to the profit-maximizing producers and the welfare-maximizing consumers. Keynes's correctives were meant to stimulate, not overthrow, the market.

Unlike conservatives, however, liberals believe that governmental intervention in the economy can achieve some goals of social justice. Liberals share with conservatives a basic faith in the capitalist system. However, they believe that inequalities based on wealth and power should and can be reduced through state action. The state can assist the poor when market mechanisms fail. The state has a role in providing basic human needs to help those who (for whatever reason) cannot compete fairly in the market system.[8]

Conservative economists argued that markets will inherently tend toward a socially beneficial equilibrium (Pareto optimum). Keynes contended that this was not the case. Rather, production and consumption can balance while unemployment remains at a relatively high level. The state must therefore intervene to stimulate both employment and investment. Keynes challenged the basic argument of laissez-faire: that economic prosperity can best be gained without state management. Keynes argued that government intervention was necessary to achieve full employment.[9]

As there were similarities between conservative economists and realist theories, one finds basic unities between liberal economists and globalist approaches to international relations. While both conservatives and liberals embrace a market economy, they differ over the role of the state in the interdependent global economy. Conservatives focus on the economic and political interests of the territorial state, adopting a realist framework. Liberals, on the other hand, prioritize the market needs of transnational business and financial institutions, embracing a globalist perspective.[10]

Globalists thus explain the politics of interdependence much better than the realists. Globalists strongly support the activities of TNCs as "engines of development" and "transmission belts" of free enterprise, efficiency, and good management. To avoid disruptions in TNC activity and threats to "orderly growth," some globalists have responded sympathetically to calls from the South for reforms of international economic governance that benefit the least developed countries (LDCs). While realists believe the international system is defined by competition alone, globalists have pushed for the creation of new international monetary and trade regimes to facilitate economic cooperation.[11]

For globalists, therefore, as for liberals, governments have a role to play. The state should direct these reforms so that the TNCs can secure and distribute the benefits from a global economy. Furthermore, globalists repudiate state action (often taken on "realist," conservative grounds) that interferes with transnational management, such as imposing tariffs and surcharges on imports, subsidizing home industries, placing embargoes on trade with particular countries, and so on. For the globalist, as for the liberal, the world is a more interdependent place than that described by a conservative realist. In this world, cooperation is not only possible but necessary.

Globalists and liberals acknowledge the emergence of a global society and argue for the development of a true global economy. Growing trade, investment, and monetary ties are a part of global "interdependence" that challenges old conceptions of national economic autonomy.

How does a globalist liberal framework provide for economic and social human rights?

Advantages: Globalists argue that the alleviation of hunger will come through the benefits of world economic integration. Integrating diverse and separate economies will result in an overall gain of output from which, over time, everyone could potentially benefit. Joel Cohen gives the following hypothetical example to demonstrate the benefits from economic integration and international trade: Countries A and B each have 1,000 acres of land. Country A has 1,000 workers and 100 mules. Country B has 100 workers and 1,000 mules. Neither a worker alone nor a mule alone can cultivate anything. However, one worker together with one mule can cultivate one acre per year. The advantages of integration are clear. Only 100 acres could be cultivated in Countries A and B if neither workers nor mules can move between countries. If, however, Country B could ship 900 mules to Country A, then combined the two countries could cultivate 1,100 acres. Or, instead of shipping mules, the migration of 900 workers from Country A to Country B would equally increase the total cultivated land.[12]

Liberal globalists thus stress ethics of utilitarianism, in that they jump to consequences, the final results. Utilitarian ethics argues for policies, institutions, and actions that improve the welfare of the most people. To act morally in the world today is to act in a way that improves the well-being of the most people. Globalists argue that in our imperfect world, the greatest number of people can benefit from an integrated, globalized economy. It may be messy getting there. The transition from a "backward" localized economy to a full merger into the international market may cause pain to many. But, over the long run, the well-being of most people will be achieved.

Disadvantages: Critics argue that the globalist perspective refuses to recognize the structural dimension of the world economy that plays a significant role in the creation of hunger and deprivation. The world economy is filled with national and international inequities in power, wealth, and consumption. Unfortunately, TNCs have often been more interested in transferring wealth out of the LDCs than in the developmental needs of the poorest sectors. For example, examine the impact of logging by Japanese TNCs on the Philippines: Since 1945, Japanese TNCs have logged and brought back to Japan a significant percentage of the Filipino forest. By 1989, only 1 million hectares remained of the original 17 million hectares of tropical forests in the Philippines. As a result of the actions of the Japanese TNCs, including Mitsubishi, Mitshi, C. Itoh, and Sumitomo, the Philippines has one of the most severe deforestation problems of any developing country.[13] Rather than serving as "engines of development," the actions of TNCs are often detrimental to the economic well-being of LDCs, as evidenced here (and in copious other examples).

TNCs produce goods and services for those who have purchasing power and create a demand in LDCs for their products. However, the poor in these nations lack the money to purchase these products and are thus unable to express their preferences in the marketplace. They become either invisible or a nuisance. A system built on the profit incentive alone has continuously failed to meet the basic human needs of those who fall behind. In the end, economic globalism creates and perpetuates enormous economic and social inequalities. The economic and social human rights of the most vulnerable are violated.

In addition, economic globalization has shifted power away from elected governments and given it to a handful of corporations and financial institutions. These organizations exist for short-term financial gain. As a result, Harvard professor Stanley Hoffmann argues that the global economy is literally out of control. There are no rules of accountability; instead, there is a huge zone of irresponsibility.[14]

Structuralist/Dependency/Egalitarian

Many structuralists believe that human beings are naturally cooperative and productive. The positive (wage increases) and negative (unemployment) incentives that liberals and conservatives advocate are considered unnecessary. Humans have the ability to mold their own destinies. Traits such as aggression, competition, passivity, uncooperativeness, and egoism are not natural. Rather, they emerge in response to an inhumane and fundamentally immoral economic system. Surviving in a capitalist economy often means becoming selfish and oblivious to the needs of others.[15]

Equality of opportunity is a myth in a society where power and wealth is in the hands of the few. According to structuralists, liberals and conservatives do not go to the root of the problem. A capitalist economy creates classes and institutional structures. All aspects of life, including personal relationships, are shaped by the pursuit of profit and human needs are subordinated to the needs of the market. According to Karl Marx, "exchange value" replaces "use value." For example, food is distributed to those who can buy it (exchange value) and not distributed on the basis of need (use value). The result is that food surpluses in the global economy often do not reach the hungry.

Structuralists see an inherent conflict between the rich and the poor. This inequality of wealth and power is the result of a system that is based on the exploitation of one class by another. Private ownership of the means of production has created a vicious system filled with contradictions and class conflict. Individual freedom to accumulate has unfortunately interfered with the freedom of the many to survive. For the liberal promise of freedom to have real meaning for the majority, socioeconomic inequality must be overcome.[16]

Structuralists thus strongly embrace egalitarian principles and critique the economic structures of capitalism that prohibit true equality of opportunity. Food, shelter, education, and medicine are essential human needs, not abstract concepts. It is a mockery to offer political rights to people who are underfed or diseased. Individual freedom may not always be everyone's primary need. As a nineteenth-century Russian radical is believed to have proclaimed: There are situations in which boots are superior to the works of William Shakespeare.

Dependency theories extend the internal dynamics of the capitalist mode of production, as originally outlined by Marx, to the world as a whole. These theorists argue that capitalism created underdevelopment in the past and generates it in the present. The world is divided between the developed center and an underdeveloped periphery and semiperiphery. The economic gap widens over time between the center and the periphery, which is reduced to a state of dependence. The position of the countries in the periphery is seen as analogous to the proletariat's situation in relation to the capitalist. André Gunder Frank and others argue further that underdevelopment is an essential condition for the survival and maintenance of the capitalist world system as a whole.[17] Samir Amin argues that these LDCs should thus "delink" from the centers of capitalism.[18] Cutting ties with the centers of capitalism is seen as perhaps the only chance the LDCs have of breaking out of the tragedy of underdevelopment. Dependency theory thus veers toward an autarkic, self-sufficient model of development.

How does a structuralist framework provide for economic and social human rights?

Advantages: The structuralist critique brings issues of class and power out of the shadows and into the open. There is a huge discrepancy between the normative framework of liberal freedom and the realities of global life in the twenty-first century. Global economic structures are responsible for a great deal of human suffering. The moral message is that this human agony is unjust. We must not delude ourselves. For those on the bottom of the global division of labor, things are getting much worse, not better. We can do better.

IPE CONCEPTS CENTRAL TO ECONOMIC AND SOCIAL HUMAN RIGHTS

Global Public Goods

Global public goods refers to those products and necessities that all people enjoy in common that are nonexcludable and nonrivalrous in consumption. Nonrivalry in consumption refers to those goods that any number of consumers may enjoy without detracting from the enjoyment of others. Nonexcludability means that no one can be excluded from enjoying the good. Clean air, for example, is a pure public good. Global public goods are outcomes that benefit all countries, population groups, and generations. Global public goods include the following: international peace and the prevention of deadly conflict; health and the eradication of disease; and environmental sustainability and the preservation of the global commons.[a]

Economic Equality

Economic equality signifies the equal provision of public goods, including nutrition, sanitation, shelter, clothing, primary and secondary education, and basic health care. Economic equality, as distinct from income equality, forms the foundation for achieving economic

Disadvantages: Many conclude from the experience of "socialism" in Russia and Eastern Europe that a major weakness in socialist theory is the lack of a theory of incentives. If the totalitarian states of Eastern Europe had been less corrupt, then perhaps the original humanist vision of a society of true equality could have provided continuous "moral incentives." But with the corrupt "nomenclature" recreating an elite class, the vast majority of the working class in these countries had no possibility for a better life. No matter how hard they worked, their families would not see an improvement in their living conditions. The result was that a general malaise, obvious to the naked eye of even the most untrained observer, gripped these nations, resulting in economic stagnation. There appeared to be no motivation or incentive to work hard and innovate under these conditions.

In sum, it does not appear that there is one approach in IPE theory that fully addresses the economic and social human rights claims embraced by international law. Effective global public policy must therefore take into account the advantages and disadvantages found within each paradigm.

and social human rights. Economic equality is contingent on public policy to ameliorate deprivations and create equal opportunity for all. Such public policy measures would focus on health care, sanitation, unemployment insurance, job retraining programs, public education, and so on.[b]

Capabilities Approach

A way to consider real equality of opportunity is through equality of capabilities. A person's capability for adequate functioning depends on being well nourished, avoiding premature mortality, self-respect, and being able to participate in the life of the community. The capabilities approach allows us to look at the actual ways in which individuals and groups are given the freedom to achieve adequate functioning. The capabilities approach examines the differences in social conditions that affect human capabilities, including public education, crime and violence, health care and infectious disease, public facilities, and community relations.[c]

a. See Inge Kaul, Isabelle Grunberg, and Marc A. Stern, eds., *Global Public Goods: International Cooperation in the 21st Century* (New York: Oxford University Press, 1999).
b. See Amartya Sen, *Development As Freedom* (New York: Knopf, 1999).
c. See Amartya Sen, *Inequality Reexamined* (Cambridge, Mass.: Harvard University Press, 1992).

To a significant extent, the debates between these IPE theories is over the provision of what economists call "public goods."

Global Public Goods

Paul Samuelson defines a public good as a product "which all enjoy in common in the sense that each individual's consumption of that good leads to no subtraction from any other individual's consumption of that good."[19] A clean and healthy environment is a pure public good. Individual enjoyment of the environment does not distract from the pleasure of others in clean air, soil, and water. Yet, as the environmental crisis so tragically illustrates, public goods are often neglected and suffer from underprovision.

To set up a business, an entrepreneur depends on critical factors such as a peaceful society, clean air, clean water, property rights, an educated workforce, and so on. A businessperson's ability to produce "private goods" or services to sell in the market depends on these other "public goods" being provided. The benefits of these public goods are clearly not limited to a single producer or buyer; once provided, many enjoy them for free. Market mechanisms have historically failed to provide for these types of goods.

The theory of market failure explains the necessity for government action to protect public goods. In some areas, the market seems to meet the needs of consumers, but yet in others it clearly fails. Why, for example, does the market continuously fail to provide the ecological balance—from nature preservation and wildlife conservation to clean air, soil, and water—that consumers (citizens) unquestionably crave? Economists call this inability of the market to provide certain goods "market failure." Market failure occurs due to the lack of financial incentives for the production of public goods. As a result, without government action, these public goods will be underproduced and threatened.

There are two qualities of these goods and services that are recognized as destroying financial incentives and contributing to market failure: nonrivalry in consumption and nonexcludability. Nonrivalry in consumption refers to those goods that any number of consumers may enjoy without detracting from the enjoyment of others. Nonexcludability means that no one can be excluded from enjoying the good, that is, the seller is unable to prevent nonpayers from consuming the good. Some examples help to clarify these concepts. Peace and national defense are often said to be pure public goods. When peace exists in a country, all citizens enjoy it; one citizen's consumption does not detract from others, and it is impossible to prevent nonpayers from benefitting from a peaceful society. Clean air is another pure public good. One cannot exclude nonpayers from enjoying the benefits of clean air, and one person's consumption does not detract from the consumption of others.[20]

Nonexcludability and nonrivalrous consumption mean that there are no market incentives to provide for public goods like peace or clean air. Why? Because nonexcludability results in what is called the "free-rider problem." A free rider is someone who benefits from a good without paying to support the good's production. It is not possible to charge the occupants of one household for the clean air they breathe if their neighbors breathe it for free. The issue of nonexcludability has long been noted. Adam Smith writes that government would have to erect and maintain "those public works, which, though they may be in the highest degree advantageous to a great society, are, however, of such a nature, that the profit could never repay the expense to any individual or small number of individuals."[21] In other words, when market incentives fail, the government must maintain those public works clearly "advantageous to a great society," such as clean air.

The idea of externalities also helps to clarify the role of public goods. "Externalities" refers to outcomes that occur when an individual or firm takes an action but does not bear all the costs (negative externalities) or receive all the benefits (positive externalities).[22] Consider, for example, the role of education. It is true that the individual person benefits from a solid education, but so does the society as a whole. Educated individuals are able to move from employer to employer without having to be retrained, comply with written laws and norms, and participate in the civil life of the country. Because of these substantial positive externalities, education is a public good.[23] Pollution, on the other hand, is a substantial negative externality and could be described as a "public bad." There is no incentive in a market economy for individual rational actors to provide for public goods or correct public bads. It is more rational to sit back and either enjoy the public good or let others pay for the public bad.

As externalities become international in reach, the issue of who provides the public good becomes even more problematic. If there is no incentive for individual businesses within global capitalism to stem negative externalities, how will the global environment and global social welfare be protected? It is not in the interest of any individual business to pay to protect our endangered oceans, atmosphere, and forests. It is not in the interest of any individual business to be concerned with the welfare of refugees and migrant workers, the poor and most vulnerable. It is also not in the narrow, immediate self-interest of any individual nation to be concerned with externalities beyond its borders.

The example of the struggle to establish global labor standards is illustrative. Unless there is a strong international organization with the ability to forge industry-wide negotiating forums across nations, individual firms have to act in isolation. The increased costs for improving working conditions are seen as jeopardizing their competitive position. In fact, there is pressure in the opposite direction—to lower working standards to become more globally competitive. The result is that even if a firm wanted to raise its labor standards it would be very reluctant to do so. Market pressures force businesses to cut costs as much as possible to stay competitive. Many LDCs have opposed attempts to establish global labor standards precisely due to this fear of losing a global "competitive edge."

A negative externality of our global economy is the overexploitation of common resources, frequently referred to as "The Tragedy of the Commons."[24] The global "commons"—the oceans, land, air, and outer space—are used without regard to the costs imposed. No one is excluded from utilizing these natural resources. Although regulatory progress has been made in international environmental law, the global commons remain threatened and endangered. The right to a healthy environment is jeopardized (see chapter 4).

Public goods are thus no longer only national in character, but global as well. Inge Kaul, Isabelle Grunberg, and Marc Stern outline three elements central to the identification of global public goods: the division of the world's population into countries, socioeconomic groups, and generations. Global public goods are outcomes that benefit all countries, population groups, and generations. "At a minimum, a global public good would meet the following criteria: its benefits extend to more than one group of countries and do not discriminate against any population group or any set of generations, present or future."[25]

The fulfillment of economic and social human rights at the national level depends on the defense of global public goods internationally. Global public goods include the following: international peace and the prevention of deadly conflict; health and the eradication of disease; financial stability and debt abatement; equitable development and poverty alleviation; refugee and migrant worker protections; and environmental sustainability and the preservation of the global commons.[26] These goods are all nonexcludable and nonrivalrous in consumption. These global public goods are frighteningly undersupplied. Furthermore, acting alone individual nations cannot provide for these basic needs of each of their citizens. It is only through multilateral action in international law and international organization that these global public goods can be fulfilled.

Fundamental needs of all human beings include a healthy environment, nutrition, shelter, sanitation, health care, and education. I believe that these economic and social human needs should be classified as global public goods. The satisfaction of these public goods makes life possible. The human needs these public goods fulfill are universal. Economic and social human rights are claims for the fulfillment of these human needs and basic public goods.

Current market mechanisms unfortunately make some of these human needs excludable and rivalrous in consumption. But, it does not have to be that way. Individual consumption of food, for example, should not reduce the amount available for consumption by others, that is, nonrivalry in consumption. There is enough food for all. The same applies to the provision of education, health care, sanitation, and shelter. Individual consumption of these human needs should not limit others' consumption.

It is true that there is a difference in excludability between, for example, health care and clean air. It is impossible to withhold clean air from the rich and the poor alike. Health care, on the other hand, can be provided only to those with money. But there are more similarities than differences between these public goods. They are both essential for the well-being of the individual, the stability of society, and the efficient functioning of the economy overall. Classifying these basic human needs—a healthy environment, nutrition, shelter, sanitation, health care, and education—as global public goods clarifies their central importance. With modern industrial production techniques and new technologies, all citizens can enjoy each of these public goods without detracting from the enjoyment of others.

A central divergence in IPE theory between conservatives, liberals, and structuralists is over the degree to which market mechanisms can provide for these basic public goods. Conservatives argue for market-based solutions with minimal state intervention.[27] Liberals, while not wanting to disrupt market efficiency, argue for state action when confronted with market failure. Structuralists assert that basic public goods should be taken out of the market altogether and, with structural reforms of global governance, guaranteed to all people.

There are clear difficulties in enforcing private property rights on these public goods. In addition to the free-rider problem already discussed, it is questionable whether markets really are the right resource allocation mechanism. My concern is with creating a system that meets basic human needs and allows each individual to live a life of human dignity. An individual with few financial resources should not be denied health care, sanitation, clean water, and so on. Is it possible to live a life of dignity when one lives in fear of homelessness, hunger, and sickness? Examine the right to food. The private market cannot be relied on to distribute food to all. The poor and hungry may not be able to command the required purchasing power and are thus denied a life of dignity. Food security should not be subject to market fluctuations, but considered a public good.[28]

There are certain public goods that governments are now empowered to enforce, including the task of providing security from external threats and the protection of citizens against force, fraud, theft, and violence. It is generally understood that the market is the wrong mechanism to provide national defense or police protection. Defense and police protection are public goods, nonexcludable and nonrivalrous in consumption. Ecological balance, nutrition, shelter, sanitation, health care, and education should be added to this list of public goods that the state has the legal responsibility to protect.

There are well-known arguments for state involvement in the provision of public goods, especially when negative externalities are produced with market failure. For example, there is strong support for government-led campaigns for immunization against contagious diseases. If left solely to individual choice, the extent of immunization in a society will typically fall short of the socially desirable amount. State involvement is necessary in order to avoid exposure of the entire population to the contagious disease. Similar arguments are made regarding sanitation and environmental protection in general.[29]

There is a class of commodities to which all people can make human rights claims: nutrition, a healthy environment, sanitation, shelter, clothing, primary and secondary education, and basic health care. If our concern is avoiding destitution and achieving equality based on the freedom to achieve and the capability to function (see the discussion of Amartya Sen later in this chapter), access to these commodities should not depend on the ability to pay. This category of economic goods and social rights deserves special attention.[30]

When judging a government's performance, we should examine the availability of those basic needs necessary for the exercise of basic freedoms. Satisfaction of basic needs simply makes life possible. It creates the possibility of living a life of dignity. Defining public goods in relation to the fulfillment of basic human needs clarifies the urgent stakes at risk. Human needs are a prerequisite for the continuation of life. Their fulfillment makes living possible.[31]

The outlined proposals for the Global New Deal in chapter 8 demonstrate the ways in which states can act through international organization and international law to protect global public goods. There are a variety of reforms and measures that can be implemented in international organizations to guarantee the provision of global public goods. Global public goods are the foundation of the Global New Deal. It is not utopian to imagine a world where these global public goods are adequately supplied. There are clear policy options to secure their attainment.

But first, a further discussion of globalization is in order. "Globalization" refers to certain structural changes in the global political economy. Some of the most significant changes include: the liberalization of national economies; the growth of world trade; innovation in information technology; the creation of new centers of authority beyond the state; and global financial insecurity.[32] Successful public policy must take into account these forces of globalization limiting state power and often harming global public goods. Does the nation-state even have the ability to protect the economic and social human rights of its citizens? How are the principles of IPE—efficiency, autonomy, equity, and order—achieved in this new interdependent era? Does the state still have the power to protect the public goods (national and global) of its citizens?

Economic and Social Human Rights and Globalization

It is undoubtedly true that more progress has been made in the area of economic and social human rights by development organizations than by human rights organizations. Economic and social rights have been a low priority within both the UN human rights machinery and the nongovernmental organization (NGO) human rights networks. This perhaps should not be surprising. Seen only as individual entitlements, human rights are a difficult conceptual framework from which to tackle structural violence in the global economy. Structural violence refers to the denial of subsistence rights to the most vulnerable sectors as a result of the workings of economic and social institutions. These economic and social human rights violations are often unintended and unanticipated. It is more difficult to shame agribusiness, the WTO, the IMF, or free trade than it is to point a finger at a brutal dictator torturing prisoners. A framework of legal positivism is particularly limiting, as there are few judicial remedies for victims of structural violence. Perhaps judicial remedies are not the answer for victims of development-induced violations. Instead, we should focus on economic policies and political remedies that challenge and reform these economic structures.

Economic and social rights create obligations for governments to enact policies and measures that create the proper environment for these rights to flourish. The duty of citizens and governments is to support the policies, institutions, and agencies that meet these social needs. These are legal obligations and not simply altruism. Ensuring the economic and social rights found in human rights law requires that states guarantee that all public and private actors respect these norms. States are bound to respect, protect, and fulfill economic and social rights (see chapter 3).

In this era of economic globalization, is the state still able to fulfill these obligations? On the one hand, globalization has diminished the ability of all states to control economic outcomes that affect the well-being of their citizens. Market forces challenge state sovereignty over economic resources including capital and labor markets. On the other hand, states remain the central actors in economic planning even as they are often pounded by these forces of economic globalization. Although their economic power has diminished, they still can enact policies to respect, protect, and fulfill economic and social rights. The legal positivist approach has continued vitality and relevance even in this economically interdependent world system.

Globalization thus reveals the following paradox:

- the relative loss of state power, and
- the growing relevance of state power.

The Relative Loss of State Power

As noted, the first contradiction about the legal positivist approach to economic and social human rights concerns the role of the state in this era of globalization. It remains true that in most of the world the state remains the most viable entity in international politics. Nevertheless, throughout the world the state's authority and supremacy has been undermined by forces that it cannot control. The state's power is particularly circumscribed in the economic arena. The promotion and implementation of economic and social rights cannot be solely limited to the realm of the state. In this new era, the specific areas of state responsibility for economic and social rights must be related to actual state power. International entities with more economic power than many states must also be held accountable for the protection of economic and social human rights.[33]

The forces of economic globalization are perhaps causing more funda-mental transformations of our planet's economic and social life than at any time since the Treaty of Westphalia in 1648. The Treaty of Westphalia marked the emergence of the nation-state as the primary sovereign unit in international relations. James N. Rosenau characterizes this current period as one of "postinternational" relations, by which he means that the world system can no longer be solely or primarily categorized as consisting of relations between nations.[34] He coins the word "fragmagration" to capture the dual process of global integration and global fragmentation. He hopes that the label "highlight[s] the large extent to which the global system is so disaggregated that it lacks overall patterns and, instead, is marked by var-ious structures of systemic cooperation and subsystemic conflicts."[35]

The commanding principles underlying economic globalization include the primacy of economic growth; the opening of borders to capital move-ments; the removal of all restrictions on trade; the removal of government regulations that infringe on the market; the promotion of voracious con-sumerism; and the elevation of the TNC as the key actor in worldwide development. New technology has allowed these principles to be rapidly implemented. As a result of this globalization process, the state's power has been weakened significantly in the economic and social realm.

These economic principles represent the dominant ideology of our time; they define the accepted way of understanding the modern world. This hegemonic ideology has been termed "neoliberalism."[36] Classical economic "liberalism"[37] emphasizes free enterprise, the market, and indi-vidual initiative and responsibility. "Neo" refers to a renewed drive to remove the state from interfering in the market. In practice, neoliberalism has meant the abandonment of efforts to reduce the economic extremes between the few very wealthy at the top and the poor majority at the bot-tom. The neoliberal agenda argues for minimal governmental actions toward the protection of public goods.

The UN has been slow to respond to the challenge of economic global-ization and neoliberalism. The UN as an organization of states embraces Westphalian principles of sovereign power in its charter.[38] Law creation at the UN revolves around measures to hold states accountable to interna-tional standards and laws. The international human rights movement to a large degree has operated within this framework. The profound impli-cations of the globalization process have not been adequately addressed through this prism of positivist international law. To be concerned about protecting international economic and social rights means expanding the focus beyond the state to other entities as well. Legal and political human rights approaches cannot be restricted to critiques of state action only. TNCs, IFIs, and other intergovernmental organizations (IGOs) must also be held accountable to meet human rights standards.

There is a destructive side to globalization that is hard to ignore. The

UN Development Program (UNDP) documents the rising poverty, home-lessness, landlessness, violence, and levels of anxiety about the future around the world. The UN Environment Program (UNEP) documents the breakdown of our natural world as evidenced by global climate change, species loss, ozone depletion, and air, soil, and water pollution.

Examine, for example, two critical economic assets necessary for generating income and production: land and capital. Three-quarters of the world's income poor depend on agriculture for their livelihood. According to the UNDP, about a quarter of the rural poor are landless or do not have adequate security of tenure or title. Furthermore, even those who have land often have holdings too small or unproductive to provide any security. Capital is necessary to take advantage of market opportunities such as investments in small business or using new farm equipment. Credit can help families through crisis without having to resort to other measures such as taking children out of school; however, according to the UNDP, only 2 to 5 percent of the 500 million poorest households in the world have access to institutional credit.[39]

What has globalization meant for the developing countries? UN statistics reveal the following:

- Two-thirds of all foreign direct investment goes to only eight developing countries. More than one-half of all developing countries receive none.[40]
- In the 1990s, real commodity prices (adjusted for inflation) were 45 percent lower than those in the 1980s, and 10 percent lower than the lowest level during the Great Depression.[41]
- Over the last twenty-five years, the terms of trade for the LDCs have declined a cumulative 50 percent.[42]
- The final result of globalization is startling. The share in global income of the poorest 20 percent of the world's people now stands at 1.1 percent, down from 1.4 percent in 1991 and 2.3 percent in 1960. The ratio of income of the top 20 percent to that of the poorest 20 percent rose from thirty to one in 1960, to sixty-one to one in 1991, and to a new high of seventy-eight to one in 1994.[43]

Jose Bengoa, the special rapporteur for the UN Commission on Human Rights, maintains that since severe inequality in income distribution is always linked to poverty, a more equitable distribution of wealth is key to the full enjoyment and realization of human rights. Thus, he argues, income distribution should become an economic and social indicator used by the World Bank, the IMF, and the UNDP. The globalization of poverty will only worsen if these devastating trends are not altered.[44]

In May 1998, the UN Economic Rights Committee issued a statement on "Globalization and Economic, Social and Cultural Rights." The Economic

Rights Committee noted ways in which economic globalization and neoliberalism are detrimental to and incompatible with economic and social rights. The right to just and favorable conditions of work, for example, is threatened by an excessive emphasis on competitiveness. The right to social security is relegated increasingly to the private sphere, providing no security to the aged. Cuts in basic health care and education for the poor are made in the name of fiscal responsibility to meet the monetary requirements and pecuniary demands from global financial institutions, including the IMF. The Economic Rights Committee calls for a "renewed commitment to respect economic, social and cultural rights" in the midst of these global forces.[45]

In this era of globalization, how do states fulfill their international legal obligations to respect, protect, and fulfill economic and social rights?

The Growing Relevance of State Power

What is the state to do in these conditions of extreme vulnerability and sensitivity to global economic forces it is unable to control? Should the state continue to be the focus of efforts to address violations of economic and social human rights? What realistic expectations can be placed on the state to uphold and implement policies and programs to fulfill the duties required by international economic and social human rights law?

While all economic actors (including TNCs and IFIs) whose actions have an impact on the lives of the most vulnerable sectors must be held accountable to economic and social human rights law, the state remains the key player. Economic globalization is not an excuse for a government to shirk its legal duties under international law to carry out its social and economic obligations. Furthermore, slowdowns in economic growth, drops in commodity prices that have a negative impact on export earnings, and even natural disasters cannot justify a refusal to protect the most vulnerable.

At this point, we must move beyond human rights law and legal positivism to the realm of international political economy. The legal approach to guaranteeing these basic subsistence rights can only take us so far. To understand why a state has these legal duties, even in times of recession and natural calamity, it is vital to examine the economic policies that can be utilized to meet these responsibilities.

In the midst of the overall negative trends in income distribution as a result of globalization (outlined earlier), there are some success stories. In fact, there are a number of key economic lessons that can be extrapolated from these cases that point to the continued centrality of the state in economic policy making. While there is no universal blueprint that states can follow to guarantee growth, equity, and justice in their development models, there are policies that can be utilized to meet the obligations found in international law to protect, respect, and fulfill economic and social human rights and, by doing so, shield the most vulnerable.

One of the most striking facets of UN statistics is that the link between meeting basic human needs and economic growth is often not very close. Human development continues to advance around the world despite periodic economic decline and worsening gross national product (GNP). This was even true in the 1980s, the "lost decade," which had a devastating impact on the lives and living standards of 1.5 billion people. The 1980s were marked by drops in incomes and living standards more severe in most cases than anything experienced in the Great Depression of the 1930s. Yet, despite these conditions in two-thirds of the developing countries, there was an acceleration in the rate at which child mortality was reduced. Richard Jolly writes: "For nearly seventy countries, child mortality was reduced at a faster rate in the 1980s than in the 1960s or 1970s. Moreover, the regions with acceleration in the rate of reduction of child mortality were the regions of economic decline—while countries with slow rates of improvement in child mortality were those of accelerating economic growth."[46]

One conclusion to be drawn is that there is no reason to wait for improvements in economic growth to attack child mortality or other dimensions of social development, such as expanding basic education, access to clean water and sanitation, and improvements in nutrition. Economic policies of social development need to be linked to the duties of states to meet their legal obligations in economic and social human rights law.

The UNDP *Human Development Report* attempts to quantify key elements of social development in its well-known index. The Human Development Index measures a country's achievements in life expectancy, education and literacy, and basic income. As outlined in chapter 3, the Human Poverty Index significantly advances these measures and presents a deeper understanding of true human capabilities.[47] Paul Streeten details social development as a three-dimensional process: (1) social services (health and education) and social transfers (social security and safety nets); (2) economic access and productive returns (livelihood generation and employment); and (3) social integration (peace and absence of violence).[48] The UN Summit of Social Development in 1995 focused on three aspects: poverty, unemployment, and social integration.

It is now abundantly clear that crucial aspects of social development can occur despite low income levels and limited industrialization and modernization. Low-income countries can achieve levels of health and education comparable to industrialized states. The low-income success stories include Sri Lanka, Kerala (India), Botswana, Barbados, and Costa Rica. In all cases, state action for social development was a priority and necessary policies were implemented regardless of the pace of economic growth.

Santosh Mehrotra outlines the common successful policies of these countries as including:

- state-supported basic public services
- investment in health and education before economic take-off
- resource allocation to health and education well above the average for developing countries
- investment in basic education that preceded the improvement in the health status
- interventions that favored the status of women
- attempts at ensuring a nutritional floor for the population, and specific health and education interventions to ensure the effectiveness of these services[49]

Rich and poor states have legal obligations to make every effort to respect, protect, and fulfill economic and social human rights. This task is clearly more difficult for resource poor states. But resource scarcity does not relieve a state from conscientiously striving to meet minimum obligations, including minimal levels of essential foodstuffs, primary health care, basic shelter and housing, and basic education. If the state of Kerala—with one of the lowest rates of economic growth in the world and very little industrialization amid a decline in agricultural production—can still ensure access to basic health care and primary education to all its citizens, then there is absolutely no reason why other states can not equally guarantee these economic and social human rights.

Despite a much larger per capita income, Brazil still has a lower life expectancy than Sri Lanka. Why? Because Sri Lanka implemented a successful public action plan for social development. Botswana managed to increase life expectancy for its population from forty-eight to sixty-seven years and Mauritius from sixty to about seventy years.[50] The UN's Economic Rights Committee is absolutely correct in its evaluation of resources and rights. The lack of resources should not be an excuse to fail to implement public policies to protect and provide basic economic and social human rights.

A key component to the success stories in human development has been the education of women. Amartya Sen focuses on the notion of women's agency, which is the freedom women have to engage in work outside the home, receive an education, have ownership rights, and earn an independent income. When these economic and social rights are protected, women's well-being is enhanced.[51] Mehrotra demonstrates the links between female adult literacy and positive health outcomes. High education indicators preceded health breakthroughs. The education of women strengthened their earning capacity, their caretaking capacity, and their control over resources.

Women's resource control and caretaking capacity comprise one of the conditions for adequate nutrition, along with household food security, access to health services, and a healthy environment. . . . Maternal literacy and schooling is known to be associated with a more efficient management of limited household resources, greater utilization of available health services, better health-care practices, lower fertility, and more child-centered caring behavior. Moreover, it raises the awareness of the means to overcome problems and generates effective political demand. In general, therefore, women's education has an enormous effect on nutrition and health, in the long run probably one of the most important.[52]

Countries that were committed to a program of social development dedicated approximately 5 to 8 percent of their gross domestic product (GDP) to health and education.[53] Defense expenditures were not significant in most of the high-achieving countries.[54] Throughout the crisis of the 1980s, government expenditures in health and education as a proportion of GDP held up in all these countries. The global economic recession and structural adjustment did not interrupt macroeconomic priority given to health and education.[55]

These conclusions were further confirmed in the 1998 *Social Watch* report published by the Instituto Del Tercer Mundo in Montevideo, Uruguay. Social Watch is a transnational coalition of organizations that gathers data on governments' compliance with their commitments made during the 1995 Copenhagen Summit on Social Development and the 1995 Beijing Women's Conference. Their country-by-country analysis and Index of Fulfilled Commitments provide useful information to assess methods of meeting economic and social human rights. These reports demonstrate again the importance of public policy and investment in human capital in any strategy to alleviate poverty. Public spending on health and education are again proven to be key ingredients to successful social development. Strategies that stressed the full utilization of human resources proved to be a sound path to poverty reduction.[56]

Compare Costa Rica and Mexico. Costa Rica has a tradition of universal coverage of basic social services. Even in economic recessions, suitable allocations for preventive health care and primary education are made so that these services continue to reach the poor effectively. Mexico has no such tradition. Instead, health expenditures focus on curative (not preventative) measures, and spending is geared to higher education. The *Social Watch* report further documents the ways in which Costa Rica supports labor-intensive development in agriculture and tourism that effectively integrated peasants and unskilled workers into the formal economy. Mexico, on the other hand, is now strongly dependent on foreign capital, employment in agriculture and manufacturing is unstable, sustainable development seems out of reach, and poverty reduction strategies have failed.[57]

The example of Costa Rica reaffirms key lessons from Southeast Asia.

Most observers have concluded that the rapid reduction of poverty in Southeast Asia was fundamentally due to public provision of social services including public education and basic health care. Compare this success in human development in Southeast Asia with South Asia. The poor in Southeast Asia have improved opportunities to escape poverty compared to the poor in South Asia.

Constanza Moreira concludes that "labour-intensive growth combined with expanded access to basic services is the best guarantee for egalitarian growth. Experience shows that support for building *human capital* (reallocation of public spending to health and education services), for the development of sectors where poverty is concentrated, and for labor-intensive growth models contributes to a positive result when dealing with poverty reduction."[58]

The legal positivist approach to international economic and social human rights may be correct in focusing attention on the role of the state. It is clear that the state must take the lead in promoting social development. Economic growth, poverty reduction, and social development cannot be left to the forces of the market and globalization. The state can institute policies to address all aspects of human development. Human rights law can be used to hold states accountable to basic norms designed to protect human dignity. And furthermore, as we will see later on, states can act through international organizations to protect global public goods.

The state's role in implementing public policies to protect the economic and social rights of its citizens is clear. Policy options exist and have proven successful. Yet debates continue and areas of unclarity linger. Disagreements remain particularly strong over the issue of equality and the relationship of equality to the fulfillment of economic and social human rights. Should state policies focus on strategies to achieve income equality? What is the difference between "income equality" and "economic equality"? I thus turn now to the relationship between equality and economic and social human rights.

Economic and Social Human Rights and Economic Equality

It is of extreme significance that all the major ethical and political proposals of the twentieth century in some form or another are justified on the basis of equality,[59] from conservative theories of equality in libertarian rights,[60] to liberal theories of equality in liberty and distribution of primary goods,[61] to Marxist theories of equality in class power and wealth.[62] Article 1 of the Universal Declaration of Human Rights declares: "All human beings are born free and equal in dignity and rights." It is in fact hard to imagine an ethical theory or a viable political program in the current period not embracing some form of equality.

Yet, differences clearly remain over conceptions of the proper subject of this equality norm. What is to be evaluated equally? How is equality in "dignity and rights" determined? What does it mean to argue in favor of equality for all? Equality of what? Resources? Abilities? Access to power? Happiness? Liberty? Property?

Human beings are not created equal. Some of us are born with physical or mental limitations while others are blessed with athletic or mental prowess and ability. Most of us are "average" or below in intelligence measurements while others score brilliantly. A lucky few have households of abundance with few monetary worries while the majority of us organize our lives around the cash nexus. Some of us are more spiritually inclined than others. Significant differences exist over requirements to achieve happiness. This list could go on and on. Combine the never-ending ways in which equality could be evaluated with the fact that we are a heterogeneous species, and the utility of the norm must be questioned. Is the concept of any use beyond rhetorical exuberance?[63]

International human rights law, drafted and adopted at the UN and ratified by states, embraces norms of equality. Certain key economic rights are to be implemented with equity and equality among all member states of the UN.

Economic and social human rights, as adopted in international law, attempt to be responsive to egalitarian, utilitarian, and libertarian ethical perspectives. Egalitarian principles rely on the ethical axiom that all human beings are to be treated as morally equal. Utilitarians seek to maximize the well-being of all people, even if in the short term that means sacrificing equal treatment and equal opportunity. Libertarians aspire to fairness in the procedures by which the world functions (e.g., no theft, no fraud, and so on), whatever the equity resulting.

The Universal Declaration of Human Rights embraces all ethical frameworks and explicitly avoids identifying with any particular moral philosophy. The document is thus a limited guide for the development of a strategy for the actual achievement of the rights it enumerates. For example, as already noted, article 1 is clearly responsive to egalitarian principles: "All human beings are born free and equal in dignity and rights." A utilitarian, on the other hand, could point to principles in articles 25, 26, and 28 that present economic and social claims for the well-being of all peoples. And libertarian principles can be found in article 12, with regard to "privacy, family, home or correspondence," and in article 17, concerning private property rights. Moral philosophers could make deontological and consequential arguments for each, or all, of the UDHR's articles.

Human rights law thus does not help to clarify or resolve the conflicts between ethical frameworks. For example, national development strategies could focus on egalitarian principles and invest in their poorest regions. An egalitarian will argue that those regions lagging behind in roads, industry, communication facilities, and agriculture should be the center of investments. Yet, from a utilitarian perspective this might not make sense. A utilitarian could argue that investment in more advanced regions might result in more rapid growth that would potentially make all areas better off. From this perspective, public investments should be made where they yield the highest return.[64]

Human rights discourse can, therefore, only take us so far. It does not help us resolve these conflicts. Egalitarians, utilitarians, and libertarians can all refer to human rights law to support their particular ethical paradigm. All base their ethical framework on some principles of "equality." The politician's personal value system—no matter what it is—can most likely find some validation somewhere in human rights law.

A useful approach to overcoming these ethical dilemmas is to try to determine what is absolutely fundamental to the principle of equality. What constitutes its base? For the equal consideration of any interest to have true meaning, economic equality, as distinct from income equality, must be upheld. Economic and social human rights are linked to the realization of economic equality.

Economic equality can be defined as the equal provision of public goods, including nutrition, sanitation, shelter, clothing, primary and secondary education, and basic health care. Economic equality forms the foundation for achieving economic and social human rights. International and national public policy should focus on the measures to guarantee to all the attainment of these public goods.

Sen emphasizes the distinction between income inequality and economic inequality. He believes that policy debates have been distorted by an overemphasis on income poverty and income inequality "to the neglect of deprivations that relate to other variables, such as unemployment, ill health, lack of education, and social exclusion." Many of the criticisms of egalitarian schemes for income equality do not apply to the broader notions of economic equality. "For example, giving a larger share of income to a person with more needs—say, due to a disability—can be seen as militating against the principle of equalizing incomes, but it does not go against the broader precepts of economic equality, since the greater need for economic resources due to the disability must be taken into account in judging the requirements of economic equality." Economic equality is contingent on "public policy issues with strong economic components: the financing of health care and insurance, provision of public education, arrangements for local security and so on."[65]

Global Social Injustice: Preventing Economic Equality

In international relations, issues of economic equality are often tied to arguments for "distributive justice." Justice usually implies a set of claims.

Equity and equality represent one set of claims that are said to be necessary for true justice. Human rights represent other types of claims to a certain kind of treatment that are also tied to conceptions of justice. Claims have also been based on such precepts as merit, need, fairness, and duty. These claims are applicable to all and impose obligations of action.

If social and economic structures produce unfair disadvantages for some while benefitting others, then claims to distributive action can be justified. The redistribution of economic benefits throughout society may be necessary to ameliorate actions of injustice and unfairness toward individuals and groups within society. Few today argue that true respect for equality requires a total egalitarian distribution of all economic goods. But then what type and extent of redistribution is required? Perhaps the answer to this question lies in the equal distribution and provision of national and global public goods—that is, economic equality.

Claims for distributive justice often are the result of what has been called "social injustice." Social injustice refers to unfair and inequitable structures and policies of the political, legal, economic, and social institutions of a society. When these structures favor some individuals or groups over other individuals and groups, a situation of social injustice exists. It is not just the case of individual action, but of the overall structures and policies of a society or state. For example, a corrupt business executive who embezzles funds and abuses his or her labor force may be committing an egregious action. But this would not be a case of social injustice unless the economic and legal system promoted and encouraged such behavior (Mobutu's Zaire comes to mind).[66]

The distribution of economic benefits is often tied to issues of social justice. Disparity of wealth itself may not be a case of injustice. However, worldwide poverty and malnutrition *as a result of national and international policies and structures* are a moral issue of social injustice. There is a relation between human suffering and the structures of the international economic system. An unfair outcome is produced; a right is violated. Equality thus involves issues of the justice of national and international economic institutions.

A minimum agenda of economic and social rights includes the right to food of an adequate nutritional value, to clothing, to shelter, to primary health care, to clean water and sanitation, to primary education, and to a healthy, sustainable environment. This "core" of rights establishes a minimum standard. Economic equality may be seen as the fulfillment of this minimum standard.

Many studies have demonstrated that there are sufficient resources and economic and technical knowledge to ensure that the basic rights of practically everyone in the world could be guaranteed within a decade or so—without huge cost to taxpayers in the developed world (see the twenty-twenty discussion in chapter 8). The right to food, for example, can be met in the modern era. Unfortunately, however, basic human needs and economic equality are often undermined and sabotaged by structural forces within the global economy.

Global Social Justice: Creating Economic Equality

To be classified as a human right, economic and social rights claims must be fundamental, universal, and clearly specifiable. "Fundamental" refers to the protection of a minimally decent, rather than a maximally comfortable, life. "Universal" implies that the right should be applicable to all, regardless of the level of development a country has reached. And "specifiable" means it is possible to determine whether a right has been upheld or violated.[67]

There has been a great deal of debate as to the "core" of economic and social rights. The UN Economic Rights Committee has set itself the task of defining a minimum core under each right, which all countries will be obliged to uphold (see chapter 3). There are certain grounds on which all human beings deserve equal respect. David Beetham argues the need to specify the most general preconditions required for a decent life. One such precondition is the material means of existence (others would include physical integrity or security and the enjoyment of basic liberties). "These necessary conditions of human agency constitute the basis of human rights."[68]

In a similar vein, Henry Shue develops a framework of "basic rights." He argues that it is fraudulent to guarantee someone a right they are unable to realize.[69] Basic rights, including subsistence, are essential because without them other rights cannot be fulfilled. Shue calls this the transitivity principle for rights: "If everyone has a right to y, and the enjoyment of x is necessary for the enjoyment of y, then everyone also has a right to x."[70] Rosa Luxemburg articulated a similar concern. She argued that to promise the working class the right to self-determination was equal to telling them they had the right to eat off of gold plates. She believed that those whose lives were at the mercy of the dictates of capital had little real control (or self-determination) over their futures.[71]

A further distinction also helps to clarify the human rights approach: obligations of conduct and of result. Obligations of conduct (active or passive) point "to behavior which the dutyholder should follow or abstain from." For example, the obligation not to torture is an obligation of conduct. Obligations of result are more concerned with achievements than with the choice of a line of action. For example, the elimination of the occurrence of hunger is an obligation of result. However, neither obligation necessarily requires state activity. The objective circumstances, the context, will determine the nature of state involvement. For example, in the case of food distribution it may be that by not interfering with market incentives and individual control over resources, the state can best avoid hunger. Yet, whether active or passive, the obligations of conduct and result require that the state uphold equal freedom from hunger.[72]

The antithesis of this human rights approach to food can be found in Emperor Haile Selassie's comments during the Ethiopian famines of 1973, explaining the absence of famine relief measures undertaken by his government: "We have said wealth has to be gained through hard work. We have said those who don't work starve." Others quote the Bible: "If any would not work neither should he eat."[73] The emperor's comments may seem extreme today. In times of famine, there are probably very few conservatives, liberals, or radicals who would argue against charitable aid of some form.

However, the reality of today's world is that there is the equivalent of an Ethiopian famine in the daily lives of millions and acute poverty affecting at least 1.2 billion people in the developing world. Is this destitution and poverty the result of laziness and refusal to work? It is perhaps easy to scoff at Emperor Selassie's comments since the plight of the tens of thousands affected in the 1970s in Ethiopia was obviously not the result of their refusal to work. Rather, the world witnessed the complete breakdown of the economic and legal structures within Ethiopia. Because of this, the obligations of conduct and obligations of result were clear. So why are the obligations of conduct and result toward the victims of structural violence in today's world not clear?

Many argue that, unfortunately, there are no alternatives to a system that produces winners and many losers. Others maintain that international and local state action to address issues of economic equality will, in the end, only make things worse. These arguments, marshaled against distributive justice and economic equality, often include the following points:

- Any large-scale redistribution would produce disincentives to production. If this occurred, the position of those on the bottom would in fact be lowered instead of raised.
- Such policies would impact negatively on capital accumulation, stifling future economic diversification and growth.
- An economic system that is centrally planned and directed by the state stifles the creativity of individuals.
- The content of economic and social rights remains extremely vague and thus not legally enforceable. As a consequence, the obligations that flow from these rights are not even rhetorically acknowledged, let alone acted on.
- Universal coverage does not restrict the benefit to those who are truly needy (i.e., those who are poor for reasons beyond their control), and it thus dulls the incentive to work.

However, these arguments are perhaps more vulnerable than they initially appear for the following reasons:

- Meeting basic human needs does not limit economic growth. On the contrary, attaining minimal economic rights for all can reinforce development objectives and strengthen patterns of growth (as demonstrated in the Republic of Korea, Japan, Sweden, and elsewhere).
- The myth of a trade-off between growth and equity has been exposed and should be forever discarded. Investment in "human capital," for example, policies based on principles of equity, can have a very positive impact on growth. Japan and Sweden, for example, have combined rapid growth with programs to meet the basic needs of all their citizens. Key to many of the economic success stories is the redistribution of wealth (not income) and attention to economic equality through land reform, rural infrastructure, primary and secondary education, health care, and so on. Investments in human capital can generate income. For example, scholars have noted how Brazil's GDP has been slowed as a result of its inattention to economic equality. One study concluded that if in 1960 the Republic of Korea had had Brazil's inequality, its GDP in 1985 would have been 15 percent lower.[74]
- The only incentive for a person who lacks freedom from hunger is to find food. One's life is consumed with survival needs. Achieving minimal economic rights creates motivational incentives because, often for the first time, the person who was destitute is now able to consider life options.
- Furthermore, special treatment to achieve economic equality will enhance motivational incentives for people with disabilities, the elderly, and groups continuously denied equal opportunity (women, minorities, and so on). Sen documents how inequality of capability is often the result of gender and age. In these situations, special treatment to create economic equality would therefore generate new opportunities and motivational incentives for these disadvantaged groups.[75]
- It is possible to establish and meet a minimum threshold for the realization of economic and social rights. Bard-Anders Andreassen proposes that all governments establish a nationwide system of identifying local needs and opportunities for the enjoyment of economic and social rights. In particular, the needs of groups that have the greatest difficulties in the enjoyment of these rights should be addressed. Different approaches most suitable to local conditions should be explored.[76] There is no general model applicable to all settings. This approach corresponds to the "Limburg Principles": "The achievement of economic, social and cultural rights may be realized in a variety of political settings. There is no single road to their full realization. Successes and failures have been registered in both mar-

ket and non market economies, in both centralized and decentralized political structures."[77]

John Kenneth Galbraith's proposal for "popular consumption criteria" to be the anchor of development strategies of the LDCs has considerable merit today. He argues that development should be organized around the living standards (consumption requirements) of the present and prospective typical citizen. Development would then concentrate on consumption that is purchasable by people with a low income. A major emphasis would be placed on food, clothing, shelter, education, and medicines—the dominant items of the low-income family. The same rule then would operate equally against automobiles, expensive dwellings, and luxury consumer goods. As a result, economic planning would be concentrated on the needs of the most numerous citizens. Those who are hungry would have a special claim on resources. Galbraith is not arguing for agriculture or for industry or even for light industry as opposed to heavy industry. Rather, he is arguing for whatever approach provides for the supplies of the typical citizen.[78]

Sen's capabilities approach deepens this discussion of economic equality and the achievement of global social justice. The capabilities approach is a clear normative framework useful for resolving some of the dilemmas in ethical theory and human rights law concerning equality and justice. It further provides a pathway for the creation of public policy to realize economic and social human rights.

Economic and Social Human Rights and the Capabilities Approach

Mary Robinson, the high commissioner for human rights, acknowledged the impact of Sen's capabilities approach in her remarks to the delegates attending the UN's Copenhagen Plus Five Conference in June 2000:

A new dialogue is taking place between development and human rights experts which has brought about convergences and given added depth to the law-based approaches of traditional human rights thinking. It has been enriched by Amartya Sen's work on capability rights. This approach recognizes that human development and human rights are mutually reinforcing in that they expand capabilities by protecting rights. This dialogue has contributed to the development of people-centered sustainable development.[79]

The link between human development and human rights was also clearly articulated in the *Human Development Report 2000*, published for the UNDP. "If human development focuses on the enhancement of the capabilities and freedoms that the members of a community enjoy, human rights represent the claims that individuals have on the conduct of individual and collective agents and on the design of social arrangements to facilitate or secure these capabilities and freedoms."[80]

Sen's capabilities approach provides a framework for the realization of economic and social human rights. Sen cogently argues that an adequate way of considering "real" equality of opportunities is through equality of capabilities. The focus is not on outcomes, but on the *ability* to function and the *freedom* to achieve. He argues that a person's *capability to achieve functions* that he or she has reason to value provides us with a general approach to assess equality and inequality. Functions include being well nourished, avoiding escapable morbidity and premature mortality, having self-respect, and being able to take part in the life of the community.[81]

Capability is directly related to the freedom to achieve valuable functionings. Sen believes that by concentrating directly on freedom as such rather than on the means to achieve freedom, we can better identify the real alternatives we have. Capability reflects a person's freedom to achieve well-being. "In the capability-based assessment of justice, individual claims are not to be assessed in terms of the resources or primary goods the persons respectively hold, but by the freedoms they actually enjoy to choose the lives that they have reason to value." Capability is thus distinguished from both the distribution of primary goods (and other resources) and final achievements.[82]

Why is this important? A person with a disability could have more primary goods, yet less capability and freedom than an individual without a disability. Or take another example from Sen: "A person may have more income and more nutritional intake, but less freedom to live a well-nourished existence because of a higher basal metabolic rate, greater vulnerability to parasitic diseases, larger body size, or simply because of pregnancy. . . . Neither primary goods, nor resources more broadly defined, can represent the capability a person actually enjoys."[83] What a person needs to achieve this freedom may vary.

To have the "freedom to achieve" means having certain needs met in one way or another. Sen mentions well nourishment and avoidance of escapable morbidity. Poverty is a result of a deprivation of "some minimum fulfillment of elementary capabilities." As a result, equality does not refer to equal incomes or even equal resources. Rather, equality is based on the equal freedom to achieve. Everyone equally should have freedom of choice and freedom to achieve. One cannot assume the same results would be obtained by looking at the resources a person commands. Valuing freedom imposes more "exacting claims."[84] To be able to live as one would value, desire, and choose requires freedom from hunger, malaria, and other maladies. Inequalities across the world lead to a loss of basic freedoms such as preventable morbidity and escapable hunger.

The relationship between income and capability is affected by age, location, race, gender, and other social factors. Sen believes that no matter what foundational structure we opt for, the reorientation from an income-centered to capability-centered view gives us a better understanding of what is involved in the challenge of poverty.[85] An African American male in Harlem may have more "resources" and live in a country with a higher overall standard of living than a citizen of the state of Costa Rica. Yet, due to social achievements in Costa Rica (or Kerala, India, or Sri Lanka), the citizen from the LDC may have more freedom to achieve and capability to function.[86] These relatively poor countries may suffer income poverty, yet their focus on communal health services, medical care, and basic education has led to remarkable life expectancy rates. These insights can inform public policy for development and poverty alleviation. A country, even with a relatively low income, that guarantees health care and education to all can achieve remarkable results in terms of the length and quality of life of their population.

Policy makers interested in achieving economic and social human rights can find direction through the capabilities approach. IPE theories can be evaluated through this lens: which theory provides for the equal distribution of resources to provide for the opportunity for adequate functioning for all peoples, including women and racial minorities? The phrase "equal distribution of resources" leads us to issues of inequality. As noted, Sen's focus is on economic equality as opposed to income equality.

Sen's capabilities approach gives us the tools necessary for policy formation to address economic and social human rights. The capabilities approach helps us focus on what individuals need for adequate functioning. Sen asks us not to merely look at low income to determine "poverty," but rather examine the "deprivation of basic capabilities," reflected in "premature mortality, significant undernourishment (especially of children), persistent morbidity, widespread illiteracy and other failures." This shift in focus also allows us to tailor public policy to meet the needs of specific groups within societies who are denied basic capabilities and, thus, denied the freedom to achieve. This approach is thus of value to women and racial minorities who often face unequal conditions, discrimination, and lack of real opportunity.[87]

The capabilities approach allows us to look at the actual ways in which individuals and groups are given the freedom to achieve adequate functioning. What are the variations in the social climate? What are the differences in social conditions, including public education, crime and violence, health care and infectious disease, public facilities, and community relations? In a situation where a particular racial minority faces a social climate that hinders basic functioning, public policy can then address these issues.

In sum, the capabilities approach is a vehicle for overcoming structural violence and oppression. The capabilities approach to the evaluation of human societies requires that they be judged in terms of how well their members are able to achieve basic universal goods, such as sound health, adequate education, greater longevity, and so on. Sen argues that development should mean more than merely industrialization and GDP growth, or the mere satisfaction of individual's preferences, because a narrow focus on economic growth alone has not helped much to increase the basic capabilities of millions in the developing world.

"Development," Sen writes, "requires the removal of major sources of unfreedom: Poverty as well as tyranny, poor economic opportunities as well as systematic social deprivation, neglect of public facilities as well as intolerance or overactivity of repressive states."[88] A person's capability is severely diminished if he or she is chronically ill and ignorant. The practical policy implications of Sen's thesis are radical and offer a direction to foreign aid agencies and international organizations that promote economic development. Development must minimally include the following measures: substantial investment in public health, substantial investment in primary and secondary schooling, the enactment and enforcement of laws to eliminate all forms of discrimination against women and minorities, and the end of all forms of authoritarianism, with open public discussion of all governmental decisions.

These measures to enhance and protect human capabilities require attention to the provision of public goods. As discussed earlier, the globalized nature of our economy and society require that we now focus on global public goods. Since markets have historically failed to provide for global public goods, they are safeguarded only through action by governments and international organizations. The enhancement of human capabilities is fundamentally linked to the protection of global public goods. I now will turn to policies to protect human capabilities, global public goods, and economic equality.

The Global New Deal and IPE

Summary Observations

The Global New Deal is based on the premise that international organization is needed now more than ever. Due to the problems of "market failure," global public goods and economic equality will be continuously underprovided unless international mechanisms are created for their provision. Every nation and

Global New Deal Proposals

Global public goods, economic equality, and the capabilities approach are integral to the protection and fulfillment of economic and social human rights in our interdependent globalized economy. There is no one theory of IPE that successfully incorporates these essential ideas into its approach.

every citizen is vulnerable to forces they cannot individually control. It is only through cooperative action at the global level that these public goods will be protected and provided. States acting alone are no longer solely responsible for their fate in the global economy. State leaders can certainly make matters worse through greed, corruption, and wasteful spending on prestigious construction projects and bloated military budgets. But even the most fiscally disciplined, democratic, and responsible governments cannot control things like terms of trade, interest rates, exchange rates, commodity prices, market access, and so on. Thus, despite their focus on national local economic policy, the IMF and the World Bank admit that to an extent, globalization undermines national policy.

It is thus necessary to strengthen international organization and global governance if we are serious about ending global suffering. International policy coordination is a minimum requirement necessary to address the "externalities" of the global economy, including threats to the global commons and the new "global apartheid" between the "haves" and the "have nots."

The proposals of the Global New Deal in chapter 8 attempt to fill this gap and formulate policy to protect global public goods, generate economic equality, and create real equality of opportunity through equality of capabilities.

The Global New Deal calls for the establishment of a UN Economic Security Council to promote economic equality and a Global Public Goods Fund to finance these under provided necessities. The Economic Security Council could hold states accountable to their pledges to eliminate malnutrition and provide safe drinking water, primary health care, population stabilization, and access to basic education. The Economic Security Council and the Global Public Goods Fund are reforms recommended in global governance to protect, respect, and fulfill economic and social human rights (see chapter 8).

These proposed reforms can help mobilize state and civil society to shape economic policy along lines of efficiency, fairness, and sustainability. This belief in the utility and promise of international organization informs the proposals of the Global New Deal. These policy proposals link human rights and IPE strategies to overcome global suffering.

3

The United Nations and Economic and Social Human Rights

How does the UN approach economic and social human rights? How are these rights defined in international law? Is it possible to develop accurate indicators of social development to measure the achievement of economic and social human rights? How does the UN monitor and enforce a state's compliance with international human rights law? Are workers' interests in developed and developing countries furthered by enforcement of international economic and social standards? Is it possible to energize the global enforcement of these basic human rights and enact effective policies to protect the vulnerable during this period of rapid economic globalization?

As part of my class on International Cooperation, I travel to Geneva with students every two years to better understand the work of various international organizations, national missions to the UN, and nongovernmental organizations (NGOs). During our 1998 meetings, a series of incidents brought into sharp focus the current UN deadlock between the North and the South over economic and social human rights and development.

This impasse was strikingly visible in the approach to the internationally recognized "right to development."[1] The human rights officer of the Pakistani mission to the UN told us that the right to development was the most important human right. As a priority, his government would fight for the right to development to be included as part of the International Bill of Human Rights.[2] His stress on the critical importance to poor countries of development rights brought back the oft-quoted words of Leopold Senghor, the former president of Senegal: "[H]uman rights begin with breakfast."[3] Two days later at the U.S. mission to the UN, the U.S. human rights officer declared that the right to development was simply rhetoric and held no real meaning. The U.S. position was that this claimed "right" was impossible to implement and was pushed by the less developed countries (LDCs) to pressure the developed countries into increasing aid levels. The U.S. acceptance of the validity of development as a human right at the 1993 Vienna World Conference on Human Rights did not appear to change U.S. policy. After leaving these two meetings, it was hard to see how even a dialogue could move forward given these diametrically opposed positions.

Conflicts between the North and the South also surfaced in meetings with the World Trade Organization (WTO), the Office of the U.S. Trade Representative to the WTO, and the World Wide Fund for Nature (WWF). Prior to these meetings, a ruling by the WTO struck down U.S. legal protections for endangered sea turtles. The Eckerd College students I traveled with were very environmentally conscious, and they were concerned not only about this ruling, but also about how intertwined trade and environmental policies have become. According to the WWF, sea turtles are an internationally protected species endangered around the world by the loss of their habitat. They became an international trade issue with the advent of mechanized shrimp trawling, which by 1990 had caused some 100,000 adult turtles to drown each year in nets. This loss is easily preventable. A turtle excluder device has proven effective in keeping turtles out of the shrimp nets. The device is inexpensive, easy to install, and standard practice in more than a dozen countries. The United States not only required its domestic shrimp industry to use turtle excluders, but applied identical standards to countries selling shrimp in U.S. markets. In response, Malaysia, Thailand, India, and Pakistan filed a complaint to the WTO claiming that the requirement deprived them of market access guaranteed under most-favored-nation status. The WTO agreed with the four Asian countries. The United States must now open its markets to countries whose fishing methods threaten sea turtles.[4]

The WTO representative characterized U.S. policy as imperialistic. She claimed that the United States had no right to impose its environmental standards on the rest of the world. She sided with the shrimp fishermen in Malaysia whose jobs, she claimed, were threatened by turtle excluder devices.[5] The U.S. trade representative said that the United States would appeal this decision and referred us to President Bill Clinton's address to the WTO the previous week. President Clinton had declared, "We must do more to harmonize our goal of increasing trade with our goal of improving the environment and working conditions. . . . International trade rules must permit sovereign nations to exercise their right to set protective standards for health, safety, and the environment and biodiversity. Nations have a right to pursue those protections—even when they are stronger than international norms."[6]

These differences toward economic rights and development between the developed and less developed countries demonstrate the difficulty of achieving a global understanding of economic and social human rights. The United States not only undermines the right to development, but also refuses to ratify the Economic Rights Treaty (the International Covenant on Economic, Social and Cultural Rights),[7] which is strongly supported by the LDCs. Many LDCs continue to see not only environmental regulations, which are often strongly supported by developed countries, but also trade-labor linkages as impediments to their economic growth. For example, in 1996 developing countries succeeded in derailing the social clause movement—in other words, the attempt to link adherence to basic labor rights with membership in the WTO. The LDCs argued that the social clause would infringe on their sovereignty and deny them a legitimate comparative advantage. This opposition allowed the WTO to declare that it would not pursue the trade-labor linkage any further. Economic and social human rights thus exist within a global framework filled with discord, fragmentation, and dissension. Progress depends on overcoming the historical legacy of exploitation, and subsequent mistrust, between the North and the South.

This chapter examines key aspects of the UN approach to economic and social human rights in the following sections:

- Defining economic and social human rights
- Measuring economic and social human rights
- Monitoring and enforcing economic and social human rights
- Strengthening global compliance with economic and social human rights

Defining Economic and Social Human Rights

The UN approaches economic and social human rights through a framework of legal positivism, that is, rights are defined by what states have actually agreed to through consent.[8] Consent is most often demonstrated either through written agreement (treaty, convention, and so on) or through customary practice. A legal positivist looks to state treaties, customs, and general principles of international law as the primary sources of international economic and social human rights. These socially constructed legal principles of rights and obligations reflect the bias of the governing elites of global politics. Thus, for the most part the poor and dispossessed do not have a voice in the formation of the international legal rights that are often proclaimed in their name.[9]

Women have also traditionally been left out of the formation of international law (see chapter 6). The distinct needs and rights of women are not reflected in most international legal instruments. The private sphere where women often face both domestic violence and economic exploitation has not been adequately addressed through existing legal norms. The specific needs of women in relation to the biological functions of raising and breast-feeding children have also been inadequately addressed. The issue here is not just equality with men, but the distinct economic and social rights of women.

Conventions on economic and social rights have been developed by the UN-affiliated International Labor Organization (ILO). The ILO has adopted 177 conventions establishing labor standards on a wide range of issues from the most general (such as freedom of association) to the specific (such as road transport). The ILO has prioritized these standards and established the following basic human rights conventions: freedom of association and collective bargaining, abolition of forced labor, equal remuneration, and nondiscrimination in employment. Virginia Leary points out that these are the most widely ratified ILO conventions and are those to which the ILO devotes most of its attention. To many scholars, the ILO's basic human rights conventions form the corpus of minimum international labor standards or internationally recognized worker rights.[10]

The UN also has a corpus of international treaties addressing economic and social rights. The distinction between the two types of rights is generally seen as follows:

- Social rights are those rights necessary for an adequate standard of living (Universal Declaration of Human Rights [UDHR], article 25; Economic Rights Treaty, article 11; and Convention on the Rights of the Child, article 27). Paul Hunt includes rights to food, shelter, health, and education as key social rights.[11] Asbjørn Eide links social rights to "necessary subsistence rights—adequate food and nutrition rights, clothing, housing, and the necessary conditions of care."[12] The right to education affirms free and compulsory primary education and equal access to secondary and higher education. The right to health ensures access to adequate health care, nutrition, sanitation, and to clean water and air. The right to housing provides guarantees against forced eviction and access to a safe, habitable, and affordable home. The right to food requires that states cooperate in the equitable distribution of world food supplies and respect and assure the ability of people to feed themselves.[13]
- Economic rights, on the other hand, refer to the right to property (UDHR, article 17), the right to work (UDHR, article 23; Economic

Rights Treaty, article 6), and the right to social security (UDHR, articles 22 and 25; Economic Rights Treaty, article 9; and Convention on the Rights of the Child, article 26). The right to work denotes the opportunity to earn a living wage in a safe environment and embraces the freedom to organize and bargain collectively.[14]

In 1986, a group of distinguished experts in international law, meeting at the University of Limburg (Maastricht, the Netherlands), drafted guidelines on the nature and scope of states' obligations under the Economic Rights Treaty. "The Limburg Principles on the Implementation of the International Covenant on Economic, Social and Cultural Rights" (hereinafter the "Limburg Principles") have been extremely useful to human rights advocates, lawyers, and diplomats attempting to interpret the legal duties of states under this convention.[15] The "Limburg Principles" comprehensively summarized the state of international law in relation to economic and social rights as of 1986.

On the tenth anniversary of the "Limburg Principles," a group of experts again met in Maastricht to elaborate on the nature and scope of violations of economic, social, and cultural rights and appropriate responses and remedies. This 1997 meeting resulted in "The Maastricht Guidelines on Violations of Economic, Social and Cultural Rights" (hereinafter the "Maastricht Guidelines"), which reflect the evolution of international law since 1986 and clearly demonstrate the emerging consensus within the legal community as to state responsibility and accountability under the Economic Rights Treaty.[16]

These principles and guidelines are intended to outline what a state must do to meet the obligations and duties that flow from the economic, social, and cultural rights articulated in the Economic Rights Treaty, that is, the right to work, the right to housing, the right to health care, and so on. The experts were able to draw on the work of many others, including the constructive role played by the UN Economic Rights Committee and various UN conferences and reports.[17] As a result, the "Maastricht Guidelines" are a very clear summary of the current understanding of economic and social rights in international law.

The following are some key principles found in the "Maastricht Guidelines":

1. The state remains the primary actor responsible for implementing international economic and social rights. The guidelines claim to recognize the global forces at work at the end of the twentieth century weakening the state's ability to control their economic destiny. However, "as a matter of international law, the state remains ultimately responsible for guaranteeing the realization of these rights."[18] The UN's approach is to hold governments accountable

for the provision of basic social services, including health care, employment, and education.

2. States have obligations to respect, protect, and fulfill. This three-part approach to explaining economic and social rights was first formulated by Henry Shue.[19] Eide, as special rapporteur on the right to food, further developed these categories.[20]

> The obligation to *respect* requires States to refrain from interfering with the enjoyment of economic, social and cultural rights. Thus, the right to housing is violated if the State engages in arbitrary forced evictions. The obligation to *protect* requires States to prevent violations of such rights by third parties. Thus, the failure to ensure that private employers comply with basic labor standards may amount to a violation of the right to work or the right to just and favorable conditions of work. The obligation to *fulfill* requires States to take appropriate legislative, administrative, budgetary, judicial and other measures toward the full realization of such rights. Thus, the failure of States to provide essential primary health care to those in need may amount to a violation.[21]

3. The guidelines outline violations through acts of commission (direct action by states) and omission (failure of states to act). Acts of commission include the formal removal of legislation and/or funding necessary for the continued enjoyment of an economic or social right, the active denial of such rights to particular individuals or groups, and the reduction of specific public expenditures to protect social welfare resulting in the denial of minimum subsistence rights for everyone. Violations of omission include the failure to enforce legislation designed to implement provisions of the covenant and the failure to utilize the maximum of available resources toward the full realization of the covenant.

4. States are allowed a "margin of discretion in selecting the means for implementing their respective obligations." However, "certain steps must be taken immediately and others as soon as possible." A state violates the covenant when it fails to satisfy what the Economic Rights Committee refers to as "a minimum core obligation to ensure the satisfaction of, at the very least, minimum essential levels of each of the rights. . . . Thus, for example, a State party in which any significant number of individuals is deprived of essential foodstuffs, of essential primary health care, of basic shelter and housing, or of the most basic forms of education is, prima facie, violating the Covenant." Resource scarcity does not relieve the state of these minimum obligations.[22]

5. States are required to ensure that private entities or individuals, including transnational corporations within their jurisdiction, do not deprive individuals of social or economic rights. "States are respon-

sible for violations of economic, social and cultural rights that result from their failure to exercise due diligence in controlling the behavior of such non-state actors."[23]

6. States are required to eliminate all forms of discrimination against women. "Discrimination against women in relation to the rights recognized in the Covenant, is understood in light of the standard of equality for women under the Convention on the Elimination of All Forms of Discrimination Against Women. That standard requires the elimination of all forms of discrimination against women, including gender discrimination arising out of social, cultural and other structural disadvantages."[24]

The Economic Rights Treaty

The Economic Rights Treaty, which entered into force on 3 January 1976, is divided into five parts. The focus of part one is the right to self-determination; part two defines the general nature of states parties obligations; part three recognizes specific substantive rights; part four addresses international implementation; and part five states specific legal provisions. Substantive provisions in part three include rights to the following: an adequate standard of living, including food, clothing, and housing; physical and mental health; education; scientific and cultural life; the opportunity to work; just and favorable conditions of work; rest and leisure; social security; special protection for the family, mothers, and children; and the right to form and join trade unions and to strike.

The challenge is to identify approaches to holding nations accountable to fulfill their obligations in the treaty. The Economic Rights Treaty demands that governments take all appropriate means and use the maximum available resources to fulfill these specific rights, but it gives no further guidance. Legislative and judicial remedies are key, but overall economic and social development planning and intervention by the government may be even more important.

Unlike the Political Rights Treaty (the International Covenant on Civil and Political Rights), which has an independent group of experts supervising implementation of the covenant's provisions (the Human Rights Committee), the UN's Economic and Social Council (ECOSOC), a body of governmental representatives, was charged with implementation responsibility of the Economic Rights Treaty. In the late 1970s and into the 1980s, ECOSOC set up a series of sessional working groups of governmental delegates to help with these responsibilities. These working groups were a failure. In 1987, ECOSOC replaced them with a body of human rights experts operating in their personal capacity, the Economic Rights Committee. The Economic Rights Committee thus began from a weaker position than its counterpart, the Human Rights Committee. The Economic Rights Committee's existence depends on the continued support of ECOSOC. Theoretically, if Economic Rights Committee decisions upset the members of ECOSOC, its continued existence could be jeopardized. The Human Rights Committee, on the other hand, exists by legal statute, as it is a part of the Political Rights Treaty.[25]

The Economic Rights Committee is charged with monitoring the compliance of states parties to the Economic Rights Treaty and is the principle UN body concerned with implementation of this treaty. The composition of the Economic Rights Committee is similar to the Human Rights Committee with eighteen independent experts elected by ECOSOC for four-year terms. Membership reflects an equitable geographic representation. States parties to the Economic Rights Treaty must submit an initial report within two years of ratification with subsequent reports required every five years. The reporting procedure involves a dialogue between the state party and the Economic Rights Committee. The Economic Rights Committee's examination of states parties' reports and their adoption of general comments have been useful and innovative.[26]

Political Rights Treaty/Human Rights Committee

As a point of comparison, it is useful to look at the reporting and implementation mechanisms established through the Human Rights Committee. The Human Rights Committee was established as an independent body of human rights experts. Human rights activists hoped that these experts would prove to be more objective and less political in assessing human rights violations than the political appointments made by nation-states to the Human Rights Commission. The Human Rights Committee conducts public examinations of reports submitted by states parties. Its power was enhanced with the passage of the first optional protocol that allows for communications from individuals whose civil and political rights have been violated.[27]

In May 2001, there were ninety-eight states parties to the optional protocol.[28] The Office of the High Commissioner for Human Rights (OHCHR) reports that by the end of January 1998 the Human Rights Committee had considered some 800 complaints and adopted 270 decisions on their merits. The views of the Human Rights Committee interpreting the substance of the Political Rights Treaty can be termed "international human rights jurisprudence." National courts that now refer to the decisions and views of the Human Rights Committee include the Supreme Court of Zimbabwe, the Judicial Committee of the Privy Council in London, and the Constitutional Court of South Africa. This interplay between UN treaty bodies and national juridical organs is a very positive development. However, it is important to note that this advance must be put in context—only about one-half of UN member states are parties to the optional protocol.[29]

The individual complaint procedures developed through the optional protocol have been refined. According to Mercedes Morales, a human rights officer to the OHCHR in Geneva, after exhausting all domestic remedies individuals may submit complaints directly to the UN. The complaint can be of any length—from one page to hundreds. Once admissibility is determined, a summary of the case is submitted to a special rapporteur. The rapporteur reports to the Human Rights Committee, which ultimately makes all final decisions. If the Human Rights Committee finds that a violation has been committed, implementation of its decision through either compensation or a change in legislation is expected to take place at the national level. Despite the fact that these judgments are not legally binding, Morales reports that there is a 30 to 40 percent compliance rate with the decisions of the Human Rights Committee. This is significant progress. The Human Rights Committee's annual report lists those countries that do not reply to complaints.[30]

Many states move to implement the views of the Human Rights Committee by releasing political prisoners, awarding compensation to victims of human rights violations, reinstating individuals in the civil service, amending legislation considered incompatible with the provisions of the Political Rights Treaty, or granting other remedies. All of these measures depend on the good will of the states parties. Colombia has been the only state to pass enabling legislation, "which elevates the decisions of UN and regional human rights bodies to the level of enforceable judgements at the national level."[31] Yet, states do seem to listen to the Human Rights Committee. The Human Rights Committee and the Committee against Torture have requested more than 200 interim measures of protection, for example, in death penalty, extradition, or deportation cases requesting stays of execution or temporary suspension of extradition. In all but five cases these requests have been respected.[32]

Economic Rights Treaty/Economic Rights Committee

In contrast to the previous complaint and enforcement system for civil and political rights, the implementation procedures of the Economic Rights Treaty are still being developed. In theory, the 144 nations that had ratified the Economic Rights Treaty as of May 2001[33] agreed that these economic and social claims had equal status to civil and political rights. In practice, these same nations have failed to take the necessary implementation steps (legislative, administrative, or judicial) to make these claims equal to civil and political rights.

Furthermore, the Economic Rights Treaty does not have a protocol equivalent to the First Optional Protocol to the Political Rights Treaty. Thus, the Economic Rights Committee may not receive formal complaints from individuals alleging violations of the Economic Rights Treaty. A proposal for a formal complaints procedure, in the form of an optional protocol to the Economic Rights Treaty, for individuals and groups who feel that their rights under the Economic Rights Treaty have been violated, has been drafted by the Economic Rights Committee. This proposal will be discussed later on in relation to proposals to strengthen global compliance with economic and social human rights law.

Louis Henkin believes that the differences in implementation procedures between the Political Rights Treaty and the Economic Rights Treaty are significant. The Political Rights Treaty calls for full and immediate realization while the Economic Rights Treaty only requires steps "to the maximum of [a state's] available resources" with a view to progressively achieving the full realization of rights. He identifies a "subtle but conscious and pervasive difference in tone and in the terms of legal prescription." The Political Rights Treaty speaks of individual rights: "Every human being has the inherent right to life. . . . No one shall be held in slavery. . . . Everyone shall have the right to hold opinions without interference." The Economic Rights Treaty, on the other hand, addresses state action and obligation, not individual rights: "The states-parties to the present covenant recognize the right to work . . . the states . . . undertake to ensure . . . the right of everyone to form trade unions . . . the states . . . recognize the right of everyone to social security . . . to an adequate standard of living . . . to education."[34]

The Economic Rights Treaty thus reflects the social reality of economic and social human rights claims. These collective human rights depend on national and global planning for their fulfillment. Within this context, the "Limburg Principles" and the "Maastricht Guidelines" provide state and nonstate actors with clear guidelines for meeting their human rights obligations in their economic planning. The Economic Rights Committee works to hold states accountable to these norms and obligations.

The Economic Rights Committee functions to a large degree in a manner similar to the Human Rights Committee described earlier. Regular reports are submitted by states parties, deliberations are held, and general comments are published. The Economic Rights Committee seeks to achieve three principal objectives: "(1) development of the normative content of the rights recognized in the Covenant; (2) acting as a catalyst to state action in developing national benchmarks and devising appropriate mechanisms for establishing accountability, and providing means of vindication to aggrieved individuals and groups at the national level; and (3) holding states accountable at the international level through the examination of reports."[35]

According to Matthew Craven, the largest problem facing the Economic Rights Committee is the substance of the covenant itself. The Economic Rights Treaty suffers from excessive generality and lack of clear responsibility for supervision. It is this void that the Economic Rights Committee has sought to fill. "The breadth of subjects covered by the Covenant, combined with the lack of case law (whether national or international) in certain vital areas such as health and nutrition, mean that significant importance has to be placed upon the Committee's 'creative' or 'interpretative' functions." Key in this effort is the drafting of general comments to "develop an understanding of the normative content" of economic and social rights.[36]

The Economic Rights Committee has devoted considerable energy to overcoming and resolving the problems of generality in the definitions of economic, social, and cultural human rights. In particular, through its general comments the committee has provided state and nonstate actors with a clearly defined understanding of the obligations and duties these rights entail. In fact, the General Comments of the Economic Rights Committee provide the clearest articulation of the economic, social, and cultural rights affirmed in international law. It is thus no longer credible to argue that economic and social rights are too vague to enforce. The general comments provide clarity and outline the substance of these rights.

Democratic Participation in the Implementation of Economic and Social Rights

In 1987, Philip Alston asserted that there is an identifiable "minimum core content of each right that cannot be diminished under the pretext of permitted 'reasonable differences.'" He wrote:

The fact that there may exist such a core (which to a limited extent might nevertheless be potentially subject to derogation or limitations in accordance with the relevant provisions of the Covenant) would seem to be a logical implication of the use of the terminology of rights. In other words, there would be no justification for elevating a "claim" to the status of a right (with all the connotations that this concept is usually assumed to have) if its normative content could be so indeterminate as to allow for the possibility that the right holders possess no particular entitlement to anything. Each right must therefore give rise to an absolute minimum entitlement, in the absence of which a state party is to be considered to be in violation of its obligations.[37]

Alston is right—there is a minimum core content to economic and social human rights that the Economic Rights Committee is valiantly struggling to refine and articulate. The Economic Rights Committee has been able to criticize governments for violations of this core content. All states have the duty to enforce these universal human rights. The Vienna Declaration of the UN World Conference on Human Rights states, "While the significance

> ### GENERAL COMMENTS OF THE ECONOMIC
> ### RIGHTS COMMITTEE
>
> General Comments of the Economic Rights Committee cover the fol-
> lowing subjects: General Comment no. 1 (1989), "Reporting by States
> Parties"; General Comment no. 2 (1990), "International Technical Assis-
> tance Matters"; General Comment no. 3 (1990), "The Nature of States
> Parties' Obligations"; General Comment no. 4 (1991), "The Right to
> Adequate Housing"; General Comment no. 5 (1994), "Persons with
> Disabilities"; General Comment no. 6 (1995), "Rights of Older Persons";
> General Comment no. 7 (1997), "The Right to Adequate Housing";
> General Comment no. 8 (1997), "The Relationship between Economic
> Sanctions and Respect for Economic, Social and Cultural Rights"; Gen-
> eral Comment no. 9 (1998), "The Domestic Application of the
> Covenant"; General Comment no. 10 (1998), "The Role of National
> Human Rights Institutions in the Protection of Economic, Social and
> Cultural Rights"; General Comment no. 11 (1999), "Plans of Action for
> Primary Education"; General Comment no. 12 (1999), "The Right to
> Adequate Food"; General Comment no. 13 (1999), "The Right to Edu-
> cation"; and General Comment no. 14 (2000), "The Right to the Highest
> Attainable Standard of Health."
>
> ### General Comments nos. 1–3:
> ### On Refining and Clarifying the State Reporting System
>
> The Economic Rights Committee notes in the first three general com-
> ments that the Economic Rights Treaty imposes two immediate obliga-
> tions on states parties: the undertaking to guarantee that relevant rights
> "will be exercised without discrimination " and the commitment "to
> take steps" within a reasonably short time after the covenant's entry
> into force to meet the recognized obligations.[a] The Economic Rights
> Committee continues:
>
> > [T]he Committee is of the view that a minimum core obligation to
> > ensure the satisfaction of, at the very least, minimum essential lev-
> > els of each of the rights is incumbent upon every State party. Thus,
> > for example, a State party in which any significant number of indi-
> > viduals is deprived of essential foodstuffs, of essential primary
> > health care, of basic shelter and housing, or of the most basic forms
> > of education is, *prima facie*, failing to discharge its obligations
> > under the Covenant.[b]

The Economic Rights Committee's attempt to establish a "minimum threshold" that should be achieved by all states at the earliest possible moment irrespective of their economic situation has appeal. It is then possible "to speak of the widespread violation of economic, social and cultural rights in a technical legal sense instead of merely as a moral injunction."[c] The burden of proof shifts to the state. It must prove that existing poverty, hopelessness, and hunger are due to factors beyond its control and that it has mobilized its resources to meet the needs of the most vulnerable. The Economic Rights Committee thus works to establish universal criteria through which states can be held accountable.

However, this approach is not without its problems. It is exceedingly difficult to establish minimum thresholds and standards for economic and social rights at the international level. Are different criteria to be applied to resource poor as opposed to resource rich countries? Should the minimum level be raised in those countries that have the ability to meet a higher level of demand? Or will the Economic Rights Committee only focus its attention on the basic needs of the developing states and ignore the developed states?

Furthermore, the Economic Rights Committee will have to address the issue of responsibility. In a globalized economy, the impact of transnational actors (e.g., global corporations and banks, international financial institutions [IFIs], and so on) often have a direct impact on the well-being and/or destitution of a population. Mechanisms must be created to hold these state and nonstate actors accountable to international human rights law.[d]

Sigrun I. Skogly notes the ways in which the Economic Rights Committee has begun to deliberate on the impact of IFIs on economic and social human rights. Reporting states are now asked whether they consider the human rights implications of proposed World Bank and International Monetary Fund (IMF) projects and programs. These states are also systematically asked whether they consider the human rights implications of their own voting behavior inside the World Bank and the IMF. The Economic Rights Committee has also attempted to draw the World Bank and IMF into its deliberations. The committee requests the assistance of these specialized agencies to help provide information on nonreporting states—that is, states that have not submitted required reports and failed to comply with their obligations under the treaty.[e]

The Economic Rights Committee has been clear about state responsibility. Through either legislation, judicial remedy, or public policy, governments are required to take immediate and targeted steps toward the realization of economic and social rights. Governments have discretion to decide what steps to take but are required, at the very least, to ensure minimum levels of basic rights to their citizens.

General Comment no. 4: On the Right to Housing

The Economic Rights Committee affirms that the right to housing applies to everyone and should "be seen as the right to live somewhere in security, peace and dignity." The Economic Rights Committee identifies certain aspects of this right that must be taken into account: legal security of tenure; availability of services, materials, facilities, and infrastructure; affordability; habitability; accessibility; location; and cultural adequacy. It states: "Regardless of the state of development of any country, there are certain steps which must be taken immediately." The Economic Rights Committee notes that certain actions require an abstention of the government from certain practices, while other actions require that priority be given to social groups living in unfavorable conditions.

> While appropriate means of achieving the full realization of the right to adequate housing will inevitably vary significantly from one State party to another, the Covenant clearly requires that each State party take whatever steps are necessary for that purpose. This will almost invariably require the adoption of a national housing strategy. . . . Effective monitoring of the situation with respect to housing is another obligation of immediate effect. . . . Measures designed to satisfy a State party's obligations in respect of the right to adequate housing may reflect whatever mix of public and private sector measures is considered appropriate.[f]

The Economic Rights Committee also considers that "instances of forced eviction are *prima facie* incompatible with the requirements of the Covenant and can only be justified in the most exceptional circumstances, and in accordance with the relevant principles of international law." And finally, the last paragraph of this general comment addresses the impact of international finance on housing by calling for international housing assistance to be targeted to the housing needs of disadvantaged groups and stating that IFIs' structural adjustment "should ensure that such measures do not compromise the enjoyment of the right to adequate housing."[g]

The state clearly has a primary role in creating conditions whereby the right to housing becomes a reality. But the Economic Rights Committee is clear that this role includes enabling strategies through which local community-based organizations and private citizens are encouraged to build houses themselves; the government must take positive steps to encourage private housing construction. "[P]rivate individuals and groups should be able to construct housing themselves without excessive conditions being placed upon them."[h] But, as Craven notes, this does not absolve states from responsibility for the provision of housing. For example, the Economic Rights Committee criticized Chile following a sharp reduction in government low-cost housing projects. By placing the housing problem entirely in the hands of the private sector, one member commented that Chile was ignoring the position of the poor. The Economic Rights Committee has directed similar criticisms toward Italy's shortage of low-income housing.[i]

General Comment no. 5: On Persons with Disabilities

The Economic Rights Committee notes that in its experience to date, states parties have devoted very little attention to persons with disabilities. States parties are called on "to take appropriate measures, to the maximum extent of their available resources, to enable such persons to seek to overcome any disadvantages, in terms of the enjoyment of the rights specified in the Covenant, flowing from their disability." States must do more than merely abstain from taking measures that might have a negative impact on persons with disabilities. "The obligation in the case of such a vulnerable and disadvantaged group is to take positive action to reduce structural disadvantages and to give appropriate preferential treatment to people with disabilities."[j]

Of particular interest is the attention that the Economic Rights Committee pays to the impact of market-based policies on the disabled. The Economic Rights Committee calls for regulation of the private sphere to

> ensure equitable treatment of persons with disabilities. In a context in which arrangements for the provision of public services are increasingly being privatized and in which the free market is being relied on to an ever greater extent, it is essential that private employers, private suppliers of goods and services, and other non-public entities are subject to both nondiscrimination and equality norms in relation to persons with disabilities. . . . In the absence of government intervention there will always be instances in which the operation of the free market will produce unsatisfactory results for persons with disabilities, either individually or as a group, and in such circumstances it is incumbent on Governments to step in

and take appropriate measures to temper, complement, compensate for, or override the results produced by market forces.[k]

The Economic Rights Committee also notes the ways in which persons with disabilities are treated as "genderless human beings," and the double discrimination faced by women with disabilities. "Women with disabilities also have the right to protection and support in relation to motherhood and pregnancy."[l]

General Comment no. 6: On the Rights of Older Persons

The Economic Rights Treaty does not specify precise rights for older persons, although article 9 does recognize the right to old-age benefits by declaring "the right of everyone to social security, including social insurance." The Economic Rights Committee "notes that the great majority of States parties reports continue to make little reference to this important issue. It therefore wishes to indicate that, in the future, it will insist that the situation of older persons in relation to each of the rights recognized in the Covenant should be adequately addressed in all reports." General Comment no. 6 develops rights relating to work, social security, the protection of the family, an adequate standard of living, education, and culture as they relate to older persons.[m]

In accordance with article 3 of the covenant, the Economic Rights Committee calls on states parties to

> pay particular attention to older women who, because they have spent all or part of their lives caring for their families without engaging in a remunerated activity entitling them to an old-age pension, and who are also not entitled to a widow's pension, are often in critical situations . . . states parties should institute non-contributory old-age benefits or other assistance for all persons, regardless of their sex, who find themselves without resources on attaining an age specified in national legislation. Given their greater life expectancy and the fact that it is more often they who have no contributory pensions, women would be the principal beneficiaries.[n]

General Comment no. 7: On Housing and Forced Evictions

The Economic Rights Committee articulates the circumstances under which forced evictions are permissible and spells out the types of protection required under the covenant: "The State itself must refrain from forced evictions and ensure that the law is enforced against its agents or third parties who carry out forced evictions." Furthermore, the Economic Rights Committee calls on states to enact legislative measures against forced evictions that provide the greatest possible security of tenure to occupiers of houses and land and designate the circumstances under which evictions may be carried out. These measures must apply to forced evictions carried out by private persons or bodies as well as governmental actions.[o]

Where forced evictions are justified, as in the case of persistent nonpayment of rent, the relevant authorities must "ensure that those evictions are carried out in a manner warranted by a law which is compatible with the Covenant. . . . Evictions should not result in rendering individuals homeless or vulnerable to the violation of other human rights."[p]

General Comment no. 8: On Economic Sanctions

The Economic Rights Committee notes the increasing frequency with which economic sanctions are being imposed internationally, regionally, and unilaterally. These sanctions have a direct impact on the rights recognized in the Economic Rights Treaty, by, for example, disrupting the distribution of food and sanitation supplies. Since insufficient attention has been paid to the impact of these acts on vulnerable groups, the Economic Rights Committee sees the need to "inject a human rights dimension into deliberations on this issue."[q]

The Economic Rights Committee outlines two sets of obligations. The first set relates to the affected state, which still "must take steps 'to the maximum of its available resources' to provide the greatest protection for the economic, social and cultural rights of each individual living within its jurisdiction." The second set relates to the party or parties responsible for the imposition of sanctions. These parties must take into account the impact of their actions on the economic, social, and cultural rights of the most vulnerable sectors of the population. Effective monitoring of the suffering caused by the sanctions must be implemented. Furthermore, action must be taken "to respond to any disproportionate suffering experienced by vulnerable groups within the targeted country."[r]

General Comment no. 9: On Domestic Application

The Economic Rights Committee notes that the Vienna Convention on the Law of Treaties obligates each state party to modify its domestic legal order to give effect to its treaty obligations. Legally binding human rights standards should operate "directly and immediately within the domestic legal system of each State party, thereby enabling individuals to seek enforcement of their rights before national courts and tribunals." It is unfortunate that the assumption is often made that there are no judicial remedies for violations of economic and social rights. The Economic Rights Committee asserts that "there is no Covenant right which could not, in the great majority of systems, be considered to possess at least some significant justiciable dimensions." The courts' capacity to protect the rights of the most vulnerable and disadvantaged groups in society should not be curtailed.[s]

General Comment no. 10: On the Role of National Human Rights Institutions

In 1998, the Economic Rights Committee issued a short statement on the role of national human rights institutions in the protection of economic, social, and cultural rights. These national institutions—from national human rights commissions to human rights advocates—can play an important role in the implementation of human rights by promoting educational programs, scrutinizing existing laws, providing technical advice, monitoring compliance with specific rights, and so on. The Economic Rights Committee urges states to ensure that the mandates accorded all national human rights institutions include appropriate attention to economic, social, and cultural rights.[t]

General Comments nos. 11 and 13: On the Right to Education

In these two general comments, the Economic Rights Committee argues that education at all levels should exhibit four essential features: availability, accessibility, acceptability, and adaptability. These concepts clarify state obligations under international law in relation to the right to education. The committee writes:

> States have obligations to respect, protect and fulfill each of the "essential features" (availability, accessibility, acceptability, adaptability) of the right to education. By way of illustration, a State must respect the availability of education by not closing private schools; protect the accessibility of education by ensuring that third parties, including parents and employers, do not stop girls from going to school; fulfill (facilitate) the acceptability of education by taking positive measures to ensure that education is culturally appropriate for minorities and indigenous peoples, and of good quality for all; fulfill (provide) the adaptability of education by designing and providing resources for curricula which reflect the contemporary needs of students in a changing world; and ful-

fill (provide) the availability of education by actively developing a system of schools, including building classrooms, delivering programmes, providing teaching materials, training teachers and paying them domestically competitive salaries.[u]

Under international law, primary education is to be "compulsory" and "available free to all." Secondary education is to "be made generally available and accessible to all by every appropriate means, and in particular by the progressive introduction of free education." And higher education "shall be made equally accessible to all, on the basis of capacity."[v]

General Comment no. 11 focuses on plans of action for primary education. "[N]either parents, guardians, nor the State are entitled to treat as optional the decision as to whether the child should have access to primary education." Primary education should be available without charge to the child, parents, or guardians. Financial difficulties arising from either the debt crisis or the impact of structural adjustment programs do not relieve a state from its obligation to adopt a plan of action for primary education. "This obligation needs to be scrupulously observed in view of the fact that in developing countries, 130 million children of school age are currently estimated to be without access to primary education, of whom about two thirds are girls."[w]

General Comment no. 12: On the Right to Food

The committee writes that the core content of the right to adequate food implies: "The availability of food in a quantity and quality sufficient to satisfy the dietary needs of individuals, free from adverse substances, and acceptable within a given culture; the accessibility of such food in ways that are sustainable and that do not interfere with the enjoyment of other human rights."[x]

Like other human rights, the right to adequate food imposes obligations to respect, protect, and fulfill.

> The obligation to *respect* existing access to adequate food requires States parties not to take any measures that result in preventing such access. The obligation to *protect* requires measures by the State to ensure that enterprises or individuals do not deprive individuals of their access to adequate food. The obligation to *fulfill* (*facilitate*) means that the State must proactively engage in activities intended to strengthen people's access to and utilization of resources and means to ensure their livelihood, including food security. Finally, whenever an individual or group is unable, for reasons beyond their control, to enjoy the right to adequate food

by the means at their disposal, States have the obligation to *fulfill* (*provide*) that right directly. This obligation also applies for persons who are victims of natural or other disasters.[y]

General Comment no. 12 illuminates clear violations of the right to food, such as

the formal repeal or suspension of legislation necessary for the continued enjoyment of the right to food; denial of access to food to particular individuals or groups, whether the discrimination is based on legislation or is proactive; the prevention of access to humanitarian food aid in internal conflicts or other emergency situations; adopting legislation or policies which are manifestly incompatible with pre-existing legal obligations relating to the right to food; and failure to regulate activities of individuals or groups so as to prevent them from violating the right to food of others, or the failure of a State to take into account its international legal obligations regarding the right to food when entering into agreements with other States or with international organizations.[z]

Large segments of the world's population face food insecurity due to a lack of access to available food. The right to food rests on the fact that hunger and malnutrition is not a product of a lack of food, but a result of crippling poverty limiting access to these abundant food supplies. The Economic Rights Committee notes that more than 840 million people throughout the world are chronically hungry. While problems of hunger and malnutrition are particularly acute in developing countries, undernutrition and other problems related to the lack of access to adequate food exist in some of the most economically developed countries. Each state party is required to "take whatever steps necessary to ensure that everyone is free from hunger and as soon as possible can enjoy the right to adequate food. This will require the adoption of a national strategy to ensure food and nutrition security for all."[aa]

General Comment no. 14: On the Right to Health

Article 12.1 of the Economic Rights Treaty recognizes "the right of everyone to the enjoyment of the highest attainable standard of physical and mental health," while article 12.2 enumerates a number of "steps to be taken by the States parties . . . to achieve the full realization of this right." The Economic Rights Committee acknowledges that for millions of people throughout the world, the full enjoyment of the right to health remains a distant goal.[bb]

As with education, the Economic Rights Committee again stresses availability and accessibility. Functioning public health and health care facilities, goods and services, and programs have to be available in sufficient quantity. These will include safe and potable drinking water and adequate sanitation facilities, hospitals, clinics and other health-related buildings, trained medical and professional personnel receiving domestically competitive salaries, and essential drugs. These health facilities and goods and services have to be accessible to everyone without discrimination and within the jurisdiction of the state. Accessibility has four overlapping dimensions: nondiscrimination, physical accessibility, economic accessibility (affordability), and information accessibility.^{cc}

General Comment no. 14 describes in detail states parties' obligations to respect, protect, and fulfill the right to health. Violations of the obligation to respect are those state actions, policies, or laws that are likely to result in bodily harm, unnecessary morbidity, and preventable mortality. "Examples include the denial of access to health facilities, goods and services to particular individuals or groups as a result of de jure or de facto discrimination; . . . the suspension of legislation or the adoption of laws or policies that interfere with the enjoyment of any of the components of the right to health."^{dd}

Violations of the obligation to protect arise from a state's refusal or failure to safeguard persons within their jurisdiction from infringements of the right to health by third parties. This includes such omissions as

> the failure to protect consumers and workers from practices detrimental to health, e.g. by employers and manufacturers of medicines or food; the failure to discourage production, marketing and consumption of tobacco, narcotics and other harmful substances; the failure to protect women against violence or to prosecute perpetrators; . . . and the failure to enact or enforce laws to prevent the pollution of water, air and soil by extractive and manufacturing industries.^{ee}

Violations of the obligation to fulfill are the result of states parties' failure to take all necessary steps to ensure the realization of the right to health.

> Examples include the failure to adopt or implement a national health policy designed to ensure the right to health for everyone; insufficient expenditure or misallocation of public resources which results in the non-enjoyment of the right to health by individuals or groups, particularly the vulnerable or marginalized; the

failure to monitor the realization of the right to health at the national level, for example by identifying right to health indicators and benchmarks; the failure to take measures to reduce the inequitable distribution of health facilities, goods and services; the failure to adopt a gender-sensitive approach to health; and the failure to reduce infant and maternal mortality rates.[f]

a. See Bruno Simma, "The Implementation of the International Covenant on Economic, Social and Cultural Rights," in *The Implementation of Economic and Social Rights: National, International and Comparative Aspects,* ed. Franz Matscher (Arlington, Va.: Engel Verlag, 1991), 88–94.

b. Committee on Economic, Social and Cultural Rights, General Comment no. 3 (1990), UN Doc. E/1991/23, Annex III.

c. Matthew Craven, *The International Covenant on Economic, Social, and Cultural Rights: A Perspective on Its Development* (Oxford: Clarendon, 1995), 143.

d. Craven, *International Covenant,* 143.

e. Sigrun I. Skogly, *The Human Rights Obligations of the World Bank and the International Monetary Fund* (London: Cavendish, 2001), 133–134.

f. Committee on Economic, Social and Cultural Rights, General Comment no. 4, "The Right to Adequate Housing" (Art. 11[1] of the Covenant) (6th sess., 1991), in United Nations, "Compilation of General Comments and General Recommendations Adopted by Human Rights Treaty Bodies," UN Doc. HRI\GEN®\Rev. 1 at 53 (1994).

g. Economic Rights Committee, General Comment no. 4.

h. Craven, *International Covenant,* 336.

i. Craven, *International Covenant,* 336.

j. Committee on Economic, Social and Cultural Rights, General Comment no. 5, "Persons with Disabilities" (11th sess., 1994), UN Doc E/C.12/1994/13 (1994).

k. Economic Rights Committee, General Comment no. 5.

l. Economic Rights Committee, General Comment no. 5.

m. Committee on Economic, Social and Cultural Rights, General Comment no. 6, "The Economic, Social and Cultural Rights of Older Persons" (13th sess., 1995), UN Doc. E/C.12/1995/16/Rev. 1 (1995), 4.

n. Committee on Economic, Social and Cultural Rights, General Comment no. 6, 4–5.

o. Committee on Economic, Social and Cultural Rights, General Comment no. 7, "The Right to Adequate Housing" (article 11[1] of the Covenant), UN Doc. E/C.12/1997/4 (1997), 1–2.

p. Committee on Economic, Social and Cultural Rights, General Comment no. 7, 3, 4.

q. Committee on Economic, Social and Cultural Rights, General Comment no. 8 (1997), "The Relationship between Economic Sanctions and Respect for Economic, Social and Cultural Rights," UN Doc. E/C.12/1997/8 (12 December 1997), 2.

r. Committee on Economic, Social and Cultural Rights, General Comment no. 8, 3.

s. Committee on Economic, Social and Cultural Rights, General Comment no. 9 (1998), "The Domestic Application of the Covenant," UN Doc. HRI/GEN/1/Rev. 4 (7 February 2000), 48–52. The committee refers to article 27 of the Vienna Convention on the Law of Treaties: "[A] party may not invoke the provisions of its internal law as justification for its failure to perform a treaty."

t. Committee on Economic, Social and Cultural Rights, General Comment no. 10 (1998), "The Role of National Human Rights Institutions in the Protection of Economic, Social and Cultural Rights," UN Doc. HRI/GEN/1/Rev. 4 (7 February 2000), 53–54.

u. Committee on Economic, Social and Cultural Rights, General Comment no. 13 (1999), "The Right to Education," UN Doc. HRI/GEN/1/Rev. 4 (7 February 2000), 75.

v. Committee on Economic, Social and Cultural Rights, General Comment no. 13, 68–69.

w. Committee on Economic, Social and Cultural Rights, General Comment no. 11 (1999), "Plans of Action for Primary Education," UN Doc. HRI/GEN/1/Rev. 4 (7 February 2000), 54–56.

x. Committee on Economic, Social and Cultural Rights, General Comment no. 12 (1999), "The Right to Adequate Food," UN Doc. HRI/GEN/1/Rev. 4 (7 February 2000), 59.

y. Committee on Economic, Social and Cultural Rights, General Comment no. 12, 60.

z. Committee on Economic, Social and Cultural Rights, General Comment no. 12, 61.

aa. Committee on Economic, Social and Cultural Rights, General Comment no. 12, 58, 61.

bb. Committee on Economic, Social and Cultural Rights, General Comment no. 14 (2000), "The Right to the Highest Attainable Standard of Health," UN Doc.E/C.12/2000/4 (4 July 2000), 2.

cc. Committee on Economic, Social and Cultural Rights, General Comment no. 14, 3–4.

dd. Committee on Economic, Social and Cultural Rights, General Comment no. 14, 13.

ee. Committee on Economic, Social and Cultural Rights, General Comment no. 14, 14.

ff. Committee on Economic, Social and Cultural Rights, General Comment no. 14, 14.

of national and regional particularities and various historical, cultural and religious backgrounds must be borne in mind, it is the duty of states, regardless of their political, economic and social systems, to promote and protect all human rights and fundamental freedoms."[38]

However, the move from merely "denouncing" violations to the actual implementation of a strategy to improve the working and living conditions of the most vulnerable sectors must involve democratic participation. The people whose economic and social rights have been violated should be a part of the implementation process. Universal standards must take account of local cultures and adjust to local conditions. This is not an argument for cultural relativism, but an argument for modesty and effectiveness. It is arrogant for any actor or any theory (e.g., neoliberal economic theory or liberal human rights theory) to claim to know the best methods for every unique culture and society to implement economic rights progressively. Rather, to be effective these approaches and theories must engage in what Abdullahi Ahmed An-Na'im describes as a "cross-cultural dialogue." An-Na'im stresses the need to verify and substantiate the genuine universality of the existing human rights standards through a process of retroactive legitimation. While existing human rights standards should be maintained, they should be respectfully implemented through a cross-cultural dialogue of mutual learning. Those of one cultural tradition "must never even appear to be imposing external values in support of the human rights standards they seek to legitimize within the framework of the other culture."[39]

State action becomes decisive. The state has a duty to open up the space for democratic participation. There is a link here between civil and political rights, and economic, social, and cultural rights. The *African Charter for Popular Participation in Development and Transformation* articulates this well:

> We believe strongly that popular participation is, in essence, the empowerment of the people to effectively involve themselves in creating the structures and in designing policies and programmes that serve the interests of all as well as to effectively contribute to the development process and share equitably in its benefits. Therefore, there must be an opening up of political process to accommodate freedom of opinions, tolerate differences, accept consensus on issues as well as ensure the effective participation of the people and their organizations and associations. This requires action on the part of all, first and foremost of the people themselves. But equally important are the actions of the State and the international community, to create the necessary conditions for such an empowerment and facilitate effective popular participation in societal and economic life. This requires that the political system evolve to allow for democracy and full participation by all sections of our societies.[40]

Democratic participation and cross-cultural dialogue are essential for the implementation of economic and social human rights. The enactment of measures to enable people to exercise economic and social rights is vital. A legal positivist human rights approach has promise if it is combined with a strategy of democratic participation. Universalism and localism need not be seen in opposition. Effective implementation of international economic and social human rights law depends on its adaptation and acceptance by local communities.

Despite the shrinking nature of our global community, the state is still central in the creation of the proper environment for the fulfillment of these rights. The state can enact measures to respect, protect, and fulfill basic human rights. The state can open up the political space so that democratic participation can become a reality. And the state can regulate the activities of other transnational economic actors whose practices violate basic human rights protections.

Without the participation and involvement of the working class and vulnerable sectors of the South, attempts by the North to impose labor and environmental regulations will continue to be viewed with suspicion. This mistrust must be conquered. Workers in both the developed and developing countries have an objective interest in seeing the fulfillment of the UN's right to development and the full implementation of the ILO's basic human rights conventions. Perhaps through a cross-cultural dialogue on universal human rights standards, the historical legacy of mistrust between the North and South can be overcome.

Measuring Economic and Social Human Rights

The UN Development Program (UNDP) has played a leadership role in the development of indices and measurements of basic economic and social human rights. The yearly UNDP *Human Development Report* consistently refines its approach and generates sophisticated, functional, and reliable statistics and analyses on poverty and human capabilities. These thoughtful reports provide all economic actors—states, IFIs, TNCs, and so on—with the critical information central to the development of public policy to achieve economic and social human rights.

The human development approach draws on three different perspectives of poverty: income, basic needs, and capabilities. The income perspective asserts that a person is poor if his or her income level is below a defined poverty line, often determined by the amount necessary for a specified amount of food. The basic needs perspective argues that poverty is the result of the lack of the resources for the fulfillment of basic human needs, including food. This approach goes beyond the lack of private income and includes the need for basic health, education, and essential services to be provided by the community to prevent individuals from falling into poverty. In the capabilities perspective, poverty is the absence of the opportunity to achieve some basic capabilities to function. As we saw in my discussion of Sen's analysis in chapter 2, capability functions include being well nourished, adequately clothed and sheltered, able to

---

PIVOTAL NGOs WORKING ON ECONOMIC AND SOCIAL HUMAN RIGHTS: BUILDING DEMOCRATIC PARTICIPATION

A myriad of NGOs have emerged in international relations organizing for economic and social human rights fulfillment. The following three organizations demonstrate the vitality and resourcefulness of these critical new players in international politics.

- Center for Economic and Social Rights (CESR)
  162 Montague St., 2nd Floor, Brooklyn, NY 11201
  Tel: (718) 237–9145; Fax: (718) 237–9147
  E-mail: rights@cesr.org; Web: www.cesr.org

"The Center for Economic and Social Rights (CESR) was established in 1993 to promote social justice through human rights. CESR works with social scientists and local partners in affected communities to document rights violations, advocate for changes in policies that impoverish and exploit people, and mobilize grassroots pressure for social change. As one of the first organizations to challenge economic injustice as a violation of international human rights law, CESR believes that economic and social rights—legally binding on all nations—can provide a universally accepted framework for strengthening social justice activism." (www.cesr.org/about2.htm)

---

avoid preventable morbidity, and able to partake in the life of the community. Poverty clearly cannot be reduced to a single dimension. The capabilities approach most fully captures this total picture.[41]

The 1996 UNDP *Human Development Report* introduced a new, multidimensional measure of human deprivation: the capability poverty measure (CPM). To a considerable extent, this device incorporated Sen's model and attempted to assess the capability to function and realize the freedom to achieve. The CPM calculated the percentage of people who lack basic, or minimally essential, human capabilities in health, nourishment, and education.[42]

The CPM provided a vehicle to measure the capability to achieve adequate functioning. It gave a more accurate assessment of deprivation and poverty than estimations based on levels of national income poverty alone. For example, the World Bank estimated in 1996 that approximately 900 million people in the developing world, 21 percent of the total, were income poor and lived below the poverty line. The corresponding figures for capa-

---

- Foodfirst Information and Action Network (FIAN)
  PO Box 102243, D-69012 Heidelberg, Germany
  Tel: 49 6221 830 620; Fax: 49 6221 830 545
  E-mail: fian@fian.org; Web: www.fian.org

"Our mission is to realize the human right to adequate food through concrete action. FIAN is a non-partisan human rights organization. It has a consultative status with the United Nations. FIAN acts when, for example, the pollution of fishing-grounds, land evictions or the non-respect of minimum wages threaten the livelihoods of the poor and their right to feed themselves is violated. We support the victims in their struggle for justice by campaigning for an end to the violation." (www.fian.org)

- Women's Environment and Development Organization (WEDO)
  355 Lexington Avenue, 3rd Floor, New York, NY 10017–6603
  Tel: (212) 973–0325; Fax: (212) 973–0335
  E-mail: wedo@wedo.org; Web: www.wedo.org

"WEDO is an international advocacy organization that seeks to increase the power of women worldwide as policymakers at all levels in governments, institutions and forums to achieve economic and social justice, a healthy and peaceful planet, and human rights for all. WEDO's program areas are Gender and Governance, Sustainable Development, and Economic Justice." (www.wedo.org/)

---

bility poverty was 1.6 billion, or 37 percent of the people in the developing countries. In Pakistan, for example, only one-third of the population were income poor, but more than three-fifths were capability poor. In Bangladesh, 55 million people were income poor, but 89 million were capability poor.[43]

In 1997, the *Human Development Report* developed these ideas further and introduced the Human Poverty Index (HPI), which refined and replaced the CPM. The HPI compiles in one index the deprivation in four basic dimensions of human life: a long and healthy life, knowledge, economic provisioning, and social exclusion. The indicators to measure these deprivations differ between developing and industrialized countries.[44]

HPI-1 brings together in one index the first three deprivations in developing countries. The deprivation of a long and healthy life is measured by the percentage of people not expected to survive to age forty. The deprivation of knowledge is measured by adult illiteracy rates. The deprivation of economic provisioning is measured by the percentage of people without access to safe water and health services and the percentage of children under five who are moderately or severely underweight.[45] Due to a lack of data and the absence of suitable indicators, HPI-1 does not reflect deprivations in social inclusion in developing countries.

HPI-2 brings together in one index these deprivations in industrialized countries. The deprivation of a long and healthy life is measured by the percentage of people not expected to survive to age sixty. The deprivation of knowledge is measured by the adult functional illiteracy rate. The deprivation of economic provisioning is determined by the percentage of people living below the income poverty line. And the deprivation of social inclusion is determined by the long-term unemployment rate of twelve months or more.[46]

HPI-1 and HPI-2 thus focus on different variables to identify human poverty in developing versus industrialized countries. First, in developing countries public provisioning is more important than private income in the determination of a decent standard of living. More than four-fifths of private income in developing countries is spent on food. Private income alone does not capture the total deprivation in economic provisioning. Lack of access to health services and safe water and the level of malnutrition provide a better description of real conditions of poverty. In industrialized countries, on the other hand, private income is the most important source of economic provisioning.[47]

Some of the conclusions in HPI-1 and HPI-2 published in the *Human Development Report 2000* are the following:

- The people in many developing countries face conditions of extreme human poverty. HPI-1 exceeds 50 percent in Burkina Faso, the central African republic, Ethiopia, Guinea-Bissau, Mali, Mozambique, Nepal, and Niger. In a third of all developing countries where the HPI-1 rate was calculated, it exceeded 33 percent, indicating that at least a third of the people in each country suffer from poverty.[48]
- Public policy can make a significant difference in lowering the poverty rate in developing countries. For example, compare Mexico and Trinidad and Tobago. Mexico has a higher gross domestic product (GDP) per capita ($7,704) than Trinidad and Tobago ($7,485). The two countries score a similar rate on the Human Development Index, with Trinidad and Tobago ahead by only 0.009 percent. But Mexico has twice the level of poverty (HIP-1 rate) compared to Trinidad and Tobago. Clearly, the public policies to address the economic provisioning of basic services have been more successful in Trinidad and Tobago than in Mexico.[49]
- A similar outcome is seen in comparing Guatemala to Tanzania. Both suffer terrible conditions of human poverty with HPI-1 rates between 29 and 30 percent. Guatemala and Tanzania rank next to each other, forty-ninth and fiftieth, respectively, in the HPI-1 overall rankings; 32

to 34 percent of the populations of both countries do not have access to safe drinking water; and 13 to 14 percent of the populations of both countries do not have access to adequate sanitation. In both countries, 27 percent of all children under the age of five are underweight. Yet, Tanzania is faced with conditions of low human development and a GDP per capita of only $480. Guatemala, on the other hand, has conditions of medium human development and a GDP per capita of $3,505. Guatemala unquestionably has the economic wealth and financial ability to implement public policies to alleviate the human suffering these poverty figures expose. Neither economic equality nor the protection of public goods has been a priority in Guatemala. In that country, the richest 20 percent consume 63 percent of the national income while the poorest 20 percent struggle to survive with only 2.1 percent.[50]

- HPI-2 reveals that poverty is not confined to developing countries. The United States has the highest levels of poverty (15.8 percent), followed by Ireland (15 percent), and the United Kingdom (14.6 percent). It is startling to learn that in the United States, Ireland, and the United Kingdom more than one in five adults are functionally illiterate. More than 17 percent of people in the United States are income poor, with the income poverty line set at 50 percent of the median disposable household income.[51]
- The HPI rates also reflect disparities within countries—between rural and urban areas, between regions and districts, and between ethnic and language groups. For example, in South Africa the unemployment rate among African males at 29 percent was more than seven times that among white males at 4 percent. And in India, the illiteracy rate among ethnic tribes is 70 percent, compared with 48 percent for the country as a whole.[52]

The HPI is a superb step forward in the evaluation of the true depths of global poverty. These data are central to the articulation of plans for the alleviation of needless human suffering. UNDP analysis of these figures demonstrates the effectiveness of public action to protect economic and social human rights. Even countries with low GDP rates have successfully provided programs to meet basic needs in sanitation, nutrition, education, and health care.

In this era of economic interdependence, how are states and other economic actors held accountable to international economic and social human rights standards? As outlined in the first part of this chapter, the obligation to respect, protect, and fulfill economic and social human rights is clearly articulated in international law. Through the HPI, the UNDP not only demonstrates the ways in which these rights are being violated, but also clearly points to policy directions for the provision of these rights. Can global governance evolve in a way that prioritizes the economic and social rights of the most vulnerable?

Monitoring and Enforcing Economic and Social Human Rights

Virginia Dandan, the chair of the Economic Rights Committee, believes that economic and social rights are so interrelated that it is totally arbitrary to draw a line between them. She notes that these distinctions were made decades ago when there was a less clear understanding of the nature of rights. The reality is that economic rights have a social basis and social rights have an economic basis. Both classifications of rights are of equal importance and interdependent. But Chairperson Dandan recognizes that the categories of "social" and "economic" have become the traditional terms to refer to these rights, and it is the way they are described in the Economic Rights Treaty. If these original definitions make things clear to the public and to states, then the division perhaps does serve a purpose. There is also no better term at the moment, so as a matter of convenience the Economic Rights Committee continues with this conceptualization. But Chairperson Dandan stresses the importance of understanding economic and social rights in their totality and not as separate items.[53]

Chairperson Dandan believes that, overall, states parties are taking the Economic Rights Committee increasingly seriously. States are concerned about their reputations, and they respond to committee requests. The Economic Rights Committee does utilize the three-part approach to economic and social human rights to respect, protect, and fulfill. Of particular importance to the committee is the issue of respect, which implies an obligation of an immediate nature. No matter what the economic condition of a state, if it has ratified the Economic Rights Treaty, it must respect the economic and social rights of its citizens. A state may not use resource scarcity as an excuse to avoid its obligations. The Economic Rights Treaty is clear: Each state must achieve the realization of economic and social human rights to the maximum of its available resources. Chairperson Dandan notes that it takes no money to desist from violations (the duty to respect). It also takes little money to review legislation to make sure that a state's laws are in conformity with the Economic Rights Treaty. And furthermore, the convention calls for progressive compliance with demonstrable progress. The Economic Rights Committee thus looks for steady improvement and does not accept a nation standing still or going backward.[54]

The Economic Rights Committee applies a single standard for rich and poor countries. The standard applied is the "maximum of its available resources." For example, the United States may have a resource base of eight while the Democratic Republic of the Congo's resource base is two.

The issue for the Economic Rights Treaty is how each country is applying its specific resource base to the achievement of economic and social human rights. More resources can be applied in one case, but each must apply the maximum available.[55]

Despite progress, the Economic Rights Committee still faces major problems in state reporting. Many states don't bother to report at all, while others' reports are inexcusably late. When a state does not report on time, the committee writes to the state's representative to inform him or her that its case will be heard with or without the state reporting. The committee again invites the state representative to submit a report. If a state claims that it does not have the resources to pull together such a detailed report, the OHCHR will help by providing technical assistance. The UN recently, for example, provided such assistance to the Solomon Islands in the preparation of its report. There is therefore absolutely no excuse for countries not to meet their reporting obligations.[56]

But, with or without the state report, the committee will eventually go ahead with the hearing. The state is invited to take part in the hearing even if it does not submit a report (e.g., the Democratic Republic of the Congo recently sent a delegation to the hearing after not submitting the required report). Information on the state's compliance with the Economic Rights Treaty is gathered from a variety of sources beyond the state, including other UN agencies (ILO, UNDP, UN Environment Program, World Health Organization, Food and Agriculture Organization, and so on), and expanded NGO participation and reporting. A special rapporteur is often assigned to conduct an independent country investigation and to submit a draft of preliminary observations to the committee. The final step is a three-hour hearing by the Economic Rights Committee on the state's compliance with the Economic Rights Treaty. The Economic Rights Committee will adopt either preliminary observations or concluding observations. Concluding observations are contingent on state submission of the required report.[57]

Unfortunately, many states parties view the process as an unwarranted intrusion and burden and try to fill the reporting requirement as superficially as possible. Many of the reports submitted are of poor quality and do not follow the reporting guidelines established by the committee. More detailed and comprehensive NGO alternative reports (also called shadow reports) have proved of enormous importance in providing the information missing from these states' reports. These alternative reports highlight inaccuracies and distortions in a government report and provide new information and ideas for appropriate policy. Scott Leckie reports that these alternative reports have also acted as a catalyst in the emergence of new coalitions and movements between previously unconnected groups in the Dominican Republic, Panama, the Philippines, Israel, and elsewhere. International human rights law, and in particular the Economic Rights Treaty, is being used by these NGO coalitions as a basis for demands on states, giving new importance and vigor to these underused legal texts.[58]

These NGO coalitions are one example of the impact of the work of the Economic Rights Committee on the national level. "Success," of course, is difficult to measure. Human rights officers at the OHCHR have assessed that the concluding observations on Canada, the Democratic Republic of the Congo, the Dominican Republic, Hong Kong, Israel, the Philippines, and the Solomon Islands have had a positive impact on government policies and actions. In a number of these cases, the Economic Rights Committee and the UN provided technical assistance so these countries could correct policies and remedy violations. In the Dominican Republic and Panama, for example, such assistance was provided in the area of housing.[59]

The Economic Rights Committee takes into account the many difficulties that governments face, such as population growth, inflation, and special circumstances like weather calamities, and tries to help states define policies to meet their human rights obligations. As a result of constantly changing conditions, every state is probably out of compliance somewhere. Yet, despite these conditions every state has a duty to keep striving for 100 percent compliance. The Economic Rights Committee sees its role as helping states define policies to progressively meet their economic, social, and cultural rights obligations.[60]

Actions recommended by the Economic Rights Committee include the adoption of new legislation, the repeal of existing legislation, the implementation of existing legislation, the encouragement of preventive actions, and the implementation of NGO-devised plans and other specific policy measures. For example, the Philippines government was urged by the committee in 1995 to give "consideration . . . to the repeal of Presidential Decrees 772 and 1818 and [the committee] recommends that all existing legislation relevant to the practice of forced evictions should be reviewed so as to ensure its compatibility with the provisions of the covenant." Belgium, on the other hand, was encouraged to implement its current legislation. In 1994, the committee expressed to Belgium "concern at the adequacy of the measures taken to actually enforce that [housing rights] constitutional provision. The Committee urges the Government to more intensively apply existing laws allowing the government to requisition properties and housing left unoccupied by owners."[61]

The Economic Rights Committee recognizes that other powerful international actors besides states are also responsible for the impact of their policies on the most vulnerable. In its 1998 statement on globalization, the committee emphasized that the realms of trade, finance, and investment are in no way exempt from human rights principles and that "the international organizations with specific responsibilities in those areas should play a positive and constructive role in relation to human rights."[62] The Economic Rights Committee directly addressed these issues in its statement to the Third Ministerial Conference of the WTO in Seattle in 1999. In this document, the Economic Rights Committee notes that the

> wave of economic and corporate restructurings undertaken to respond to an increasingly competitive global market and the widespread dismantling of social security systems have resulted in unemployment, work insecurity and worsening labour conditions giving rise to violations of core economic and social rights set forth in articles 6 to 9 of the Covenant.
>
> It is the Committee's view that WTO contributes significantly to and is part of the process of global governance reform. This reform must be driven by a concern for the individual and not by purely macroeconomic considerations alone. Human rights norms must shape the process of international economic policy formulation so that the benefits for human development of the evolving international trading regime will be shared equitably by all, in particular the most vulnerable sectors. The Committee recognizes the wealth-generating potential of trade liberalization, but it is also aware that liberalization in trade, investment and finance does not necessarily create and lead to a favourable environment for the realization of economic, social and cultural rights. Trade liberalization must be understood as a means, not an end. The end which trade liberalization should serve is the objective of human well-being to which the international human rights instruments give legal expression.[63]

The Economic Rights Committee is thus clearly aware of the profound impact of the policies and decisions of IFIs and TNCs on the economic well-being of citizens in most states. Yet, Chairperson Dandan insists that this changing role of the state does not relieve it of its human rights obligations. A state cannot argue that the WTO or the IMF made it do X, nor can it claim that a TNC forced it to do Y. It is the state's responsibility to protect the resources that are critical to the livelihood and environmental balance of its territory. The Economic Rights Committee asks states to take their obligations for meeting economic and social human rights into their negotiations with IFIs and TNCs. The state must make sure that its obligations are not compromised by the conditions of external aid and foreign investment.[64]

However, this attempt to link human rights to IFIs and TNCs has so far failed to produce significant results. On the one hand, it has proven to be very difficult to get the IFIs to engage with the Economic Rights Committee or to define their work in human rights terms. The World Bank is currently the most human rights sensitized—attending more meetings of the Economic Rights Committee than other IFIs and demonstrating a greater willingness to define its message in human rights terms. For example, the recent World Bank publication *World Development Report 2000/2001: Attacking Poverty* presents a "poverty reduction agenda" that focuses not only on income deprivation, but also on low achievements in education and health, that is, social human rights.[65] The IMF remains distant and attends few meetings. And there has been absolutely no cooperation between the WTO and the Economic Rights Committee. The WTO has ignored the invitation of the Economic Rights Committee to "collaborate . . . on these matters and thereby be active partners towards the realization of all the rights set forth in the Economic Rights Treaty."[66] Overall, IFIs continue to show a disregard for economic and social human rights. The LDCs with the greatest need of financial support to meet these rights are often ignored. Structural adjustment programs and debt payment plans often deepen poverty and worsen social conditions for the poor, in particular for women and children in the LDCs.

On the other hand, the LDCs themselves are hesitant to bring their legal obligations under the Economic Rights Treaty into their negotiations with IFIs and TNCs. Some of these states fear the creation of new social conditionalities on aid and loans needed for development. Some fear losing a competitive advantage in global wage rates. For these reasons it is hard to convince LDCs to link economic and social rights to relations with IFIs and TNCs.[67] And it is up to the states to take this action. Legally, the Economic Rights Committee has little influence and no actual power to force IFIs to take these rights seriously. States, however, command this authority, and state pressure could make a difference.[68]

There is thus plenty of opposition to the Economic Rights Committee expanding its focus to include actors beyond states. Yet, Chairperson Dandan argues that there are "many ways to skin a cat." She believes that if we keep "chipping away at the tall wall" (IFIs and TNCs), with persistence and patience, eventually it will not be able to ignore these critical issues of rights and justice. All efforts in this direction—from the Economic Rights Committee statement to the WTO meeting in Seattle to the work of NGOs—help focus the global community on the plight of the voiceless.[69]

Incorporating Economic and Social Rights into UN Development Programs

UN Secretary General Kofi Annan initiated a process of mainstreaming human rights into all UN activities, including its development programs. The Economic Rights Committee contends that development activities that do not contribute to respect for human rights are not worthy of the name. Mary Robinson, the UN high commissioner for human rights, endorsed this approach when she suggested that decisions as to appropriate priorities in the quest for development "can be made easier by

using the language and standards of human rights and placing the decision making process firmly in the context of the government's international human rights obligations. These obligations stretch also to international organizations."[70]

The integration of human rights into the UN's development programs
can be seen in the work of the UN Development Assistance Framework
(UNDAF), Common Country Assessments (CCA), and the Human
Rights Strengthening (HURIST) project. These programs are part of the
secretary general's efforts to enhance the UN's capacity to implement a
rights-based development mandate. It is too early for an overall evaluation of the effectiveness of these initiatives. Hopefully, these programs
will provide clear mechanisms and solid support for individual countries
to base development policy on the achievement of economic and social
human rights.

The UNDAF is an attempt at bringing greater coherence to the UN's
assistance programs at the country level. It establishes a planning framework for the development operations of the UN system. The CCA is
viewed as the first step in the preparation of the UNDAF. It articulates a
common understanding of the causes of the development problems,
needs, and priorities of a country. The CCA process includes the participation of UN agencies (UNDP, OHCHR, and so on), the national government, civil society (NGOs, research institutes, and so on), the private sector (companies, business associations, and so on), the donor community,
and the Bretton Woods Institutions (World Bank and IMF). These partners
in the development of the CCA work together to develop a consensus on
the development problems, priorities, and needs of the country requesting assistance. The common understanding, agreed to by these development partners, becomes the key document used to define the overall purpose and strategy of UN system support to the country.[71]

The UNDAF–CCA helps the UN establish a unified voice in its development work. It is moving the UN away from a top-down process to a
country-led and country-managed approach to development. It builds
partnerships within the UN system and with national authorities, civil
society, the private sector, and so on. And most significantly, human rights
criteria form the base of its indicators for development.

The UNDAF–CCA process provides an entry point for a human
rights–based approach to development assistance for the UN system as a
whole. UN agencies have for years worked in the areas of education,
housing, poverty eradication, and health. This work "for the promotion of
the economic and social advancement of all peoples," as stated in the UN
Charter, continues. But the UNDAF–CCA strategy represents a shift to a
rights-based approach.[72]

An advantage of a rights-based approach to development is that it equips
the UN with a whole range of legal instruments to utilize in negotiations

and discussions with state and nonstate actors. The normative framework in international law that impacts on the development area includes rules covering nondiscrimination, education, social security, health, participation, and an adequate standard of living, which minimally entails access to food, water, and housing. Many of the human rights agreements are binding on states and thus require compliance. Through this linkage of international law to development planning, the UN is trying to move beyond the human rights standard setting and into human rights enforcement and monitoring. This program represents significant maturation and advancement in the understanding and approach to human rights at the UN.

UNDAF–CCA guidelines include references to human rights and guide country teams to learn where to find general information on human rights in general and on the human rights situation in a given country. Development is assessed through the CCA Indicator Framework, which embraces a human rights core. Framework indicators for economic and social human rights include income poverty, food security and nutrition, health and mortality, reproductive health, child health and welfare, education, gender equality and women's empowerment, employment and sustainable livelihood, housing and basic household amenities and facilities, the environment, and drug control and crime prevention. Framework indicators for civil and political human rights include ratification of international human rights instruments, democracy and participation, administration of justice, and liberty and security of person.[73]

Through the CCA Indicator Framework, states are able to establish specific benchmarks to measure their own performance in the realization of economic, social, and cultural rights. The UN system can respond with technical assistance and aid in an integrated and holistic manner.

The OHCHR, in particular, helps countries adopt a human rights approach to development programming. The OHCHR helps translate development issues into human rights terms. This places these development issues within a normative framework of internationally agreed on and binding human rights law. The OHCHR links development issues to their "human rights substance" in terms of content, minimum standards, and benchmarks according to the various human rights instruments (including the Economic Rights Treaty). Through this adoption of a human rights–based approach, the UN is able to identify progress in the enjoyment of human rights and identify areas where work remains to be done.[74]

For example, after reviewing the progress in the enjoyment of key economic and social human rights in areas of health, education, water and sanitation, standard of living, food, and gender, the OHCHR can point to remaining obstacles to the enjoyment of these rights by vulnerable populations. Public policy can then be identified for action to overcome these obstacles. Examples of such policy include establishing of community monitoring systems to ensure that resources meant for development are used effectively and efficiently; developing local area planning systems to reflect the demands and priorities of the poor; expanding the economic opportunities of women; addressing the much-neglected area of violence against women and children; and promoting education programs to alter mindsets that perpetuate antifemale biases.[75]

Sylvie Saddier, a human rights officer at the OHCHR, notes the many obstacles that occur at the country level in implementing the CCA. Most governments are not familiar with human rights indicators and do not know how to integrate this approach into development planning. Some states are openly hostile to the ideas and object to even using the words "human rights." The OHCHR has shared with country teams various concrete experiences that demonstrate not only the successful implementation of this approach, but also that there is not one way to integrate human rights into development. The process must be sensitive to the specifics of a given culture and country. Despite these hurdles, the UNDAF–CAA rights-based approach to development programs clearly holds much promise.[76]

HURIST is a joint program of the UNDP and the OHCHR designed to support the implementation of the UNDP's policy on human rights presented in the 1998 document *Integrating Human Rights with Sustainable Development*. The purposes of HURIST are to help in the development of national capacities for the promotion and protection of human rights and the application of a human rights approach to development programming. It supports government requests for assistance in the field of human rights by helping to develop action plans at the country level. The goal is to link development and human rights in practice through the integration of human rights into the work of the UNDP.

The UNDP has identified four focus areas for its programming in sustainable human development: the eradication of poverty, the creation of jobs and sustainable livelihoods, the advancement of women and gender equity, and the protection and regeneration of the environment. The importance of an enabling environment for the enhancement of the well-being of people, including the rule of law, the maintenance of peace, security and political stability, and a stable legal and political framework, is also recognized as a key to sustainable human development. Participatory approaches to development, good governance, and human rights are also UNDP priorities.[77]

The UNDP and the OHCHR have programmed the activities of HURIST into five windows. The first window tests guidelines for the development of national human rights plans and the development of human rights capacity in institutions of governance. Mongolia, Nepal, Jordan, Cape Verde, Lithuania, Moldova, Ukraine, and the Dominican Republic are participating in this window. The second window tests guidelines for a human rights approach to sustainable human development, focusing on develop-

ment areas like poverty, gender, environment, water, and sustainable livelihood. Cambodia, Yemen, Botswana, and Mali are participating in this window. The third window focuses on the ratification of human rights treaties.
The fourth window examines the human rights implications of globalization. And the fifth window supports country and regional initiatives in
human rights.[78]

Since HURIST is so new, it is also too soon to evaluate its progress toward
achieving these objectives. But, as with the UNDAF–CCA, HURIST is
clearly a positive step toward a more thorough integration of human rights
into the UN development programs. HURIST contributes to the creation of
a rights-based development model useful for the true actualization of economic and social human rights.

This integration of human rights into UN development programs has
greatly enhanced the importance and stature of the OHCHR. Under the
leadership of Annan and Robinson, the OHCHR has truly become the
lead human rights agency within the UN system. The office was formerly
seen as having a narrow mandate to solely serve the UN's Human Rights
Commission. The expertise of the staff of the OHCHR is now seen as central to the success of the UN's newly adopted rights-based framework for
human development. Unfortunately, the budget and staffing of the
OHCHR does not match its new prominence. The dedicated OHCHR
staff works valiantly with limited resources. Without more support from
the states of the UN, the promising rights-based development framework,
and the other critical work of the OHCHR, will not be realized.[79]

Strengthening Global Compliance with Economic and
Social Human Rights

As can be seen, the OHCHR and the Economic Rights Committee effectively encourage states to adopt and enforce economic and social human
rights. However, the limitations of these efforts are also clear, resulting in
calls for measures to strengthen global compliance with economic and
social human rights. This section critiques two proposals to enhance the
enforcement of these rights: an optional protocol to the Economic Rights
Treaty and a social clause to the WTO.

Optional Protocol

As noted earlier, it is currently not possible for individuals or groups
who feel that their rights under the Economic Rights Treaty have been
violated to submit formal complaints to the Economic Rights Committee.
The absence of this procedure denies victims of abuses the means of
achieving international redress. It further constrains the ability of the Eco-

nomic Rights Committee to develop jurisprudence and case law in economic, social, and cultural rights. The arguments in favor of an optional protocol are compelling: a strengthening of international accountability of states parties; increased congruence in the legal standing accorded to both principal international human rights treaties (since, as outlined earlier, the Political Rights Treaty already has an optional protocol); a refinement of the rights and duties emerging from the Economic Rights Treaty; and, overall, a strengthening of international accountability of states parties.[80]

The 1993 World Conference on Human Rights in the Vienna Declaration and Programme of Action "encourage[d] the Commission on Human Rights, in cooperation with the Committee on Economic, Social and Cultural Rights, to continue the examination of optional protocols to the Covenant on Economic, Social and Cultural Rights."[81] After in-depth discussions and broad consultation, the Economic Rights Committee at its fifteenth session in 1996 adopted a draft optional protocol for submission to the Human Rights Commission. In its work, the Economic Rights Committee took careful note of the oral and written submissions of the ILO, the UN Division for the Advancement of Women, representatives of various NGOs, and the work of an expert meeting convened in Utrecht by the Netherlands Institute for Human Rights in January 1995. The draft optional protocol has yet to be officially adopted by the Human Rights Commission or other relevant UN organs.[82]

The report of the Economic Rights Committee to the Human Rights Commission emphasized a number of key aspects to the draft optional protocol. First, the protocol is strictly optional and thus applicable only to those states parties who agree to it by way of ratification or accession. Second, this procedure is in no way new nor especially innovative. In addition to the First Optional Protocol to the Political Rights Treaty, similar precedents exist within the Minority Rights Treaty, Women's Rights Treaty, Convention against Torture, ILO, UN Educational, Scientific, and Cultural Organization, the American Convention on Human Rights in the Area of Economic, Social and Cultural Rights (the Protocol of San Salvador of 1988), and the Council of Europe. Third, the experiences to date with these existing individual petition procedures indicate that there is no basis to fear that an optional protocol would result in large numbers of complaints. Individuals must first exhaust all domestic remedies before appealing to the regional and international bodies. And fourth, the state party concerned retains the final decision as to what will be done in response to any views adopted by the Economic Rights Committee in response to individual complaints.[83]

An optional protocol providing an individual complaints procedure could improve the effectiveness of UN supervisory mechanisms by adding additional pressure on states parties to comply with international economic, social, and cultural rights standards. This approach makes it clear to states that economic and social rights are justiciable, that is, that these are real legal rights, appropriate for court trial, and not mere "wishes." States parties have legal obligations to respect, protect, and fulfill these rights and individuals have legal recourse to hold their individual state accountable. If an individual has exhausted all recourse for remedy within the state, he or she can then appeal through the optional protocol for redress through the Economic Rights Committee. The existence of this process alone should pressure states parties to be more attentive to their legal obligations in regards to these issues.

The success of the optional protocol to the Political Rights Treaty is strong evidence that a similar procedure attached to the Economic Rights Treaty would also be beneficial. The recommendations and suggestions from the Political Rights Treaty have been followed up by the affected states parties. National legislation has been modified and amended following Political Rights Treaty decisions. These decisions also give NGOs in civil society additional tools to pressure governments to change policy. The optional protocol represents a realistic strengthening of the UN system for monitoring and implementing international economic and social human rights.

Unfortunately, this thoughtful proposal has become overly politicized, resulting in a dampening of enthusiasm for it by states. Developed countries have opposed the adoption of this optional protocol out of concern for the financial commitments involved. Some of these states have also expressed concerns about the difficulty of measuring progress in state fulfillment of economic and social rights obligations. The LDCs, on the other hand, have in general supported this effort, even though these states may be the most affected. It is likely that there would be more individual complaints from citizens in the LDCs than from elsewhere. The LDCs, however, may welcome this attention to their economic plight. It could provide a way to dramatize requests for aid and reform of international economic structures that contribute to perpetuating these unacceptable conditions. Due to these differing perspectives, the optional protocol has become a contentious issue between the developed and underdeveloped nations. It is very close to being permanently shelved.[84]

It is necessary to break through these divisions and create a means for individual and group complaints to be adjudicated at the international level. The Global New Deal (outlined in chapter 8) picks up on these ideas and embraces an expanded optional protocol as one mechanism for respecting, protecting, and fulfilling economic and social human rights in a globalized economy.

Social Clause

A second device designed to hold states accountable to international economic and social human rights standards is a proposed social clause to the rules of the WTO. Economic globalization has seriously impacted the autonomy of the state and has made it more difficult for governments to protect their citizens' public goods (see chapter 2). The goal of the social clause is to utilize positivist international law to require compliance with key ILO conventions by all members of the WTO. WTO membership and benefits would be contingent on ratification and implementation of the social clause. The objective of the social clause is to link the campaign to liberalize trade with a drive to eradicate brutal violations of working and living standards in all countries of the world.

Contemporary neoliberal economic policy, however, calls for unrestrained access to global labor markets and labels attempts to establish fixed labor standards as nothing more than protectionism (as discussed in chapter 2). Establishing minimum wages, neoliberals argue, is an attempt to equalize differences in the costs of production between a domestic article and a similar foreign article that will take away incentives for investments in the LDCs and thus shrink the world economy. The resulting stagnation and unemployment would cause much greater hardship for the working class and the poor than is currently the case in a world of free trade.

Critics of neoliberalism, on the other hand, argue for fair trade and criticize current international economic structures that pressure countries to lower their labor standards and practice social dumping. Membership in the WTO requires that a country abolish the practice of dumping (i.e., actions by governments, such as subsidies and tax breaks, designed to artificially lower the price of an export commodity in order to undercut a comparable product abroad). By dumping cheaper export products into the market, the exporting country hopes to drive competitors out of business and capture the market. Social dumping is a similar phenomena. A state utilizes unacceptable labor practices to lower the price of production and undercut competitors. Labor and social activists contend that these practices should also be banned under the existing rules of the WTO.

Erika de Wet argues that a social clause does not necessarily imply either protectionism or cost equalization. She uses the example of ILO Convention no. 131 on Minimum Wage Fixing to demonstrate how global standards work. This ILO convention is not an attempt to establish a uniform minimum wage across countries. Its intent is to establish the universal principle of a minimum wage. The ILO recognizes that it is unrealistic to expect comparable wages to be paid in the highly industrialized countries and LDCs. The point of Convention no. 131, however, is to require every country to establish at least a minimum wage. This bare minimum demand clearly will not create cost equalization, nor will it eliminate the competitive advantage of low wages and large labor pools in many LDCs. However, the hope is that it would prevent a country from implementing a strategy to create competitive advantage by suppressing wages.[85]

A pivotal hurdle holding up progress toward implementing a social clause is disagreement over which economic and social standards should be included. The standards advocated by the International Confederation of Free Trade Unions (ICFTU), the World Confederation of Labor, and the European Trade Union Confederation include rights to freedom of association and collective bargaining (ILO Conventions nos. 87 and 98), the prevention of forced labor (ILO Conventions nos. 29 and 105), prohibition of discrimination (ILO Conventions nos. 100 and 111), and the introduction of a minimum work age (ILO Convention no. 138). Other advocates add standards on occupational safety and health (ILO Convention no. 155) and minimum wage fixing (ILO Convention no. 131).[86]

The idea of enforcing these standards through universal or regional trading agreements has not moved forward. Developing countries, in particular, have opposed the social clause in the WTO. Some LDCs see this list of labor standards as disguised protectionism and an attempt to undermine their competitive advantage in lower labor costs. Furthermore, some LDCs argue that these universal standards are not sensitive to the specific cultural environment of a poor nation.

Examine, for example, the issue of child labor. A number of these labor standards attempt to end the exploitation of children through the elimination of child labor. Yet, in some cases working outside the home may be an attractive alternative, in particular to young girls. A 1998 report by Population Council researchers suggests that in some cultures child labor for young girls may actually prolong their adolescence. Working outside the home delays the birth of their first child, gives their reproductive systems time to mature, and gives them some independence and self-esteem.[87]

However, the use of child labor often involves brutal exploitation. Garment factory work in Bangladesh, for example, is low paying and grueling. Some 90 percent of the factory workers are female and they range in age from ten to nineteen. A typical monthly wage for the youngest and most inexperienced is $15. Yet, the researchers conclude that despite this exploitation, female factory workers live better, more emancipated lives than their sisters who stayed behind in the villages. The girls working in the factory were able to not only support themselves, but also to learn complex machinery, work alongside men, and challenge authority by demanding higher wages. They were able to put off marriage and childbirth and overcome naivete and ignorance. They were thus liberated as well as exploited.[88]

International human rights law has been attentive to the issue of child labor. The ILO Convention on Child Labor establishes that "the minimum age . . . should not be less than the age of compulsory schooling and, in any case, shall not be less than 15 years. . . . [C]ountries whose economy and educational facilities are insufficiently developed [are allowed] to initially specify a minimum age of 14 years and reduce from 13 years to 12 years the minimum age for light work." It is critical to advocate this minimal standard as the abuse of child labor takes many forms including poor wages, long workdays, unhealthy working conditions, abuse, and the lack of education. According to the ILO, 95 percent of the approximately 200 million child workers around the world are in the LDCs. Clearly, the exploitation of children must end.[89]

However, in a situation where children contribute needed income to their households, face increased poverty if they leave their factory job, and gain valuable vocational skills, the course of action becomes complex. Ending child labor must be combined with an overall program to provide further options and opportunities to these children. If ending child labor means eliminating the primary vehicle through which literally tens of thousands of families avoid poverty, then an alternative road to paid work must be created. Accompanying the elimination of child labor must be a commitment to education, health care, and job creation (for adults) so that these families have alternatives. All of this testifies to the importance of democratic participation in this process. A top-down directive from the Economic Rights Committee to the LDCs to abolish child labor will go nowhere. A grassroots effort in the community to alter exploitative practices, on the other hand, has a chance of success. The ICFTU stated it most clearly: "We seek a commitment to the progressive elimination of child labour as poverty is reduced and education expanded and prosperity rises."[90]

Stephen Herzenberg notes that the fight for minimum labor standards in the United States did not simply revolve around an effort to abolish child labor, but around eliminating the sweatshop as a way of doing business. The overall strategy was to push business away from a reliance on low wages, high levels of physical effort, and worker vulnerability. The strategy incorporated "promotive, preventive, and participative" standards, with the abolition of child labor as a key component.[91]

As with child labor, the issue of night work for women also exposes regional differences in approach and understanding of universal rights. Examine the different understanding of women's human rights in Europe and East Asia in relation to this issue. The European Court ruled that the ban on night work for women violated the regulations guaranteeing equality of women. European governments were compelled to redraft laws forbidding such night work and distance themselves from the ILO convention on this subject. Compare this decision to conditions in East Asia, where upholding the ban on night work for women is seen as a victory for the rights of women workers. In East Asia, the ban is an affirmation of the human right to decent working conditions for women. In Europe, the ban is seen as a denial of a woman's right to access to the same jobs as men. The objective real differences in the lives of working women in Asia and Europe result in differing attitudes toward night work for women. It is clearly not easy to draw up a list of universal social and economic rights.[92]

The examples of child labor and night work for women point to difficulties in implementing the social clause proposal. A social clause imposed through international law and international organization is fundamentally problematic as it does not incorporate any degree of local involvement or democratic participation. Furthermore, such action is often not responsive to the local context and the ways in which rights are prioritized by victimized groups to address the most acute forms of human suffering. To be effective, the implementation of economic and social rights must incorporate local perspectives and strategies, as dramatically demonstrated in the campaign to abolish child labor. For many of these reasons, strong opposition to a social clause has emerged from governments of developing countries and many civil society groups.[93]

The Global New Deal and the United Nations

Summary Observations

The UN has been remarkably effective in defining the core content of economic and social human rights. The Economic Rights Committee has established key criteria to monitor state's compliance with international human rights law. Powerful new global economic actors, including IFIs and TNCs, are also beginning to be held accountable to economic and social human rights law. Accurate indicators of social development to measure the achievement of economic and social human rights are being refined at the UNDP. Furthermore, the UN has incorporated human rights into its development programs, including the UNDAF, CCA, and HURIST projects.

However, global compliance with economic and social human rights is often weak or nonexistent. Thus, new mechanisms have been drafted to strengthen enforcement,

Global New Deal Proposals

The Global New Deal attempts to build a bridge and be responsive to both the concerns of the developed and less developed countries. It calls for enhancing the powers of the Economic Rights Committee. It seeks to provide a place in international organizations for the voices of the victims denied economic and social human rights to be heard. The expanded Optional Protocol to the Economic Rights Treaty outlined in chapter 8 could be key to the successful adjudication of violations of economic and social human rights.

The current draft optional protocol approved by the Economic Rights Committee provides the basic framework for a workable system. It gives legal standing to the victims of abuse and those organizing for social change. The voices of those individuals denied economic and social human rights can be

including an optional protocol to the Economic Rights Treaty and a social clause to IFIs, like the WTO.

The global community seems divided on these two reform proposals. On one side, the developed states oppose the optional protocol, while giving some support for a social clause and the linking of trade and workers' rights. On the other side, the LDCs oppose the social clause and any trade–rights linkage, while stating support for the optional protocol. Is there a way to span this divide?

heard through these proposed procedures. The legal cases of the vulnerable deserve adjudication.

In addition, under the expanded optional protocol the Economic Rights Committee would also be authorized to examine the work of IFIs and TNCs. Individuals and groups would be able to raise violations of economic and social human rights by IFIs and TNCs as well as states. Thus, instead of a social clause, the Global New Deal calls for the enhancement of the power of the Economic Rights Committee to be able to hold all global economic actors accountable to human rights law.

4

The Environment and Economic
and Social Human Rights

Is there a human right to a healthy environment? What are environmental rights? What are the links between international human rights law and international environmental law? Is a rights-based approach a clear pathway to achieve ecological balance? Does the existing corpus of international human rights law provide the tools to force states and all economic institutions to account for environmental costs and correct harmful practices? Does a human rights approach provide the best avenue to bridge the perceived gap between economic development and ecological balance? How does a program for economic justice take into account environmental justice? How do the UN Environment Program (UNEP), the Commission on Sustainable Development (CSD), and the Global Environment Facility (GEF) approach these issues? What public policy successfully links ecological balance to economic and social human rights?

The late twentieth century brought new awareness of the ecological fragility of our planet. Following the 1972 UN Conference on the Human Environment in Stockholm (hereafter the Stockholm Conference), the international community enacted multiple measures in international law designed to protect the environment. Further action was formulated in 1992 at the UN Conference on the Environment and Development in Rio de Janeiro (hereafter the Rio Conference). It is now estimated that there are over 300 multilateral treaties and approximately

900 bilateral treaties dealing with the protection and conservation of the biosphere. This international regulation has led to conventions covering the oceans, atmosphere, wild life, toxic substances, radioactive waste, and other key sectors or areas.[1]

Yet, despite this action the global environment continues to be under siege. This progress in international environmental law has unfortunately not been adequate to protect our biosphere. Examine, for example, just one critical issue confronting the global community: climate change. In 1988, the UN created the Intergovernmental Panel on Climate Change (IPCC), an organization made up of hundreds of the world's leading scientists, to assess the scientific evidence for global warming. In late 2000, the IPCC produced its latest report on human-induced global climate change. Fossil fuel combustion was estimated to have raised atmospheric concentrations of carbon dioxide to their highest levels on record. This scientific body stated that societies' release of carbon dioxide and other greenhouse gases "contributed substantially to the observed warming over the last 50 years." The warming in the twentieth century was likely to have been the greatest of any century in the last 1,000 years for the Northern Hemisphere. The 1990s was the warmest decade of the last millennium. Snow cover since the 1960s has been cut by 10 percent. The sea level rose at a rate ten times faster than the average rate over the last 3,000 years. The IPCC concluded that by the end of the twenty-first century temperatures will be approximately eleven degrees higher than in 1990. This increase is greater than the change in temperature between the last Ice Age and today.[2]

Despite this evidence, when 170 nations met at The Hague in November 2000, they were unable to come to agreement on a treaty to limit the production of greenhouse gases. The global warming talks collapsed despite the recognized heating of the oceans and melting of the world's glaciers. The Kyoto Protocol, debated at The Hague Conference, would have required countries to reduce greenhouse gas emissions, primarily coal and oil, to 7 percent below 1990 levels. According to the U.S. Energy Department, Americans produce 12 percent more carbon dioxide annually than they did when President Bill Clinton took office (1992). Voluntary measures to reduce this have failed. Americans used 1.3 percent more fossil fuel in 1999 than in 1998. The Kyoto Protocol would at least force participating countries to slow these harmful trends.[3]

Our oceans, wildlife, and entire biosphere face severe threats from industrialization, modernization, and globalization. It is now estimated that up to one-fifth of all known living species are threatened with extinction. In areas like species preservation, biodiversity, and global warming, some scientists believe that it may already be too late. We may have set forces in motion that we cannot now control. Despite the scientific certainty of the depths of our environmental problems, few leaders are willing to call for appropriate policies to curb destructive human behavior. The priority for political leaders around the world is economic growth, not ecological balance.

Tragically, economic development and modern living have often conflicted with environmental protection. On the one hand, developed countries have shown an unwillingness to limit ingrained patterns of nonsustainable consumption. The U.S. economy and society, for example, are structured around the heavy consumption of fossil fuels, which significantly contribute to global warming. Adhering to the limits of the Kyoto Protocol would require fundamental changes in both economic planning and the U.S. lifestyle. On the other hand, underdeveloped countries, facing massive problems of poverty and destitution, have had difficulty prioritizing ecological balance. The priority for the poor is often seen as economic development and growth based on an industrialization model that is environmentally destructive. Thus, both the developed and underdeveloped nations have shown little motivation to mobilize either international law or international organization for environmental protection and ecological renewal.

The tragic results of this global stalemate in contemporary environmental politics was dramatically documented at the Earth Summit Plus Five Conference held in New York in 1997. Not one of the important commitments made at the Rio Conference had been kept. Instead of bringing down carbon dioxide emission to the 1990 levels by the year 2000 as promised, emissions in 1997 were higher than ever before (and are now even higher in 2002). The stated intention of raising Northern aid for the sustainable development of the Southern underdeveloped countries to 0.7 percent of the gross domestic product (GDP) was ignored. In fact, less foreign aid was available five years after the Rio Conference than at the time of the summit itself. Forest cover continued to decline, water resource management failed, and the commitment to defend biodiversity faded. The economic growth that many countries experienced simply led to more pollution.[4]

UN Secretary General Kofi Annan challenged this inertia in his report to the UN Millennium Summit in September 2000. Annan's report highlighted key environmental challenges, including global climate change, land degradation, and diminished freshwater resources. In a rebuke to the General Assembly, he wrote: "The nearly 18 months during which the General Assembly debated which subjects to include in the Summit's agenda makes it plain how little priority is accorded to these extraordinarily serious challenges for all humankind. Leadership at the very highest level is imperative if we are to bequeath a liveable earth to our children—and theirs."[5]

This chapter explores the links between economic and social human rights and environmental rights in the following sections:

- Human rights and the environment, an analysis of a human rights approach to ecological balance
- UNEP, a review of some of its key programs aimed at global environmental monitoring and information sharing
- The CSD, an appraisal of its progress since the Rio Conference
- GEF, an inquiry into this new model of international environmental organization
- The marriage of economic and environmental health, an evaluation of key dimensions to public policy that successfully links ecological balance to economic and social human rights

Human Rights and the Environment

Environmental and human rights issues converge in a myriad of ways. Environmental degradation carries a high human cost. Unfair distribution of the costs of ecological damage, often referred to as "environmental racism" or "environmental injustice," raise human rights issues of equality and discrimination. Environmental organizations in civil society depend on such human rights as the right to associate and freedom of speech to lead a successful environmental movement. In countries where civil and political rights are weak, such as the former Soviet Union, ecological damage is often high.

The links between human rights and the environment were vividly brought to the public's awareness in the 1980s and 1990s with the brutal killings of Chico Mendes in Brazil and Ken Saro Wiwa in Nigeria. Mendes was murdered by ranchers with close ties to government officials because of his efforts to protect the rain forests of Brazil from deforestation. Mendes saw that the livelihood and economic human rights of the Brazilian rubber tappers was linked to the preservation of the natural ecosystem. To silence Saro Wiwa, the former Nigerian dictatorship had him hung. His crime was protesting the oil development in his native Ogoni lands. In these and other cases, the international human rights movement has organized and protested against these acts of internal repression.[6]

Both human rights and environmental law have an overriding ambition: the modification of human activity through norms that trump all other considerations. The importance and normative value of protecting human beings and the environment constitutes a common concern of all humankind. Yet, despite the growing awareness of the links between their work, tensions remain between human rights and environmental activists. The priority of the human rights movement is the protection and development of the human species. The priority of the environmental movement is the protection and survival of all species and all natural ecosystems. Although it appears on the surface that these priorities collide, it is possible to see how they can support each other.

On one side, some environmentalists fear that the anthropocentric focus of human rights law will lead to environmental destruction. Human rights law privileges the life, health, standard of living, and overall welfare of human beings. A likely consequence of economic development focused on growth and increasing human consumption is the rapid depletion of natural resources. Fulfilling economic rights for a global population of over 6 billion people could have devastating repercussions on the environment. A response to these concerns, however, is to see human rights protection as a vehicle for the realization of environmental protection. The protection of civil and political rights creates the political space for organizing and speaking out for environmental protection. A human right to a satisfactory environment, and the creation of the legal means to support this right, could provide tools to achieve ecological balance.

On the other side, some human rights activists fear that the urgency of ending existing human suffering becomes muted and displaced when the priority becomes long-term ecological balance and the rights of future generations. The environmental movement is seen as neglecting pressing human needs while privileging the rights of other species and the protection of the natural global ecosystem. The economic rights of the sick and hungry are seen as a human rights priority that environmentalists often ignore. A response to these concerns, however, is to see environmental protection as a vehicle for the fulfillment of human rights. Human rights to health and life cannot be achieved in a degraded physical environment. Acts leading to a degraded environment (deforestation, oil spills, toxic dumps, and so on) can be a violation of internationally recognized human rights. Such acts can literally deprive local populations of the ability to survive. Environmental law is thus of assistance not just to future generations, but also to those who depend on natural resources for their survival, including indigenous groups.[7]

The Right to a Healthy Environment in International Law

Although most human rights treaties do not explicitly mention a general right to a healthy environment, a case can be made that such a right exists in international law. International law includes both "hard law" and "soft law." Hard law refers to treaties, customary law, and general principles of international law (as defined by article 38 of the Statute of the International Court of Justice). Hard law is considered binding on states and is often incorporated into national jurisprudence. Soft law refers to actions by state and nonstate actors that fall between law in this strict sense and a mere political statement with no consequences. Soft law can take many forms including recommendations, declarations, clarifications, directives, standards, and so on. In both hard and soft law, the international community has endorsed the human right to a healthy environment.

Hard Law

The following two agreements specifically call for a right to a healthy environment: the African Charter on Human and Peoples' Rights (African Charter) and the San Salvador Additional Protocol to the American Convention on Human Rights in the Area of Economic, Social and Cultural Rights (San Salvador Protocol). In addition, the linkage between fundamental human rights, such as the right to life and the right to health, and a healthy environment can be drawn directly from the International Bill of Human Rights,[8] international humanitarian law, and other human rights treaties. And finally, individual nations have expressed a concern for the protection of the environment in their national laws and constitutions.

Article 24 of the African Charter states: "All peoples shall have the right to a general satisfactory environment favourable to their development."[9]

Scholars often situate the claims that the African Charter defines as peoples' rights within third-generation rights. First-generation rights are seen as civil and political rights, whereas economic, social, and cultural rights are classified as second-generation rights. Third-generation rights are frequently called "solidarity rights" as they are based on norms of fraternity. These rights include the right of peoples to self-determination, full sovereignty over their natural resources, development, and a general satisfactory environment.

As seen in article 24, the African Charter links a satisfactory environment to development. The implications of this linkage are not clear. In a conflict between conservation and development, for example, which would prevail? There is also no clear definition of a "general satisfactory environment." Overall, the African Charter focuses much more on issues of development than on the environment. The preamble calls on states to "pay . . . particular attention to the right to development." And, article 22(1) states: "All peoples shall have the right to their economic, social and cultural development with due regard to their freedom and identity and in the equal enjoyment of the common heritage of mankind." Ecological balance is not on equal footing with the "right to development" in the charter.

In 1989, the African Commission on Human and Peoples' Rights noted that the main purpose of article 24 "is to protect the environment and keep it favourable for development." The commission suggested that states parties should "establish a system to monitor effective disposal of waste in order to prevent pollution." The commission urged states to report on legislation and other measures taken to prohibit pollution on land, in water, and in the air, to prevent the international dumping of toxic wastes, and to curb wastes generally. Critics have noted that the commission took a narrow, largely anthropocentric, view of what is meant by a "satisfactory environment," since there was no reference to the conservation of species or habitats, global climate change, and so on.[10]

Article 11 of the San Salvador Protocol recognizes:

1. Everyone shall have the right to live in a healthy environment and to have access to basic public services
2. The states parties shall promote the protection, preservation, and improvement of the environment[11]

The San Salvador Protocol, which entered into force on 16 November 1999,[12] does not define a "healthy environment." Article 1 maintains that the parties "undertake to adopt the necessary measures, both domestically and through cooperation, especially economic and technical, to the extent allowed by their available resources, and taking into account their degree of development, for the purpose of achieving progressively and pursuant to their internal legislations, the full observance of the rights recognized in the Protocol." This implies that states parties should do what they can to promote a healthy environment only as far as their resources allow. They need do nothing if they lack the resources. But if they have the resources, they must take some measures to protect the human environment. Article 11 thus represents a weak environmental right. States parties essentially must do no more than they feel able to do to promote a healthy environment. Given the extensive poverty and poor economic conditions prevailing throughout Latin America, it is hard to see nations transferring scarce resources to environmental protection.[13]

Environmental protection can also be found in the International Bill of Human Rights and other human rights conventions in calls for the right to life, the right to good health, the right to healthy working conditions, and the right to adequate living standards. There is a direct link between these concerns (life, health, and adequate working and living conditions) and a healthy environment. This connection is made clear, for example, in article 24 of the 1989 "Convention on the Rights of the Child." Children have the right to enjoy the highest attainable standard of health, and states are to take measures to "combat disease and malnutrition . . . through . . . the provision of adequate nutritious foods and clean drinking water, taking into consideration the danger and the risks of environmental pollution."[14] These human rights treaties thus bind states to address environmental protection in their development policies.

In regard to international humanitarian law, concern for the protection of the environment is found in articles 35(3) and 55 of the 1977 Additional Protocol I to the 1949 Geneva Conventions (prohibition of methods or means of warfare severely damaging the environment) and the 1977 UN Convention on the Prohibition of Military or Any Other Hostile Use of Environmental Modification Techniques.[15]

The right to a healthy environment has thus been clearly recognized in positivist international law. It has also been recognized in national legislation and national constitutional provisions. Clauses related to environmental protection—either as a duty of the state or as an individual right or both—are found in at least forty-four national constitutions and in those of a dozen state members of federal states. General laws of several countries also embrace environmental rights. The constitution of Brazil, for example, states: "Everyone has the right to an ecologically balanced environment, an asset for the common use of the people and essential to the wholesome quality of life. This imposes upon the Public Authorities and the community the obligation to defend and preserve it for present and future generations."[16]

Soft Law

Since the 1972 Stockholm Conference, there have been numerous instruments of soft law (resolutions, declarations, and so on) embracing a human right to a healthy environment. Principle 1 of the "Stockholm Declaration of the United Nations Conference on the Human Environment" declares: "Man has the fundamental right to freedom, equality, and adequate conditions of life, in an environment of a quality that permits a life of dignity and well-being, and he bears a solemn responsibility to protect and improve the environment for present and future generations."[17]

In 1974, the UN Charter of Economic Rights and Duties of States declared in article 30 that the "protection, preservation and enhancement of the environment for the present and future generations is the responsibility of all States. . . . All States have the responsibility to ensure that activities within their jurisdiction or control do not cause damage to the environment of other States or of areas beyond the limits of national jurisdiction."[18]

The 1982 World Charter for Nature reaffirms that humanity must "acquire the knowledge and enhance [its] ability to use natural resources in a manner which ensures the preservation of the species and ecosystems for the benefit of present and future generations."[19]

In 1989, the UN General Assembly, in its call for the convening of the Rio Conference, recognized the global character of environmental problems, and affirmed that the protection and enhancement of the environment were major issues that affected the well-being of peoples everywhere.[20]

In 1992, the Rio Conference adopted "Agenda 21," an 800-page detailed blueprint for launching an ambitious "global partnership for sustainable development." "Agenda 21" refers directly to two human rights instruments—the Universal Declaration of Human Rights (UDHR) and the UN

Covenant on Economic, Social and Cultural Rights (Economic Rights Treaty). Furthermore, it parallels the concern for vulnerable groups (women, indigenous populations, children, and so on) found in human rights documents.[21]

In 1993, the World Conference on Human Rights adopted the "Vienna Declaration and Programme of Action," which establishes in point eleven that: "The right to development should be fulfilled so as to meet equitably the developmental and environmental needs of present and future generations." The declaration further declares that the "illicit dumping of toxic and dangerous substances and waste potentially constitutes a serious threat to the human rights to life and health of everyone."[22]

In July 1994, Fatma Zohra Ksentini, the UN's special rapporteur on human rights and the environment, released her final report. "Human Rights and the Environment" (hereafter the Ksentini Report) argues that there has been "a shift from environmental law to the right to a healthy and decent environment."[23] The Ksentini Report proposes a set of "Draft Principles on Human Rights and the Environment."[24] Part one of the draft principles declares the following:

1. Human rights, an ecologically sound environment, sustainable development and peace are interdependent and indivisible
2. All persons have the right to a secure, healthy, and ecologically sound environment
3. All persons shall be free from any form of discrimination in regard to actions and decisions that affect the environment
4. All persons have the right to an environment adequate to meet equitably the needs of present generations and that does not impair the rights of future generations to meet equitably their needs

The draft principles conclude by calling on all states to "adopt administrative, legislative and other measures necessary to effectively implement the rights in this Declaration." Such measures shall include the

- collection and dissemination of information concerning the environment
- regulation or prohibition of activities and substances potentially harmful to the environment
- public participation in environmental decision-making
- monitoring, management and equitable sharing of natural resources
- measures to reduce wasteful processes of production and patterns of consumption
- measures aimed at ensuring that transnational corporations, wherever they operate, carry out their duties of environmental protection, sustainable development and respect for human rights[25]

The combined impact of the Ksentini Report with the other soft law environmental instruments (resolutions, declarations, and so on) should not be underestimated. Soft law is important in providing a means for articulating a new normative international program. As soft law norms evolve, it becomes increasingly difficult for international actors to ignore internationally accepted normative guidelines and human rights principles. The soft law case for a human right to a healthy environment is potent and persuasive.

These rights can be effectively utilized in the struggle for ecological balance. They establish a standard from which to judge the behavior of all economic organizations. This human rights approach is useful for clarifying definitive claims that should not be violated. They provide a link to the UN international legal framework of reporting and accountability. Existing environmental treaties have already established supervisory institutions (e.g., the Convention on International Trade in Endangered Species [CITES] and the Convention on Biological Diversity). The human rights treaty monitoring bodies also play a significant role in supervising state adherence to international norms. Environmental protection and human rights protection are linked, as both strive to guarantee basic human survival. A human right to a healthy environment embraces claims to sustain life over months and generations for individuals and groups. It pertains to biological necessities (access to food, water, and shelter) and the management of ecosystems in a way that ensures their continuous viability.

The United Nations and Ecological Balance

Institutions are needed for the development and implementation of human rights. At the local level, for example, huge state bureaucracies exist to enforce civil and political human rights. State welfare agencies are often committed to the protection of basic economic and social human rights. At the international level, the UN Human Rights Commission and the UN Human Rights Committee primarily attend to state violations of civil and political rights. The work of the UN Economic Rights Committee to monitor state actions of omission and/or commission that may violate the Economic Rights Treaty was reviewed in chapter 3.

Global institutions are particularly relevant to the achievement of ecological balance. Pollution readily crosses borders with impunity. Acting after the environmental damage has been done is often of little help. The protection of the oceans, seas, land, forests, and atmosphere involves managing the affairs between state and nonstate actors. Public and private international organizations, both in and outside of the UN system, are key to increasing the cooperation and coordination among all these stakeholders. Creating global environmental management through international organization is central to achieving a healthy environment.

There exists no single institution in control of the management of global environmental affairs. Yet, international organizations committed to the development and implementation of the right to a healthy environment have grown in strength and scope since the 1972 Stockholm Conference. The chief international environmental organization is UNEP, initially created at Stockholm. Twenty years later at the 1992 Rio Conference, the CSD was born. Also in the 1990s, GEF was established. There are a myriad of other intergovernmental organizations (IGOs) and nongovernmental organizations (NGOs) working globally on environmental protection. In addition, bodies created under specific international environmental treaties monitor states parties' compliance with the agreed on global environmental rules and norms. Due to their overall importance, this section focuses on the work of UNEP, the CSD, and GEF.

UN Environment Program

UN General Assembly Resolution 2997 created UNEP in 1972 as the first UN agency with a specific environmental agenda. The following functions and responsibilities for UNEP were articulated by the General Assembly:

- To promote international co-operation in the field of the environment
- To provide general policy guidance for . . . environmental programmes within the UN system
- To keep under review the world environmental situation in order to ensure that emerging environmental problems of wide international significance receive appropriate and adequate consideration by Governments
- To promote the . . . acquisition and exchange of environmental knowledge and information
- To maintain under continuing review the impact of national and international environmental policies on developing countries[26]

UNEP was established as a coordinating body acting to encourage environmental cooperation between member states.

UNEP was also intended to be a catalyst for environmental activities throughout the UN system. It was meant to spur the larger UN specialized agencies, such as the UNDP and the Food and Agriculture Organization, to incorporate environmental protection and planning into their projects. Since it would not be engaging in projects of its own, UNEP was given a modest staff and small budget. Governments promised an "environment fund" for UNEP to utilize in promoting environmental action throughout

---

KEY ENVIRONMENTAL
INTERGOVERNMENTAL ORGANIZATIONS

- UN Environment Program (UNEP)
  www.unep.org/
  UNEP was established in 1972 as the first UN agency with a
  primary focus on the environment. UNEP encourages sustainable development and sound environmental practices. Its
  activities include the gathering and sharing of environmental
  science and information, an early warning and emergency
  response capacity to deal with environmental disasters and
  emergencies, enhanced coordination and implementation of
  international environmental treaties, and the development of
  new international environmental law and policy instruments. UNEP is headquartered in Nairobi, Kenya, and has
  regional offices in Paris, Geneva, Osaka, The Hague, Washington, New York, Bangkok, Mexico City, Manama, Montreal, and Bonn.
- UN Commission on Sustainable Development (CSD)
  www.un.org/esa/sustdev/csd.htm

---

the UN. Unfortunately, the environment fund was never given significant
revenues, and UNEP's total resources over its first twenty years amounted
to only $1 billion. Its resources are anemic compared to the programs of the
World Bank or the International Monetary Fund (IMF). (In 1998, for example, total World Bank expenditures totaled over $28 billion and IMF expen-
ditures surpassed $27 billion.) UNEP's location in Nairobi also makes
coordination with other UN agencies difficult.[27]

Despite its limited budget—smaller than many private environmental
organizations—and small staff, UNEP is credited with some significant
accomplishments. For example, UNEP's Division of Programs includes a
specific unit dedicated to promoting international environmental law. The
work of this unit has to be judged a success. Once a draft legal instrument
is agreed on by the working group, UNEP may then convene a diplomatic
conference to consider adoption. The Vienna Convention for the Protection of the Ozone Layer (Vienna Convention) and the Montreal Protocol
on Substances that Deplete the Ozone Layer (Montreal Protocol) were
both adopted through this technique. In fact, more than forty multilateral

The CSD was created in December 1992 to ensure effective follow-up of the Rio Conference. The CSD monitors the implementation of the Rio agreements at the local, national, regional, and international levels. The CSD is a functional commission of the UN Economic and Social Council. The CSD consistently generates a high level of public interest. Over fifty ministers attend the CSD each year and more than a thousand NGOs are accredited to participate in the commission's work. The commission attempts to ensure a high visibility of sustainable development issues within the UN system.

- Global Environment Facility (GEF)
  www.undp.org/gef/
  GEF was created to assist developing countries tackle global environmental problems. GEF is mandated to financially help underdeveloped countries implement existing international environmental treaties, such as the Conventions on Climate Change and Biodiversity. The World Bank, UNEP, and the UN Development Program (UNDP) work cooperatively through GEF to address these issues. GEF has become the largest multilateral source of grant funds available for environmental protection. The hybrid organizational and governing structure of GEF attempts to balance the interests of countries from both the North and the South.

environmental treaties have been negotiated under UNEP's leadership, including the Basel Convention on the Control of Transboundary Movements of Hazardous Waste and Their Disposal (Basel Convention), the UN Convention to Combat Desertification, and CITES.[28]

In the area of soft law, UNEP has developed some important agreements, including the World Charter for Nature[29] and the Declaration of Environmental Policies and Procedures Relating to Economic Development.[30] This latter declaration was signed by the World Bank, the UNDP, UNEP, the Organization of American States, and six other development assistance agencies. UNEP played a central catalytic role in bringing these IGOs together to coordinate environmental action. By signing the declaration, the participating organizations agreed to submit all development activities to systematic environmental assessment and evaluation. In addition, these organizations agreed to support projects that enhanced the environment of developing nations. These IGOs then established the Committee of International Development Institutions on the Environment to regularly review the implementation of the declaration.[31]

UNEP also plays a significant role in monitoring, gathering, assessing, and disseminating data regarding the earth's environment. For example, the Global Environmental Monitoring System (GEMS), part of UNEP's Earthwatch system, enlists thousands of scientists around the world to assess the health of the world's ecosystems. Additionally, UNEP established INFOTERRA as a global environmental information exchange system. The Global Resource Information Database was organized to disseminate environmental information to assist the African, Mediterranean, and West Asia Environment Research and Information Networks. UNEP maintains a global chemicals information clearinghouse, including an International Register of Potentially Toxic Chemicals, designed to increase awareness about the hazards of chemical production.[32]

Despite this progress, the UN system as a whole did not keep up with the serious environmental threats confronting the planet in the final decades of the twentieth century. Scholars have documented the ways in which UNEP failed to keep pace with the dramatic changes in international environmental policy making. When UNEP was created in the 1970s, there were few other international actors trying to influence the environmental agenda. As noted earlier, since the Stockholm Conference over one hundred environmental treaties have been negotiated, establishing implementation mechanisms and state obligations to protect biodiversity and the ozone layer, to combat desertification, and so on. Due to its limited budget and size, UNEP has been unable to manage and direct this widening scope of global environmental politics. This, of course, has produced disappointment with the organization among some environmentalists.[33]

As the management of global environmental affairs has grown, UNEP's mission has remained broad and unfocused. For a financially constrained organization, UNEP is criticized for taking on too many tasks. For example, the UNEP's Governing Council reported to the June 1997 Earth Summit Plus Five special session of the General Assembly on significant activities relevant to every single chapter of "Agenda 21."[34] Former UNEP executive director Elizabeth Dowdeswell acknowledged UNEP's lack of clear priorities: "A rigorous review of current activities reveals a number that are no longer on the leading edge or represent sufficient added value given the scarce resources of UNEP. Others are self-perpetuating, continuing long after 'catalysis' should have been completed. Furthermore, activities once undertaken by UNEP, such as certain types of coordination, may now be better accomplished by others."[35]

UNEP has been a clear success in (1) negotiation management of international environmental law and (2) gathering, disseminating, and assessing environmental information. UNEP can build on the past strengths it has demonstrated in both of these areas. These two functions could provide the future focus for a streamlined, directed UNEP with a clear mission. With adequate staff and resources, UNEP could fulfill both of these tasks more effectively. As David L. Downie and Marc A. Levy write: "Doing so would meet all the relevant criteria for what a streamlined UNEP ought to focus on—UNEP is good at it, the world needs it, and no one else is doing it."[36] UNEP could continue to carry out these two critical functions as a division within the new environmental IGO, the World Environment Organization, proposed in chapter 8 as part of the Global New Deal.

In partial recognition of the limitations of UNEP, the Rio Conference in 1992 called for the creation of the CSD.

Commission on Sustainable Development

Chapter 38 of "Agenda 21," adopted at the Rio Conference, recommended the establishment of the CSD, a high-level, intergovernmental forum to oversee the implementation of the promises made at Rio and to pursue avenues toward sustainable development. Rio Conference delegates felt the need to improve the institutional arrangements at the international level for the UN system to be able to adequately address sustainable development. "Agenda 21" strives to integrate environmental and development goals and thus requires extensive coordination between various UN agencies and other international bodies. The CSD was designed to provide the institutional framework for this coordination to take place. Additionally, the CSD was envisioned as providing a forum for the continued debate on sustainable development and the search for solutions to problems of the environment and development.[37]

In response to these recommendations from the Rio Conference, the UN General Assembly created the CSD in January 1993. The General Assembly empowered the CSD with the expansive functions recommended in "Agenda 21." The CSD is charged with monitoring progress in implementing "Agenda 21" both within the UN system and by states parties through a review of their national reports regarding activities undertaken to implement "Agenda 21." Through the power of publicity and peer pressure, the CSD can encourage states parties to implement "Agenda 21" and other Rio agreements. The model, of course, is the UN Commission on Human Rights, which, although lacking formal enforcement powers, has been able to embarrass and shame countries into changing unacceptable practices. The CSD approach is similar although it focuses on positive recommendations and reinforcements as opposed to censure. UN Resolution 47/191 gave three broad responsibilities to the CSD:[38]

- To review progress toward the implementation of the recommendations and commitments contained in the final documents of the Rio Conference, including "Agenda 21," the "Rio de Janeiro Declaration on Environment and Development," and the Forest Principles

- To develop policy options to follow up on the Rio Conference and achieve sustainable development
- To build partnerships for sustainable development with governments, IGOs, NGOs, and others with a major role in the transition to sustainability (including women, indigenous peoples, the scientific community, farmers, and so on)[39]

The implementation of "Agenda 21" was reviewed by delegates to the Earth Summit Plus Five Conference held in New York in 1997. This follow-up conference adopted a "Programme for the Further Implementation of Agenda 21" that called on the CSD not only to continue with the three broad responsibilities previously outlined, but also to provide a forum for the exchange of experiences on national, regional, and subregional initiatives and collaborations for sustainable development. In addition, the Earth Summit Plus Five delegates called on the CSD to strive to attract the greater involvement of ministers and high-level national policy makers in their work and to establish closer interaction with international financial, development, and trade institutions.[40]

The CSD must mediate divergent views on the relationship between the environment and development. There remain, for example, strong disagreements on these issues between the developed North and the underdeveloped South. Although all can agree that the environment should be protected, strong divergences exist on appropriate solutions. The North has argued that by protecting the environment, development can be enhanced. In this view, the first priority is to halt and prevent the environmental degradation that contributes to poverty and underdevelopment. The South, on the other hand, has argued that the first priority should be economic development. Such development could enhance the protection of the environment. Development can alleviate poverty, which contributes to environmental depletion. For example, with the elimination of poverty there would be no need to exhaust environmental resources for food. The challenge before the CSD is to reconcile these views.[41]

The CSD is made up of fifty-three member states elected on a carefully balanced political and geographical quota system for three-year terms with one-third elected annually. Although only members may vote, other states, UN organizations, and accredited IGOs and NGOs may attend the sessions as observers.

Unfortunately, the CSD was given modest resources to achieve its ambitious agenda of reconciling the environment and development. It has no resources of its own and depends on funding from the shrinking UN budget. It has no regulatory power and is unable to force change at the national or local level. Its mandate is so broad it is difficult to distinguish clear priorities. And finally, the CSD relies on voluntary self-reports of states parties. According to Hilary French from the Worldwatch Institute, when they do reply, the tendency has been for governments "to deliver documents that are long on self-congratulations and short on substantive analysis of remaining challenges." French argues that these structural defects in the formation and operations of the CSD greatly impede substantive progress on environmental protection.[42]

National governments have used the CSD to share information on the implementation of the Rio agreements. "Agenda 21" called on all nations to formulate national sustainable development policies and programs. As of January 2000, 140 nations had created national organizations or governmental units with the responsibility of implementing "Agenda 21." Governments have been able to use the CSD to exchange views on difficult issues, including trade, unsustainable production, and consumption patterns. In addition, CSD sessions now attract environmental activists and organizations from around the world. Over 800 NGOs participated in the 1999 session of the CSD. These participants have helped push forward a progressive agenda of environmental protection.[43]

In a review of the first five years' work of the CSD, Pamela S. Chasek finds a mixed record in relation to the three major goals of its mission. First, in relation to reviewing the progress of the implementation of "Agenda 21," national reporting has been problematic. Although the CSD did adopt overall reporting guidelines, it is up to individual governments to decide on the degree of detail and the regularity of their reports to the CSD. A comprehensive reporting process was not established. Submitted self-reports are often vague, difficult to compare, and hard to verify. On a more positive note, the CSD was able to develop a set of indicators to monitor progress toward sustainable development. At its third session in April 1995, the CSD adopted a working list of 134 indicators for sustainable development and related methodology sheets. The goal is to have these indicators adopted by all countries, thus providing for more effective monitoring.[44]

Second, the CSD in its first five years has a mixed record in the area of policy guidance and options for future activities. Two CSD successes were the establishment of the Intergovernmental Panel on Forests (IPF) and the Comprehensive Freshwater Assessment (CFA). The IPF helped focus an international dialogue on forests that successfully led to an international consensus on approaches for action.[45] The CFA's comprehensive overview of major water quantity and quality problems helped clarify the nature of the water problem facing various regions of the world and the implications of not dealing with these problems. The UN assessment study showed that two-thirds of humanity will suffer from shortages of clean freshwater within thirty years unless action is taken.[46] Yet, most CSD debates do not result in mobilizing action that could achieve such results. Too often, the discussion does not reach real policy makers at the national level and only remains in the halls of the UN itself.

Third, Chasek believes that the CSD has accomplished the most in its goal of promoting dialogue and building partnerships for sustainable development. The CSD has brought together governments, IGOs, NGOs, and other major stakeholders into dialogue sessions on sustainable development. The CSD has become one of the central UN bodies to incorporate civil society into its deliberation in an effective manner. NGOs dissatisfied with the position of their government's representatives can put on pressure at home. As a result, governments are paying more attention to CSD issues to hold off a potential domestic political backlash. Many governments, of course, are not listening, and some do not have NGOs to worry about. But these dialogue sessions do bring a sense of urgency and reality into the CSD.[47]

The CSD is such a relatively young environmental IGO that it is perhaps premature to draw final conclusions about its viability and ultimate effectiveness. Thus far, its decisions and recommendations have often been vague and unhelpful, a result of difficult negotiations between parties with divergent interests. The split between the developed and underdeveloped nations over environmental priorities is unresolved and hampers bold CSD action. Until the developed nations fulfill their commitment of increasing official development assistance aid to the UN target of 0.7 percent of the gross national product (GNP), these global divisions will not heal. At the 1997 Earth Summit Plus Five Conference, it was noted that official development assistance has "drastically declined" since Rio, from an average 0.34 percent of the GNP in 1992 to 0.27 percent in 1995. At the conference, Northern and Southern countries disagreed on basic wording as to whether provisions on finance and technology transfer in "Agenda 21" were "commitments" or "objectives." The CSD will have to pay more attention to the link between the environment and development and work to resolve these global tensions.[48]

Global Environment Facility

International legal agreements, negotiated to create cooperation in environmental affairs, are to be implemented at the national level by the ratifying states. As reviewed earlier, UNEP helps facilitate the bargaining process among sovereign states critical to the achievement of agreement on these hard law instruments. The CSD receives self-reports from the states parties on the implementation of international environmental law. This process clearly gives a lot of flexibility to states. They can agree on relatively weak international treaties (e.g., the 1992 Framework Convention on Climate Change) and only move to strengthen the covenants after building domestic political support for the environmental regime. The success of this process has led to the creation of a large body of treaty law designed to regulate international environmental affairs.

However, problems have emerged. Developing countries, in particular, do not have the resources or capacity to implement the profusion of environmental agreements. This inability to implement international environmental law has been called "treaty congestion." The solution lies in mobilizing significant international financial resources to help developing countries implement the agreements. Yet, most environmental treaties make no such arrangements and only establish small budgets for administrative expenses. Implementation then depends solely on national wealth. Developed, resource rich countries can cooperate on the implementation of international environmental law, while underdeveloped, resource poor countries cannot move forward.

GEF was created to assist developing countries in tackling these global environmental problems. In its organization and mandate, GEF is a unique IGO that may serve as a model for strengthening international environmental governance. First, the facility is designed to serve existing international treaties, such as the Conventions on Climate Change and Biodiversity negotiated at the Rio Conference. Its mandate is to financially help the underdeveloped countries implement these instruments. This focus of providing funds for global, as distinct from national, priorities is indeed novel. Everyone on the planet would ultimately benefit from these actions. Second, the facility is structured to integrate global action on environmental problems. It brings together three key established formal organizations— UNEP, the UNDP, and the World Bank—to work collaboratively and cooperatively on these environmental issues. It is designed to transform the words of the environmental law treaties into action programs at the local level. The attempt here is to establish a bridge between the World Bank and UN agencies and to overcome historic distrust on both sides that has prevented previous cooperation.[49]

There is a clear division of labor between the three implementing agencies. The UNDP is to provide technical assistance and to ensure the development and management of capacity-building programs drawing on its broad network of representatives within recipient countries. UNEP is to ensure that GEF's actions are consistent with other international environmental agreements and to provide scientific and technical expertise. UNEP is also to promote environmental management in GEF-financed activities. The World Bank is to review and monitor all investment projects of GEF and is the trustee of the GEF Trust Fund. The World Bank is to ensure the development and management of all GEF projects and to mobilize private-sector resources for projects consistent with GEF objectives.[50]

GEF has become the largest multilateral source of grant funds available for environmental protection. It provides "new and additional grant and concessional funding to meet the agreed full incremental costs of measures to achieve agreed global environmental benefits in the following four focal areas: (a) climate change, (b) biological diversity, (c) international waters, and (d) ozone layer depletion." In addition, the "agreed incremental costs of activities concerning land degradation, primarily desertification and deforestation, as they relate to the four focal areas shall be eligible for funding."[51] This means that GEF covers the difference between the costs of a project undertaken with these global environmental objectives in mind, and the costs of an alternative domestic project that the country would have implemented in any case.

The participating governments agreed in March 1994 to make GEF permanent and to provide $2 billion in new resources. In 1998, donor countries agreed to another $2.8 billion to continue funding into the twenty-first century. As of June 1999, GEF had committed grants totaling $2.5 billion. The distribution of these grants between the four principal areas was roughly as follows: 39 percent for biodiversity conservation, 36 percent for climate change, 15 percent for international waters, 6 percent for ozone depletion, and 4 percent for multiple focal areas.[52]

In the negotiations on the creation of GEF, the developing countries fought for the concept of "additionality"; they argued that funds for the environment should be additional to, or at least separate from, development assistance. These countries did not want limited development aid suddenly diverted away from national priorities and funneled to these global environmental concerns. They argued GEF should also not replace national environmental planning nor create an excuse for not improving environmental practices generally; rather, the facility should finance the incremental cost to help projects achieve global environmental benefits.[53]

At the Rio Conference, countries from the South had proposed a large green fund to finance the activities of "Agenda 21." The developed countries offered GEF as the vehicle for additional funding for global environmental problems. NGOs and others were very concerned about the link between GEF and the World Bank. The World Bank has a long history of environmentally destructive projects and development approaches. Speaking for the South, the Group of 77 joined with the NGO network in expressing disapproval of the World Bank's initial dominance of GEF. The negotiations that ensued led to a restructuring of GEF along the tripartite lines outlined earlier with GEF more independent from the World Bank than it was in its pilot phase.

The structure of GEF emerged as a result of compromise and balance between the interests of the North and South. The South, arguing for legitimacy, favored a UN-style system on the basis that it was more democratic. The North, arguing for efficiency, endorsed the decision-making system of the IMF and World Bank, where votes are weighted according to contribution. The negotiations resulted in an assembly, a governing council, and a secretariat. The GEF Assembly is composed of all affiliating countries and meets every three years to review the all-encompassing policies. The GEF Governing Council is responsible for operational policies and programs. The thirty-two seats on the council are divided as follows: sixteen for developing countries, fourteen for developed countries, and two for "transitional economies." The council normally will arrive at decisions by consensus. However, if this proves impossible and a vote is required, decisions are made on a double-majority basis. Sixty percent of the votes of all countries (UN system / one nation = one vote) and 60 percent of the votes of the contributors (IMF / World Bank system / one dollar = one vote) must be obtained. The chair of the council's meetings also rotates between a government representative elected by the participants (UN system) and the chief executive officer of GEF (IMF/World Bank).[54]

If this hybrid system works, it may be a model for future international organizations to accommodate the perspectives of the North and the South. Compared to the traditional composition and decision making of the Bretton Woods institutions (IMF/World Bank), the final GEF structure gives much more voice to the South. A clear test of this system will be the degree to which the donor nations continue to fund and support this amalgam. Although funding has grown, it is not close to the level of the amounts entrusted to the Bretton Woods system.

The first full assembly of GEF members took place in New Delhi in April 1998 with 119 member governments, 16 IGOs, and 185 NGOs participating. An independent team of consultants presented to the assembly a report on the fund's overall effectiveness. The report highlighted the limited ability of GEF to leverage its modest resources in support of environmentally sound development strategies. As mentioned earlier, the facility is mandated to finance only the "incremental" costs of investment projects for global benefits in the four areas of focus: biodiversity, climate change, ozone depletion, and the seas and waters. GEF is not to finance the costs that nations would normally expect to encounter in their national project. This is problematic in two regards. First, the developing countries see this as a tendency of the donor states to care more about global as opposed to national environmental threats. Second, it seems to serve as a disincentive for countries to invest in projects that offer global and local benefits at the same time (e.g., biological diversity). The expectation would be that GEF would fund such priorities. The consultants' report also noted that the mere existence of GEF could serve to reduce the pressure on other UN agencies and the World Bank to integrate environmental issues overall in their programs. The report, for example, noted that the World Bank spent more in one year on carbon-emitting fossil fuel projects ($2.3 billion) than GEF's entire replenishment funding for 1994–1998.[55]

GEF remains a promising but controversial international funding agency. As noted, there are difficulties both measuring the "incremental costs" of global benefits and in ensuring that GEF funds are being provided in addition to existing development assistance. In addition, there are criticisms of the lack of involvement of local communities and NGOs in the designing of GEF projects.[56] And finally, there seems to be a lack of effectiveness in bringing about environmental gains in World Bank projects.[57]

But despite these problems, the model of breaking down the top-heavy decision making of the World Bank and IMF has merit. The voice of the less developed countries at least can be heard within GEF. Global environmental priorities can be negotiated and action plans can be forthcoming. However, funding will have to be increased. At the Rio Conference, the total estimated costs for implementing "Agenda 21" in the developing countries was over $600 billion annually to the year 2000.[58] Obviously, GEF current level of funding is grossly insufficient.

Assessing Environmental Governance at the UN

This review of a human right to a healthy environment and the activities of UNEP, the CSD, and GEF reveal the strengths and weaknesses of the UN system of international environmental governance. The strengths of this environmental regime can be seen in the following areas:

1. The successful establishment of a global human rights framework that includes a right to a healthy environment. This right is found in both hard law (e.g., the African Charter) and soft law (e.g., the Ksentini Report).
2. The successful negotiation of global agreements and treaties to preserve and protect the environment. These norms and rules are extensive and range from "soft" principles (e.g., the World Charter for Nature and the Common-Heritage Principles) to "hard" rules (e.g., the Montreal Protocol and the Basel Convention). UNEP, in particular, has been a key catalyst and critical organizer in the creation of this body of international environmental law.
3. The accumulation, interpretation, and distribution of critical data on the global environment (e.g., GEMS and INFOTERRA). Scientists and environmentalists on all continents are able to share information and results.
4. The establishment of certain inspection and compliance regimes to monitor adherence to international environmental treaties (e.g., the compliance procedures of the Montreal Protocol and the liability scheme for environmental damages established by the Law of the Sea Convention).
5. The incorporation of the concept of a "global civil society" into the dialogue within international organizations on environmental governance. Around 7,000 NGOs and between 15,000 to 20,000 citizens from around the world participated in the NGO forums at the Rio

Conference. Environmental organizations have played the vital role of pressuring governments, providing information, and mobilizing public opinion on critical environmental issues. Thousands of NGOs work on environmental issues on an ongoing basis. Some NGOs, like Greenpeace, have thousands of members around the world and a budget that surpasses that of UNEP.[59]

The weaknesses of the UN system of global environmental governance are also very clear:

1. There is no global institution with adequate authority to mobilize the financial resources to protect the global commons. Such actions could include the creation of financial incentives for responsible environmental behavior and fines and taxes for irresponsible behavior.
2. There is no independently powerful global authority able to operate with impartiality and even-handedness and to name and publicize nation-states in violation of the norms and rules codified in international environmental law.
3. There is no global authority in charge of coordinating and integrating all the programs and agencies engaged in global environmental governance.
4. There is a lack of integration of environmental and development concerns in policy planning at the global level. The powerful international agencies (World Bank/IMF) pursue an agenda of economic liberalization with environmental concerns often an afterthought. The environmental IGOs lack the resources and power to balance the development agenda. A full integration must be a priority.

The Marriage of Economic and Environmental Health

"Sustainable development" has emerged as the expression to encompass the integration of environmental concerns with economic planning. The most popular and perhaps widely accepted definition for the term "sustainable development" is in *Our Common Future*, the report of the UN-sponsored 1987 World Commission on Environment and Development (WCED). The WCED was chaired by Gro Harlem Brundtland, the former prime minister of Norway, and the report is known as the Brundtland Report. The Brundtland Report defines sustainable development as "development that meets the needs of the present without compromising the ability of future generations to meet their own needs."[60] Sustainability is thus the ability of a process or practice to be carried on indefinitely without undermining current or future environmental quality.

Yet, the term "sustainable development" is controversial and means

different things to different constituencies. There are now over 300 definitions of the term.[61] Many believe that the phrase is an oxymoron. Skeptics
view the term as nothing more than development with an adjective in
front of it, a dangerous magical two-word slogan. Anthony D'Amato, for
example, writes:

> What the executive board came up with in Rio was an ultimate reduc-
> tion of all ideas and themes and reports into a magical two-word slo-
> gan. If someday the human race is wiped out because there is no oxy-
> gen left in the atmosphere, or fried to death due to the depletion of the
> ozone layer, God might look down and draw a little cartoon about the
> folly of planet earth. The cartoon should show a now-gray little planet
> with a tombstone sticking out of it. On the tombstone is emblazoned
> the two-word slogan of the Rio conference: SUSTAINABLE DEVEL-
> OPMENT, R.I.P.[62]

Sharachandra Lélé writes that "sustainable development is a 'metafix'
that will unite everybody from the profit-minded industrialist and risk-
minimizing subsistence farmer to the equity-seeking social worker, the
pollution-concerned or wildlife-loving First Worlder, the growth-maxi-
mizing policy maker, the goal-orientated bureaucrat, and therefore, the
vote-counting politician."[63] But is it really possible to synthesize all these
different views into a "metafix" that successfully links economic growth
with ecological balance?

Numerous disturbing questions confront policy makers, including: Will
the sustainable development of capitalism safeguard ecological diversity?
How does one guarantee that the pursuit of profit will not trample on
social equity and environmental health? Is unlimited economic growth
compatible with the preservation of the biosphere? Can economic growth
and environmental protection go hand in hand?

On the one hand, some environmentalists believe that the answer is
no; economic growth, as currently practiced, is not ecologically sustainable. These environmentalists fear that development will be privileged
over sustainability, resulting in business as usual. In fact, some argue that
the idea of sustainable development has led the environmental movement astray. It offers current industrial and technical developers a new
lease on life without changing the life-destroying economic arrangements supporting "growth" models. No one has to reconsider basic capitalist assumptions and operating procedures of efficiency and profit.
Rather, the major institutions would suddenly adopt a more "environment friendly" way of operating. Yet, some argue that the ecological crisis in essence is a result of capitalism's insatiable drive for economic
growth and new markets. The global environment is under assault from
this economic model. Any honest program of sustainability must at least

acknowledge the environmental harm created and perpetuated by an economic system based on the unlimited pursuit of profit.

On the other hand, both former president Clinton and President George W. Bush believe that economic growth and environmental protection go hand in hand and, in fact, prioritize economic growth above all else. President Clinton explicitly defined sustainable development as a form of economic growth in his 1993 executive order (no. 12852) setting up the President's Council on Sustainable Development. The council stated that "[t]he issue is not whether the economy needs to grow but how and in what way."[64] The hope that economic growth will alleviate poverty and suffering also leads many social activists concerned about equity and the welfare of the poor to support industrial models of development based on incremental growth. They believe arguing against economic growth to protect the environment works against the interests of the poor.

Environmental activists respond, however, that the drive for economic growth and unrestricted free trade has led to unsustainable consumption patterns in the North and a spreading gap between the world's rich and poor. All of these trends militate against environmental protection and sustainability. In practice, they believe, economic growth has worked against ecological balance.

Economist Herman Daly argues that the pursuit of growth masks an unwillingness to address social and economic inequities. Daly writes:

> Our system is hooked on growth per se, and does *not* see growth as a temporary *means* of attaining some optimum level of stocks, but as an *end* in itself. Why? Perhaps because, as one prominent economist so bluntly put it in defending growth: Growth is a substitute for equality of income. So long as there is growth there is hope, and that makes large income differentials tolerable. We are addicted to growth because we are addicted to large inequalities in income and wealth. To paraphrase Marie Antoinette: Let them eat growth. Better yet, let the poor hope to eat growth in the future.[65]

If we focus economic policy on the protection of life, rather than growth, it is possible to recognize the fundamental interdependence of environmental and development issues. The natural environment is composed of all life, including human life. Environmental sustainability must therefore also include the protection of human life—which requires economic development. Environmentalists too often ignore these connections. John Nichols, author of *The Milagro Beanfield War*, addresses these issues:

> The tragedy in "environmental action" is often seen only as an effort to save the spotted owl . . . without giving a hoot about the

ghettos of Houston, Cleveland, North Philadelphia and the situation of the *people* on this globe, which is atrocious. Until environment is seen as the entire picture, both natural and human, we're
going to have a real problem. . . . [I]f you're a member of National
Wildlife Federation you should also be worried about the total
destruction of our inner cities and the fact that unemployment
among black children between 15 and 24 is 80 to 90 percent. Otherwise, it becomes irrelevant to worry about sea turtles. The clue to
any kind of survival of the planet is training people to the macro-
scopic overview, to understand how their lives are connected to
everything else, to understand that if you kill one species you're
endangering all others.[66]

Leslie Paul Thiele writes of the "threefold nature of interdependence,"
across space, species, and time. Interdependence across space is connected to Nichols's plea for environmentalists to relate their efforts to the
well-being of all human and natural life, a concern for environmental justice. The benefits to be derived from our biologically rich, life-supporting
planet should be equitably shared. Everyone has obligations to his or her
neighbor, regardless of nationality, class, gender, race, or sexuality, and to
the development of lives and livelihoods that can be environmentally sustained. Interdependence across species refers to the obligation of the
human species to integrate ourselves harmoniously with other life-forms
on our planet, a concern for ecological justice; that is, to respect our ecological connectedness and the web of ecological relationships that sustain
us. Interdependence across time refers to the rights and duties of the present generation to future (and past) generations. The concern here is for
intergenerational justice.[67]

The ideas of intergenerational justice were powerfully developed by
Edith Brown Weiss in her call for the incorporation of "intergenerational
equity" into international law. Weiss writes:

[E]ach generation receives a natural and cultural legacy in trust from
previous generations and holds it in trust for future generations. This
relationship imposes upon each generation certain planetary obligations to conserve the natural and cultural resource base for future
generations and also gives each generation certain planetary rights as
beneficiaries of the trust to benefit from the legacy of their ancestors.
These planetary obligations and planetary rights form the corpus of
a proposed doctrine of intergenerational equity, or justice between
generations. For these obligations and rights to be enforceable, they
must become part of international law, and of national and subna-
tional legal systems.[68]

Sustainable development must incorporate the rights and duties that flow from norms of environmental justice, ecological justice, and intergenerational justice. As we saw in chapter 2, development is not synonymous with economic growth. Development refers to the improvement of human well-being as measured by a healthy environment, increasing life expectancy, food security, education opportunities, health care provisions, and so on. Globalization, economic growth, and an increase in per capita income can either contribute to or subtract from human development. Sustainable development requires that improvements to human well-being are ecologically renewable. Current global economic growth has not only failed to facilitate sustainable development, but has also generated as much poverty as wealth.

David Reed of the World Wide Fund for Nature elaborates clear public policy to implement this understanding of sustainable development. Reed divides sustainable development into three components—economic, social, and environmental—and articulates viable national and international policy in all three areas.[69]

Policies to address the economic component include poverty-alleviating growth, such as labor-intensive economic policies that maximize employment generation for the poorest sectors; strengthening domestic food security; state action to defend the public well-being, including welfare and social security protection; and the elimination of distortions in existing pricing structures to include environmental and social costs in order to achieve true efficiency.

Policies to address the social component include institutionalizing mechanisms to ensure both participation of the poor in income-generating activities and their access to social wealth and productive resources; improving social services, including education and health care; providing gender equity in the public and private spheres; and fostering population stabilization strategies and providing family planning services.

Policies to address the environmental component include limiting the consumption of renewable natural resources to regenerative rates; ensuring nonrenewable resource consumption rates that do not exceed the provision of substitutes; decreasing the discharge of atmospheric contaminants, water pollutants, and toxic wastes to not exceed the environment's absorptive capacity; enforcing the "precautionary principle," that is, refraining from pursuing activities whose potentially irreversible impacts are not fully known; and establishing clear, enforceable legal and regulatory standards for the private sector to protect the environment.

One approach to sustainable development is the call for full-cost accounting and full-cost pricing. The idea is that the price paid for goods and services should include their long-term social and ecological costs (what economists often call "externalities"). Thus, the expenses for pollution prevention, natural resource depletion/preservation, health maintenance, and waste disposal would all be incorporated into actual production costs. The air, water, and land are not "free" to be spoiled and/or used up by development. Businesses using full-cost accounting would pay social and ecological costs up front, and, of course, pass these expenses on to the consumer. By overwhelming numbers, citizens in developed countries have consistently expressed a willingness to pay higher prices for electricity and gasoline to protect the environment.[70]

The internalization of environmental costs through pricing reform and tax policy is perhaps the single most important environmental measure governments can enact. It is unfortunate that Bush made light of Al Gore's attention to photovoltaic cell-derived solar electricity in the 2000 election campaign. Solar energy, as an alternative to fossil-fuel based energy sources, is a way to combat the threat of global warming. A tax on carbon dioxide emissions combined with increasing the price of coal-based electricity would give photovoltaic solar electricity a chance of being competitive domestically and internationally. Tax policy can thus help the transition to new energy sources and prevent global warming.

Paul Hawken, Amory Lovins, and L. Hunter Lovins call critical environmental resources "natural capital." Natural capital includes not just familiar resources like water, minerals, oil, trees, fish, air and so on, but also encompasses living systems, including grasslands, wetlands, oceans, coral reefs, and rain forests. It is these living systems that are deteriorating at an alarming, unprecedented rate. Inside these threatened living systems live the ecological communities that make life possible, including amphibians, bacteria, insects, mammals, ponds, fungi, and flowers. Prosperity and industrial growth have put enormous strains on these living systems that support all forms of life.[71]

Hawken, Lovins, and Lovins argue that an economy needs "four types of capital to function properly:

- human capital, in the form of labor and intelligence, culture, and organization
- financial capital, consisting of cash, investments, and monetary instruments
- manufactured capital, including infrastructure, machines, tools, and factories
- natural capital, made up of resources, living systems, and ecosystem services

The industrial system uses the first three forms of capital to transform natural capital into the stuff of our daily lives: cars, highways, cities, bridges, houses, food, medicine, hospitals, and schools."[72]

Traditional liberal economics ignores natural capital; thus, this paradigm has created a nonsustainable form of economic development. The argument here should be made very clear. Hawken, Lovins, and Lovins are not claiming that the world is running out of commodities and raw materials. Supplies for most raw materials are abundant and prices are relatively cheap as a result of the

> globalization of trade, cheaper transport costs, imbalances in market power that enable commodity traders and middlemen to squeeze producers, and in large measure the success of powerful new extractive technologies, whose correspondingly extensive damage to ecosystems is seldom given a monetary value. After richer ores are exhausted, skilled mining companies can now level and grind up whole mountains of poorer-quality ores to extract the metals desired. But while technology keeps ahead of depletion, providing what appear to be ever-cheaper metals, they only appear cheap, because the stripped rainforest and the mountain of toxic tailings spilling into rivers, the impoverished villages and eroded indigenous cultures—all the consequences they leave in their wake—are not factored into the cost of production.[73]

Ignoring the rates at which natural capital is being consumed has brought us to the precipice. There is no longer any scientific dispute about the decline of every living system in the world. One-third of the planet's resources, its natural wealth, were consumed over the last three decades. The ongoing destruction rates are staggering: If current trends continue, 70 percent of the world's coral reefs, host to 25 percent of all marine life, face extinction in our lifetimes, freshwater ecosystems are disappearing at the rate of 6 percent a year, and marine ecosystems by 4 percent a year. The capacity of the natural system to recycle carbon dioxide has been exceeded and it is building up in our atmosphere.[74]

Generally Accepted Accounting Practices should clearly include natural capital as an exhaustible resource and a valuable factor of production. Businesses could start to operate as if such principles were in force. Assigning a monetary value to natural capital deserves further consideration as a means of slowing the destruction of our living systems.

Other proposals to protect natural capital include increasing resource productivity to slow resource depletion, redesigning industrial systems to eliminate waste, and shifting economic planning to sustainable human services instead of unsustainable goods. All of these proposals have merit and are doable.[75] Yet, such changes would have to be enacted globally so that no nation became disadvantaged in global markets as a result of environmental cost internalization measures—which leads to the Global New Deal proposal for a World Environment Organization.

The Global New Deal and the Environment

Summary Observations

While innovative thinking on possible solutions to environmental problems did not stop after the 1992 Rio Conference, cooperative international environmental action certainly slowed down, and, in some cases, ceased altogether. Environmental activist Vandana Shiva argues that during the 1990s the "Rio process and the sustainability agenda were subverted by the free-trade agenda." Following the Earth Summit, the Uruguay Round of the General Agreement on Tariffs and Trade was completed in 1993. In 1995, the WTO was established and the "rule of trade" overtook the normative political commitment to sustainability proclaimed at Rio. Globalization and liberalized trade and investment create growth, Shiva argues, by destroying the environment and local, sustainable livelihoods. "The new globalization policies have accelerated and expanded environmental destruction and displaced millions of people from their homes and their sustenance base."[76]

Shiva points to an absolute truth about the 1990s. Economic neoliberalism was presented as "the only game in town." The free trade agenda did usurp the sustainability agenda of the Rio Conference. Policy to enhance free trade—from NAFTA to the Association of the Southeast Asian Nations to the EU to the WTO)—dominated global politics and international relations at the end of the century. Our chal-

Global New Deal Proposals

There is a clear need for high-level coordination of global environmental programs and the integration of development and environment decision making within the UN system. There is an urgent need to resolve the fundamental financial needs necessary to address environmental protection and ecological balance. Numerous proposals have been made to reform the UN system to address these concerns. The Global New Deal calls for ecological balance and economic human rights to be linked through the creation of a World Environment Organization (WEO) to replace UNEP. The proposed WEO, described in chapter 8, could strengthen the enforcement mechanisms of international environmental law and facilitate the integration of economic and environmental priorities into development planning.

The evaluation of the work of UNEP, the CSD, and GEF demonstrates clear programmatic successes, but also significant limitations. Nations need a central organization to address transboundary environmental externalities and other environmental problems accompanying globalization. A central WEO could consolidate research and information sharing. A WEO could help nations bring national policies in balance with other countries and in compliance with international standards. Just as the World Health Organization helps nations eradicate infec-

lenge now is to reinvigorate international organizations with ecological priorities and to link ecological balance with economic human rights and overcome the perceived distance between these two priorities. tious diseases, and just as the International Labor Organization helps nations implement programs that protect workers rights, so too could a WEO help nations to rectify transboundary pollution.

5

Race and Economic and Social Human Rights

Why are most of the people in the world who experience a life of severe destitution people of color? What political and economic structures perpetuate racial bias in economic outcomes? How is it possible to overcome and reverse the historical record of racial bias? What policies can be implemented at the national and international level to create real economic opportunity for all races? How has the UN Committee on the Elimination of All Forms of Racial Discrimination (Minority Rights Committee) approached these issues of the economic and social rights of minorities?

Simplified racial categories can be misleading and dangerous since individuals are not only members of a race, but also of a class, a gender, and a sexuality. Thus, broad generalizations about race can be deceptive and groundless in individual cases. In the real world, a person does not exist only as a racial category.[1]

According to the Minority Rights Treaty,[2] race encompasses color, descent, and national or ethnic origin. "Descent" suggests social origin: heritage, lineage, and/or parentage. "National or ethnic origin" denotes linguistic, cultural, and historical roots. This broad concept of race is clearly not limited to objective, mainly physical elements, but also includes subjective and social components. The ingredients considered central to a person's race may, in fact, vary from place to place. Some may emphasize linguistic and cultural factors while others emphasize social determinants.

Certain castes, for example, are discriminated against for social and not ethnic reasons. Furthermore, nothing is permanent about any of these aspects of race. Anthropologists have shown that environmental influences can profoundly change even the physical appearance of a human being in a relatively short time.[3]

Recent scientific research on the human genome—the aggregate of genetic material encased in the heart of almost every cell of the body—has confirmed that the racial categories recognized by society are not reflected on the genetic level. Most of the scientists studying the human genome are convinced that the standard labels used to distinguish people by race have little or no biological meaning. The human species does not divide itself into separate biological groups or races. J. Craig Venter, the head of the Celera Genomics Corporation, concludes: "Race is a social concept, not a scientific one. We all evolved in the last 100,000 years from the same small number of tribes that migrated out of Africa and colonized the world." Harold P. Freeman, the chief executive, president, and director of surgery at North General Hospital in Manhattan, who has studied the issue of biology and race, states: "If you ask what percentage of your genes is reflected in your external appearance, the basis by which we talk about race, the answer seems to be in the range of .01 percent. This is a very, very minimal reflection of your genetic makeup."[4]

Therefore, race, most certainly, cannot be understood simply in terms of skin color. Racial classifications, racist bigotry, and racial hatred have often not relied on skin color. Historical examples abound. The German Nazis' belief that the Russians (as white as the Germans) were subhuman led to a massacre of millions of Russian citizens. The white Irish farmers looked like the white British landlords in Ireland in the 1840s; yet the white British elite exported food and gave no concessions to the white Irish farmers and laborers after crop failures in 1846–1847, and thus, "imposed" the Irish potato famine. The issue here was not skin color, but political power and religion. The white Irish farmers had no political or economic power. The powerful white British elite exported the food that could have saved hundreds of thousands of Irish lives. It was easier for the British to justify these policies by classifying the Irish as a backward and inferior people.[5]

The genocide in Rwanda in the mid-1990s was led by black Hutus against black Tutsis. In fact, ethnographers have come to agree that Hutus and Tutsis cannot properly be called distinct ethnic groups. The two groups speak the same language, follow the same religion, intermarry, and share the same social and political culture. Rwanda is one of the few nations that shares one language, one faith, and one law. Yet, the leaders of "Hutu power" mobilized their people around the idea that the Tutsi were "scum" and "cockroaches" and had to be destroyed. Hutu power attempted the organized extermination of an entire people and succeeded in killing between 800,000 and 1 million Tutsi. The program of massacres that decimated the Tutsi of Rwanda in 1994 cannot be understood through a lens of skin color or ethnicity.[6]

A definition and understanding of race and racial discrimination analysis should, therefore, include more than a mere difference of skin color. Race is also tied to power differentials, social status, and other distinctions. Differences in power give one group the ability to declare the less powerful group "inferior." In fact, those in power may share the same skin color and ethnic characteristics as those they oppress, yet use "race" and "ethnic" differences to consolidate their rule.[7]

Those most vulnerable to economic and social deprivations (hunger, illiteracy, disease, and so on) are those groups without wealth and political power, the majority of whom are women and children. Skin color alone will not tell you who will suffer. For example, the numerical majority of U.S. citizens living in poverty are white, the color of most U.S. policy makers.

Yet, most of the people in the world who experience a life of severe destitution are people of color. Suffering continues to be related to the politics of race. According to the administrator of the UN Development Program (UNDP), among the 4.4 billion people in developing countries around the world at the end of the twentieth century, three-fifths lived in communities lacking basic sanitation, one-third went without safe drinking water, one-quarter lacked adequate housing, and one-fifth were under-nourished. In addition, nearly one-third of the people in the poorest countries, mostly in sub-Saharan Africa, could expect to die by age forty.[8] Of the world's 6 billion people, 2.8 billion—almost half—live on less than $2 a day, and 1.2 billion—a fifth—live on less than $1 a day, with 44 percent of these living in South Asia.[9] Overwhelmingly, these impoverished people are people of color. A glance at a map of global hunger, for example, graphically shows that the preponderance of the chronically under-nourished are peoples in Africa, Asia, and parts of Latin America and the Caribbean. In early 2001, the UN World Food Program distributed a map calling attention to "hot spots" where hunger is most severe. The map identifies huge areas in Asia and sub-Saharan Africa where tens of millions of people of color, most of them women and children, cannot get enough to eat. The UN agency estimates that of the 830 million undernourished people in the world, 791 million live in developing countries.[10]

Racial minorities inside the United States also continue to suffer a lack of economic security compared to their white counterparts, despite a "booming" economy at the end of the twentieth century. The following statistics from the 1990s reveal the economic divide between black and white Americans: According to Census Bureau statistics, there was a stark $14,000 per household income gap between blacks and whites ($25,050 a year versus $38,970; income stated in 1997 dollars).[11] The unemployment rate for young black men at all education levels was more than twice that for young white men. In addition, twice the number of young black men between the ages of sixteen and twenty-four were not in school or working.[12] One out of every three black men in their twenties was under the supervision of the criminal justice system, either imprisoned or on probation or parole.[13] Blacks in the United States were six times more likely than whites to be held in jail.[14] This vast disparity in economic opportunity between blacks and whites in the United States continues in the twenty-first century.[15]

A similar disparity in economic security exists between whites and Hispanic Americans. The National Council of La Raza reports that Hispanic workers were disproportionately concentrated in low-wage jobs that offered few benefits throughout the 1990s. As a result, married Hispanics with children continued to have higher poverty rates compared to black and white families. In 1997, for example, 21 percent of Hispanic married couples with children were poor, compared with 6 percent of white and 9 percent of black families. That same year only 55 percent of Hispanics twenty-five and older had graduated from high school, and 7.4 percent had graduated from college.[16]

Any serious program for the protection of economic and social rights must address this reality. These conditions are the result of history, especially the heritage of four major historical processes: conquest, state building, migration, and economic development. Modern states have been built by powerful groups at the expense of the less powerful, with racial prejudice underlying the entire process. For those concerned with economic justice, these issues must be confronted.

This chapter examines how the UN approaches these issues of economic injustice and race. The work of the Minority Rights Committee is analyzed in the following sections:

- The Minority Rights Treaty and economic and social human rights
- The Minority Rights Committee: states parties reports and concluding observations
- Strengthening the UN's approach to minority rights

In 2001, the UN held a World Conference against Racism, Racial Discrimination, Xenophobia and Related Intolerance in South Africa. It is thus an appropriate time to evaluate how the Minority Rights Committee and the UN can more fully address the economic and social human rights of racial minorities. The Global New Deal in chapter 8 recommends steps for the Minority Rights Committee to incorporate Amartya Sen's capabilities approach into its work to more effectively combat racial injustice in the economic and social realm.

The Minority Rights Treaty and Economic and Social Human Rights

A committee of experts was established under the Minority Rights Treaty, which entered into force on 4 January 1969. Article 8 of the Minority Rights Treaty calls for the committee to consist of eighteen "experts of high moral standing and acknowledged impartiality elected by States Parties from among their nationals." Members of the Minority Rights Committee are not representatives of the states whose nationality they bear. They are elected by secret ballot of the states parties to the convention, and they serve in their personal capacity.[17]

Despite its growth from 41 to 161 states parties,[18] the Minority Rights Committee continues to meet for just two sessions a year, each three weeks long. With two three-hour meetings each day, there are thirty meetings possible in one session. The Minority Rights Committee divides up these thirty sessions as follows: twenty-two for the consideration of new state reports; two for the review of the implementation of the convention in states whose reports are overdue by five years or more; two to review urgent and early warning procedures regarding the prevention of racial discrimination; and four for other business, including individual communications.[19]

Economic and social rights are covered extensively in the Minority Rights Treaty. Article 1(1) considers bigotry to be a form of racial discrimination, indicating the power of bigotry to nullify economic and social human rights. The Minority Rights Committee asks governments to report on legislative, judicial, administrative, and other measures that give effect to article 5(e). This article of the Minority Rights Treaty obliges states parties "to prohibit and to eliminate racial discrimination in all its forms and to guarantee the right of everyone" to economic and social rights, including the following:

- The right to work
- Free choice of employment
- Just and favorable conditions of work
- Protection against unemployment
- Equal pay for equal work
- The right to housing
- The right to public health
- Medical care, social security, and social services
- The right to education and training

Thus, the Minority Rights Treaty does not oblige a state party to protect these rights, but to make sure that discrimination with respect to the enjoyment of these rights does not occur.[20]

THE WORLD CONFERENCE AGAINST RACISM, RACIAL DISCRIMINATION, XENOPHOBIA AND RELATED INTOLERANCE

Durban, South Africa
31 August–8 September 2001
The final Declaration from the UN World Conference against Racism, Racial Discrimination, Xenophobia and Related Intolerance included the following regarding globalization, racism, and economic and social human rights:

- "We note that the process of globalization constitutes a powerful and dynamic force which should be harnessed for the benefit, development and prosperity of all countries, without exclusion. We recognize that developing countries face special difficulties in responding to this central challenge. While globalization offers great opportunities, at present its benefits are very unevenly shared, while its costs are unevenly distributed. We thus express our determination to prevent and mitigate the negative effects of globalization. These effects could aggravate, *inter alia*, poverty, underdevelopment, marginalization, social exclusion, cultural homogenization and economic disparities which may occur along racial lines, within and between States, and have an adverse impact. We further express our determination to maximize the benefits of globalization through *inter*

Hence, the Minority Rights Committee is concerned with discriminatory practices only, and not with the absence of economic or social rights in general terms. Therefore, the absence of an economic or social right in the country as a whole is not a focus of the Minority Rights Committee. The Minority Rights Committee is troubled, however, if these rights are given to one racial group as opposed to another; if, for example, the majority racial/ethnic group receives higher health care benefits compared to the minority group.[21]

In fact, Karl Josef Partsch asserts that the Minority Rights Committee has been very cautious in its application of article 5. The Minority Rights Committee has asked "reporting States whether the rights listed in the article are guaranteed by their national legal systems, but it has not indicated that the absence of such guarantees constitutes a failure to comply

> *alia,* the strengthening and enhancement of international cooperation to increase equality of opportunities for trade, economic growth and sustainable development, global communications through the use of new technologies and increase intercultural exchange through the preservation and promotion of cultural diversity, which can contribute to the eradication of racism, racial discrimination, xenophobia and related intolerance. Only through broad and sustained efforts to create a shared future based upon our common humanity, and all its diversity, can globalization be made fully inclusive and equitable." (para 11)
>
> • "Urges States to take or strengthen measures, including through bilateral or multilateral cooperation, to address root causes, such as poverty, underdevelopment and lack of equal opportunity, some of which may be associated with discriminatory practices, that make persons, especially women and children, vulnerable to trafficking, which may give rise to racism, racial discrimination, xenophobia and related intolerance." (para 174)
>
> • "Urges States to adopt and implement social development policies based on reliable statistical data and centered on the attainment, by the year 2015, of the commitments to meet the basic needs of all . . . with a view to closing significantly the existing gaps in living conditions faced by victims of racism, racial discrimination, xenophobia and related intolerance, especially regarding the illiteracy rate, universal primary education, infant mortality, under-five child mortality, health, reproductive health care for all and access to safe drinking water." (para 176)

with the Convention." The Minority Rights Committee thus seeks to establish whether minority rights are protected in the state's legal order.[22]

The Minority Rights Treaty, however, does not stop there. It also advocates state action in order to eliminate disparities and secure de facto equality.[23] Such affirmative action programs are authorized in both articles 1 and 2(2) of the Minority Rights Treaty. Article 2(2) states:

States Parties shall, when the circumstances so warrant, take, in the social, economic, cultural and other fields, special and concrete measures to ensure the adequate development and protection of certain racial groups or individuals belonging to them, for the purpose of guaranteeing them the full and equal enjoyment of human rights and fundamental freedoms. These measures shall in no case entail as a consequence the maintenance of unequal or separate rights for different racial groups after the objectives for which they were taken have been achieved.[24]

However, as with the International Convention on the Elimination of All Forms of Discrimination against Women (Women's Rights Treaty), there is a tension here between equal treatment (obligation of means) and equal outcome (obligation of result). According to Theodor Meron, the Minority Rights Committee regards equality of result as the principal objective of the convention. In a major policy statement, the Minority Rights Committee states that the Minority Rights Treaty aims "at guaranteeing the right of everyone to equality before the law in the enjoyment of fundamental human rights, without distinction as to race, colour, descent or national or ethnic origin, and *at ensuring that the equality is actually enjoyed in practice.*"[25]

The Minority Rights Treaty intends to address de facto as well as de jure equality. Legal equality is only the first step toward authentic social equality. The preamble refers to the enjoyment of human rights "without distinction of any kind"; article 5 demands the right to equality before the law; article 1(4) allows for distinction for the purpose of affirmative action "to ensure . . . groups or individuals equal enjoyment or exercise of human rights." Combined with the article 2(2) endorsement of affirmative action, this demonstrates that the Minority Rights Treaty promotes not just de jure but de facto equality, not just color-neutral values but racial equality. States are required in article 2(1) to take policy measures to eliminate any laws or regulations that have the effect of creating or perpetuating racial discrimination. Economic and social policies that have the effect of sustaining the disadvantaged position of certain racial groups must be remedied. The costliness or burdensome nature of such actions cannot be used as excuses for inaction. The goal is the equal development of all citizens.[26]

Individual Complaints System

Article 14 of the Minority Rights Treaty establishes an individual complaints system. However, by March 2002, out of the 161 parties to the Minority Rights Treaty, only 37 states had accepted this complaints system.[27] Cecilia Möller, the human rights officer with the Minority Rights Committee, notes that states are hesitant to endorse the complaint system because of the perceived vagueness of the issues. Racial discrimination is not as clear cut as torture. Discrimination is often hard to define and the issues frequently hard to prove. For example, proving employment discrimination in the interview process or verifying a bank's discrimination in the denial of a loan are both very difficult. Additionally, Möller notes that the Minority Rights Committee had received a total of only twenty individual complaints since the system has been in operation. The low number is partially the result of the fact that individuals must first exhaust all local procedures before submitting a complaint to the Minority Rights Committee. The low rate of ratification of the individual complaint procedures and the lack of knowledge about these procedures among national lawyers are additional factors limiting the use of these mechanisms. Once it is submitted, the complaint goes to the Minority Rights Committee as a whole body.[28]

However, even this abridged use of the individual complaint system has had reverberations and demonstrates the potential effectiveness of the expanded Optional Protocol to the Economic Rights Treaty (proposed in chapter 3). Michael Banton, a member of the Minority Rights Committee since 1986 (rapporteur, 1990–1996, and chairperson, 1996–1998), calls attention to the influence of article 14 on states' behavior. Banton notes that if the Minority Rights Committee finds a violation of the convention, the state is to revise its law or practice in the light of the committee's opinion. During Banton's tenure, the Minority Rights Committee considered and adjudicated ten individual complaints/communications in private session. Banton argues that this judicial approach has been successful in affecting state behavior. The Minority Rights Committee,

> like a national court, benefits from the prior refinement of issues and from the adversarial nature of the proceedings. If the petitioner is legally represented there will be a systematic account of the fact alleged, or the relevant national law, and an argument that some part or parts of the Convention have been breached; there will be a legal argument from the state designed to clarify the issues and perhaps a response from the petitioner to the state's submission. If the petitioner is not legally represented the secretariat helps in the process of refining the issues to be put before the Committee which has then simply to adjudicate on them.[29]

Some of these judicial decisions involve issues around the economic and social human rights of minority populations. A Minority Rights Committee decision on an individual complaint in these areas has ramifications beyond the individuals directly affected by the case. It establishes case law that is to be consistently upheld by the state. For example, at its fifty-seventh session, 31 July–25 August 2000, the Minority Rights Committee issued Communication no. 13/1998 concerning a complaint submitted by Anna Koptova against Slovakia. Koptova, a Slovak citizen of Romany ethnicity, was represented by the European Roma Rights Center, a nongovernmental organization (NGO) based in Budapest. In her complaint, Koptova asserted that Slovakia engaged in acts of racial discrimination against her and other Roma and failed to ensure that all public authorities and public institutions refrained from acts or practices of racial discrimination. In the 1980s and 1990s, Koptova alleged that anti-Roma hostility on the part of local officials and/or non-Romany residents forced Romany families to flee causing unemployment and homelessness. She claimed to be a victim based on articles 2, 3, 4, 5, and 6 of the Minority Rights Treaty. The Minority Rights Committee, after ascertaining admissibility, determined that local municipal ordinances prohibiting Roma from settling in Rokytovce and Nagov were a clear violation of the Minority Rights Treaty article 5. However, the committee noted that the Slovak government finally rescinded these resolutions in April 1999 and that article 23 of the constitution of Slovakia guarantees freedom of movement. Thus, the action of the Minority Rights Committee was to recommend that the Slovak government "take the necessary measures to ensure that practices restricting the freedom of movement and residence of Romas under its jurisdiction are fully and promptly eliminated."[30]

Clearly, the Slovak government was under pressure from a variety of sources to revoke discriminatory laws directed against the Roma. Koptova's complaint to the Minority Rights Committee was only one of many actions taken to bring about this change. Yet, the importance of such international pressure should not be dismissed. Koptova's effort brought international attention to the plight of the Roma in Slovakia, impacting on the reputation and international standing of the Slovak government. The efforts of Slovak citizens to enforce their laws on nondiscrimination and freedom of movement received external support from this UN body. In the future, it will be very difficult for these laws to be revoked or ignored. Through working in this manner with individuals and victims in civil society, the UN has a window of opportunity to help enforce human rights. It is difficult for the UN to force change and adherence to international norms from the outside. Through Minority Rights Treaty article 14, individuals and groups who are victims of racial discrimination can raise their complaints directly to the Minority Rights Committee for arbitration. This is a promising process for the peaceful settlement of these racial and ethnic disputes that cause so much pain and suffering. It is to be hoped that more states will soon accept the jurisdiction of the Minority Rights Committee and accede to article 14 and permit the victims' voices to be heard.

The Minority Rights Committee: States Parties Reports and Concluding Observations

The main work of the Minority Rights Committee, however, is not the arbitration of individual complaints, but the review of states parties reports. Article 9 of the Minority Rights Treaty requires states parties to submit an initial report within one year of the entry into force of the treaty, with periodic reports submitted at two-year intervals.[31] Since 1988, the Minority Rights Committee has nominated one of its members to serve as a country rapporteur for each report. The country rapporteur thoroughly evaluates the state report and prepares a comprehensive list of questions to put to the representative of the reporting state. The Minority Rights Committee makes final recommendations and concluding observations to a great extent on the basis of its examination of country reports. Since 1972, the Minority Rights Committee has invited states to send representatives to respond to questions by committee members. This procedure, not foreseen in the treaty, has subsequently been adopted by all other human rights treaty bodies. The intent is to open a "constructive dialogue" between the reporting state and the Minority Rights Committee. Through such a dialogue, the Minority Rights Committee hopes to exert a positive influence on states' policies to ameliorate racial discrimination.[32]

Obvious weaknesses in this structure include the focus on self-reporting and the lack of enforcement or "power" to bring about positive change. The Minority Rights Committee relies on states parties to follow through on their commitments under the Minority Rights Treaty and to remedy racial injustice in this area of economic and social rights. But if states parties aren't willing to address these issues, there is, in fact, little that the Minority Rights Committee can do. Public pressure and the mobilization of shame may have an impact in dramatic (often media exposed) cases of abuse, such as apartheid, ethnic cleansing, and torture. But it has been less effective in pressuring policy change to address ongoing, systemic abuse—daily practices that lead to a denial of economic and social rights to the world's racial and ethnic minorities.

Some states parties to the Minority Rights Treaty claim that it is contrary to their national law to provide data requested by the Minority Rights Committee; in particular, the demographic composition of the population. Several African states declared the act of gathering data based on ethnicity to be a form of discrimination and contrary to policies of nation building. This can provide a convenient way for majority groups to hide the information that would reveal racial bias.[33]

Many states parties do not even bother to report. The Minority Rights Committee has the ignominious distinction of having the largest number of late reports of any of the treaty bodies. As of March 2002, there were 447 overdue reports to the Minority Rights Committee among the states parties to Minority Rights Treaty.[34] "Overdue" means nonexistent; these states will not be submitting these past-due reports. The most that can be hoped for at this point is that these delinquent states try to get back on schedule and submit updated reports and meet future deadlines.[35]

When a state party does not fulfill its reporting obligations, the Minority Rights Committee examines the state's practice anyway. The Minority Rights Committee waits at least five years before proceeding on its own.

When this occurs, the committee must independently gather information on the delinquent state. For example, if previous reports on the state exist, it will look at them. The committee will also invite the noncomplying state to participate, which may push it to produce a report. Furthermore, outside sources do provide data and, when they do, the committee must then determine the credibility of this information. Likewise, NGOs submit shadow reports on many countries. All of this becomes part of the data that the committee examines.[36]

On 10 October 1994, the United States ratified the Minority Rights Treaty (with reservations), and it entered into force on 20 November 1994. The initial report from the United States was due on 20 November 1995, the second periodic report on 20 November 1997, and the third periodic report on 20 November 1999. The United States did not submit any of these reports. It is perhaps understandable when a small country, which lacks the required technical expertise and resources, submits its report late to the Minority Rights Committee. But it is impossible to justify late reports from the United States.[37]

Finally, in September 2000, the U.S. government submitted the "Initial Report of the United States of America to the Committee on the Elimination of All Forms of Racial Discrimination." The report documents the many ways minority groups in the United States face economic disadvantage and are disproportionately at the bottom of the income distribution curve. U.S. government statistics disclose that members of minority groups are more likely to be poor than are nonminorities, a consequence of persistent discrimination in employment and labor relations, especially in the areas of hiring, salary and compensation, tenure, training, promotion, layoffs, and in the work environment generally. The report also documents violations of minorities' social rights, including the lack of educational opportunities and inadequate access to health insurance and health care. The report notes, for example, that in 1998 the poverty rate among blacks was more than triple the poverty rate of white non-Hispanics. And the poverty rate among Hispanics was not statistically different from that of blacks.[38]

Thus, the U.S. government clearly acknowledges the vast disparities in economic and social rights fulfillment that exist between ethnic and racial groups in the United States. The well-documented report is a useful tool for exposing the effects of ongoing discrimination and bigotry in the United States. However, in the report the U.S. government sidesteps its responsibility to respect, protect, and fulfill economic and social rights.

The U.S. government makes two key points in its discussion of these human rights. First, it makes it clear that it does not view these claims as human rights claims at all. Concerning the Minority Rights Treaty article 5, the U.S. government writes: "Some of these enumerated rights, which may be characterized as economic, social and cultural rights, are not explicitly recognized as legally enforceable 'rights' under U.S. law." By denying their legal status, the United States does not have to accept the state obligations and duties that correspond to these categories of human rights. Within this limited view of human rights, the United States is not legally required to develop strategies to respect, protect, and fulfill the economic, social, and cultural rights of minorities. And, since the Minority Rights Treaty does not require states parties to provide for these rights, but only to prohibit discrimination in their enjoyment, the United States argues it is, in fact, in full compliance with the requirements of the convention.[39]

Second, while the United States does acknowledge severe problems in the economic and social well-being of its minority citizens, it dodges its duty under international law to enact policies to ameliorate this situation. This position reinforced a key U.S. "reservation" made to the Minority Rights Treaty on ratification in 1994: "[T]he United States does not accept any obligation under this Convention to enact legislation or take other measures under . . . Article 5 with respect to private conduct."[40] While acknowledging that "significant disparities continue," the U.S. government writes in 2000 that "the sources or causes of socio-economic differences are complex and depend on a combination of societal conditions, such as the state of the national and local economies, continued racial and ethnic discrimination in education and employment, and individual characteristics, such as educational background, occupational experiences, and family background."[41] Clearly, all of these areas must be examined. Yet, as a matter of international law, the state remains ultimately responsible for guaranteeing the realization of economic and social human rights. It is the state's responsibility to guarantee the maximum utilization of its available resources to meet the "right of everyone to an adequate standard of living," including rights to food, housing, and clothing.[42] It is unfortunate that the U.S. government does not accept this legal responsibility. The United States has the wealth and prosperity to fulfill its legal and moral duty to protect the vulnerable and to provide a basic level of economic security for all its citizens.

In its concluding observations on the U.S. report, the Minority Rights Committee expressed its concern "about persistent disparities in the enjoyment of, in particular, the right to adequate housing, equal opportunities for education and employment and access to public and private health care. The Committee recommends the State party [the United States] to take all appropriate measures, including special measures . . . to ensure the right of everyone, without discrimination as to race, color, or national or ethnic origin to the enjoyment of the rights contained in article 5 of the Convention."[43]

The Minority Rights Committee's Concluding Observations

In its review of states parties' reports, the Minority Rights Committee does not act as a judicial body with the power to determine state violations of international law governing economic and social rights of racial minorities. Rather, the Minority Rights Committee's function is to assist states in their efforts to fulfill their obligations under the Minority Rights Treaty. The point is not to focus on the issue of the compliance or noncompliance of a state with its obligations under the Minority Rights Treaty. Rather, committee members see their role as helping states recognize and ameliorate racial discrimination within their borders.

The concluding observations of the Minority Rights Committee to the states' reports provide a record of the opinions and actions of the committee. These observations summarize the Minority Rights Committee's evaluation of the state party report and contain recommendations the committee hopes the state will follow. The country rapporteur drafts the concluding observations for the committee, which are normally adopted by consensus. The concluding observations represent the most definitive record of the Minority Rights Committee's approach to its mandate.

A review of the Minority Rights Committee's concluding observations for the past five years reveals a glaring meekness in its approach to the economic and social rights of minority racial groups. Economic and social rights have clearly not been a priority for the committee. The language employed is mild, and there appears to be little pressure placed on states to change policy.

For example, in March 1997 the Minority Rights Committee considered the periodic reports from Panama and adopted the following as part of its concluding observations:

> Concern is expressed that some groups living in Panama, such as indigenous people and members of the black and Asian minorities, do not fully benefit from the rights recognized under the Convention. . . . In the light of article 5 of the convention, it is noted with concern that the issue of land rights of indigenous people has remained unsolved in a great majority of cases. These land rights seem also to be threatened by the mining activities which have been undertaken— with the approval of the central authorities—by foreign companies, and also by the development of tourism in these regions.

To overcome these problems, the committee recommended that Panama

> take appropriate measures to allow full enjoyment by different groups of society, such as indigenous people or members of the black and Asian minorities, of the rights enumerated by the Convention . . . [and] strongly recommends that the State party actively pursue its current efforts to implement fully the right of indigenous people to own property and land. It especially recommends that the State party investigate and monitor the impact of the work of mining companies, including

foreign ones, as well as the impact of the current development of tourism, on the enjoyment of basic rights by indigenous peoples.[44]

It is hard to see how these comments are very helpful to Panama. The Minority Rights Committee has not identified any new specific measures for Panama and merely endorses the government's current efforts regarding property and land rights. The Minority Rights Committee recommendations for "investigating" and "monitoring" corporate activities are superficial and safe.

Keep in mind that the Panamanian government reports one of the worst distributions of income in the world, with very high rates of unemployment, and estimates that about half the population of the country lives in poverty. The proportion of the Panamanian population that is undernourished has skyrocketed from 12 percent in the early 1970s to 19 percent in the 1990s.[45] The indigenous population, which is composed of five ethnic groups, accounts for between 8 and 10 percent of the population. According to the UN Economic Rights Committee, these ethnic groups are among the poorest and most vulnerable sectors of Panamanian society.[46]

Yet, the Minority Rights Committee does not address the economic plight of these racial minorities. The Minority Rights Committee does not help Panama develop policies that can protect the economic and social rights of these indigenous peoples. The Minority Rights Committee's recommendations should be better informed and specific. It is not that useful just to "express concern" or call for more "monitoring" of the problem. These flimsy and ineffectual reports from the Minority Rights Committee contribute to the sense of futility and cynicism concerning UN human rights efforts.

In 1999, the Minority Rights Committee held its fifty-fourth session (1–19 March) and its fifty-fifth session (2–27 August). During these meetings, the committee considered reports, comments, and information submitted by twenty-eight states parties, independent organizations, and knowledgeable individuals. It is instructive to analyze all the references to economic and social human rights made by the Minority Rights Committee in its twenty-eight concluding observations in response to these state reports in its 1999 sessions. In almost every case, the Minority Rights Committee "expresses its concern" about a given problem and then makes "suggestions and recommendations" for the state party to follow.[47]

The expressions of concern deal with issues of critical importance, such as the absence of sanctions against racial discrimination in the private sector (Austria), discrimination against the Roma (Italy and Romania), the close relationship between socioeconomic underdevelopment and racial discrimination (Peru), the vulnerable status of refugees and immigrants (Costa Rica), and disadvantaged ethnic and tribal minorities (Iran, Mongolia, and Uruguay). The committee often exposes a critical issue of eco-

COMMITTEE ON THE ELIMINATION OF ALL FORMS OF RACIAL DISCRIMINATION

54th (March 1–19, 1999) and 55th (August 2–27, 1999) Sessions

Concluding Observations Relating to Economic and Social Rights of Minorities/Indigenous Peoples (Principal Subjects of Concern and Suggestions and Recommendations)

Austria

- "34. The Committee expresses its concern that, seven years after it drew the attention of the State party to the absence of sanctions against racial discrimination in the private sector, little progress has been made in fully implementing the provisions of articles 5(e) and (f). In addition, the Committee empresses its concern that non-citizens are not currently eligible for participation in work councils."

Republic of Korea

- "61. While acknowledging the fact that the State party has recently taken measures to improve the status of foreign 'industrial trainees' and other foreigners working in the country, the Committee suggests that the Government of the Republic of Korea take further measures against discrimination in the labor conditions of foreign workers. The Committee also recommends that measures be taken to improve the situation of all migrant workers, particularly those with irregular status."

Finland

- "80. The Committee recommends that the State Party redouble its efforts towards the resolution of the land dispute concerning the Sami as soon as possible, in a manner that does justice to the claims of the Sami."
- "81. Additional measures should be taken at the state and municipal levels to alleviate the situation of the Roma minority and of immigrants with respect to housing, employment and education."

Portugal

- No specific mention of economic or social human rights of minority populations.

Congo

- No state report submitted to the committee.
- No specific mention of economic or social human rights of minority populations.

Italy

- "126. In light of reports indicating discrimination against persons of Roma origin, including children, in a number of areas, in particular housing, concern is expressed at the situation of many Roma who, ineligible for public housing, live in camps outside major Italian cities. In addition to a frequent lack of basic facilities, the housing of Roma in such camps leads not only to physical segregation of the Roma community from Italian society, but to political, economic and cultural isolation as well."
- "130. The Committee also recommends that State authorities give more attention to the situation of Roma in Italy, with a view to averting discrimination against them."

Peru

- "148. The Committee notes with concern the close relationship between socio-economic underdevelopment and the phenomena of ethnic or racial discrimination against part of the population, chiefly the indigenous and peasant communities. In this respect, the Committee regrets the absence in the periodic report of information on the socio-economic indicators relevant to the situation of populations of indigenous, peasant or African origin. It nevertheless notes that the report acknowledges shortcomings in areas such as housing and health."
- "156. With regard to the right to employment, the committee takes note with concern of the reports that access to jobs and promotions is often influenced by racial criteria, while certain minor or disparaged jobs are left to persons of indigenous or African origin."
- "158. The Committee is concerned about reports that the 1993 Constitution no longer totally guarantees that the communal property of indigenous populations is inalienable and unavailable for use."

- "160. Measures should be taken to guarantee the right of the most underprivileged members of the population to benefit from all the rights listed in article 5."
- "164. In its next report, the State party should provide information on, inter alia: . . . (b) socio-economic indicators relevant to the situation of populations of indigenous, peasant or African origin."

Syrian Arab Republic

- "177. The Committee encourages the State party to continue to explore ways of providing protection to all ethnic or national groups living in the Syrian Arab Republic and recommends that the State party include in its next report data on the ethnic composition of the population and on persons residing in the Syrian Arab republic who are non-Palestinian refugees. Information on their socio-economic situation would also be appreciated."

Costa Rica

- "193. [T]he Committee also expresses its concern about the vulnerable status of refugees and clandestine immigrants, who often live and work in the country in precarious conditions, and who frequently become victims of discrimination in the terms of article 5 of the convention, in particular paragraph 5 (e)."
- "194. The Committee remains concerned at the situation with regard to the land rights of indigenous peoples in the State party. Despite the efforts made, problems relating to the allocation of land and/or compensation persist. Of special concern have been confrontations arising over the ownership of property, in the course of which indigenous people were killed and vandalism occurred, as in the case of Talamanca."
- "201. It is also recommended that the State party take immediate and appropriate measures to ensure the enjoyment of the provisions of article 5 of the Convention also by the indigenous populations, the black minority, refugees and immigrants."
- "202. The Committee recommends that the State party intensify its efforts to ensure a fair and equitable distribution of land, taking into account the needs of the indigenous population."

Kuwait

- No specific mention of economic and social human rights of minority populations.

Mongolia

- "246. The Committee further recommends that the State party include in its next report statistical data on the socio-economic situation of the different ethnic minority groups."

Haiti

- "264. The Committee recommends that the State party in its next periodic report provide full information on the demographic composition of the population . . . together with socio-economic indicators on the situation of the various ethnic communities."

Romania

- "286. Measures of affirmative action should be adopted in favour of the Roma population, especially in the areas of education and vocational training, with a view, inter alia, to placing Roma on an equal footing with the rest of the population in the enjoyment of economic, social and cultural rights, removing prejudices against the Roma population and enhancing its capacity in asserting its rights. A coordinated effort by the various State bodies competent in this area, working in conjunction with representatives of the Roma population, is required."

Antigua and Barbuda

- No state report submitted to the committee.
- No specific mention of economic or social human rights of minority populations.

Islamic Republic of Iran

- "307. The Committee recommends that the State party continue to promote economic, social and cultural development in areas inhabited by disadvantaged ethnic and tribal minorities and groups, and to encourage the participation of these minorities in such development."

Maldives

- No state report submitted to the committee.
- No specific mention of economic or social human rights of minority populations.

Mauritania

- "329. With regard to article 5 of the Convention, allegations are noted to the effect that some groups of the population, especially the black communities, are still suffering from various forms of exclusion and discrimination, especially where access to public services and employment is concerned. While the Committee notes with satisfaction that Mauritanian legislation has abolished slavery and servitude, it also notes that in some parts of the country, vestiges of practices of slavery and involuntary servitude could still persist, despite the State party's efforts to eradicate such practices."
- "332. The Committee recommends that the State party include information in its next report on legislative measures and practices introduced by the authorities to give effect to the provisions of article 5 of the Convention, especially with a view to promoting the struggle against discrimination affecting the most vulnerable groups of the population, in particular the black communities, and to eradicating vestiges of practices of slavery and involuntary servitude."

Iraq

- The committee appealed to the UN Security Council to lift the economic embargo due to the loss of lives resulting from the economic sanctions.
- "348. Concern is also expressed over allegations that the non-Arab population living in the Kirkuk and Khanaquin areas, especially the Kurds, Turkmen and Assyrians, have been subjected by local Iraqi authorities to measures such as forced relocation, denial of equal access to employment and educational opportunities and limitations in the exercise of their rights linked to the ownership of real estate."
- "353. Allegations concerning discrimination against members of ethnic minorities in the Kirkuk and Khanaquin areas, as mentioned above, should be examined by the State party. The Committee requests to be informed about the result of such investigations."

Central African Republic

- No state report submitted to the committee.
- No specific mention of economic or social human rights of minority populations.

Chile

- "375. The Committee is concerned about land disputes which occurred during the period under examination between the Mapuche population and national and multinational private companies, resulting in tension, violence, clashes with law enforcement officials and, allegedly led to arbitrary arrests of members of the indigenous population."
- "376. The Committee expresses its concern about the situation of migrant workers, in particular of Peruvian nationality."
- "381. In its forthcoming report, the State party should include detailed information relating to the following: the work and activities of the Indigenous Development Corporation; the system of land distribution; the judicial system in place for the indigenous population; the situation of migrant workers, the implementation of articles 4 and 5 of the convention and, ongoing legislative reforms."

Latvia

- "397. Concern is also expressed about reports that there are still unjustified differences of treatment between citizens and non-citizens, mostly members of minorities, in the enjoyment of the rights provided for in article 5 (e) of the Convention."
- "406. It is also recommended to the State party to review the differences of treatment between citizens and non-citizens, mostly persons belonging to ethnic groups, in the light of the provisions of article 5 (e), so as to eliminate any unjustifiable differences."

Uruguay

- "423. The Committee remains concerned about the insufficient information on the situation of ethnic groups living in the State party's territory. Concern is also expressed about the lack of information on special measures, such as affirmative action programmes, taken for the protection of the rights of disadvantaged ethnic groups such as Afro-Uruguayans and indigenous groups."
- "424. The Committee remains concerned about the lack of information on the effective enjoyment of the rights provided for in, especially, article 5 (c) and (e), and in particular by members of the Afro-Uruguayan and indigenous communities. In addition, concern is particularly expressed about the situation

of women belonging to the Afro-Uruguayan community, who are victims of double discrimination on grounds of both their gender and race."

- "429. The Committee also recommends that the State party take immediate and appropriate measures to ensure the enjoyment of all the rights enumerated in article 5 of the Convention in particular by members of the Afro-Uruguayan and indigenous communities and provide further information on the subject. With respect to employment, education and housing, the Committee recommends that the State party take steps to reduce present inequalities and adequately compensate affected groups and persons for earlier evictions from their houses."
- "430. The Committee recommends that the State party establish special programmes aimed at facilitating the social enhancement of women belonging to the Afro-Uruguayan community, who suffer double discrimination on grounds of both their gender and race."

Mozambique

- No state report submitted to the committee.
- No specific mention of economic or social human rights of minority populations.

Kyrgyzstan

- "447. The Committee wishes to receive further information regarding the practical enjoyment by persons belonging to ethnic and national minorities of the rights listed in article 5(e) of the Convention, in particular the right to work, including the right to equal opportunities of promotion and career development, the rights to health, education and to housing."

Colombia

- "475. Recognizing that many Afro-Colombians live in extreme poverty in urban slum areas, the Committee recommends that the State party take steps to address de facto racial segregation in urban centres. The Committee also requests additional information in the next periodic report on housing patterns in urban areas and on legislation that may address discrimination in the housing sector."
- "476. The Committee recommends that the State party implement affirmative and effective measures to ensure increased

employment opportunities for minority and indigenous communities in both the public and private sectors and to advance the social, political, economic, and educational status of historically marginalized communities."

Azerbaijan

- "491. Although the Committee notes that the State party's Constitution guarantees the enjoyment, without discrimination, of most of the rights mentioned in article 5 of the Convention, it remains acutely concerned about the effective enjoyment of these rights by persons belonging to ethnic groups, in particular by persons belonging to the Armenian, Russian and Kurdish minorities when seeking employment, housing and education."
- "497. The Committee recommends that the State party utilize all available means, including international cooperation, to ameliorate the situation of displaced persons and refugees, especially regarding their access to education, employment and housing, pending their return to their houses under conditions of safety."

Dominican Republic

- "514. The Committee recommends that the State party take urgent measures to ensure the enjoyment by persons of Haitian origin of their economic, social and cultural rights without discrimination. Efforts should be made, in particular, to improve their living conditions in the *bateyes* (shanty towns)."

Guinea

- "533. Concern is expressed about the lack of information regarding the practical implementation of article 5 of the convention. In this connection, the Committee is concerned about the destruction by the State of more than 10,000 homes in the Conakry Ratoma neighborhood, belonging mainly to members of the Puhlar ethnic group; the resulting riots which led to the death of eight persons; and the inter-ethnic tension which remains in that area. The Committee is also concerned about the lack of compensation for those persons whose property was expropriated."
- "538. [T]he State party is invited to provide further information on the effective enjoyment of the political, economic and social rights enumerated in article 5 of the Convention, in particular by persons belonging to ethnic groups."

nomic and social injustice within the state party. This is a critical first step since exposure can help identify the path forward.

Where the Minority Rights Committee is weak, however, is in helping to find solutions. Its suggestions and recommendations are uniformly unsubstantial. To address these violations of the economic and social human rights of minorities, the committee calls on states parties to "redouble its efforts," take "additional measures," "give more attention" to the issue, "provide information," "take immediate and appropriate measures," "intensify its efforts," "continue to promote" economic development, "take steps to address" economic discrimination, and so on. These "recommendations" are void of any content. What measures should states parties take? What types of policies are effective in addressing economic discrimination? How can a program of economic growth also incorporate policies to address the needs of the most vulnerable minority groups? These questions should be the main focus of the committee.

Thus, the Minority Rights Committee is adept at identifying the economic and social issues confronting racial minorities within the states parties to the Minority Rights Treaty, but it is not very resourceful in identifying the actions that these nations need to take to address these issues. The Minority Rights Committee's role could be strengthened by spending more time assisting nations in the formulation of effective policy in these areas. It is difficult to construct appropriate and workable policy to ameliorate racial bias in economic development. Yet, as will be seen later on, there are successful programs that can guide policy makers.

These criticisms of the work of the Minority Rights Committee are directed at the complacency of the states parties to the Minority Rights Treaty, and not at the expert members of the committee. These individuals receive no payment for the work they do on the committee and have no research or secretarial assistance. Other difficulties include translation delays and a lack of access to sources of information beyond the state's self-report. Most members have full-time jobs elsewhere, which limits the amount of committee work they can undertake. Overall, committee members' efforts to breathe life into this process have been stymied by a lack of support from nation-states.[48]

The Minority Rights Committee has even had difficulties getting its minimal budget funded. To overcome the committee's financial difficulties resulting from the nonpayment of contributions by states parties, the committee approved an amendment to article 8(6) of the convention, which was later adopted by the General Assembly of the UN. The amendment calls for expenses of the members of the committee to be borne by the regular UN annual budget. However, this amendment is not in force as it awaits the prescribed number of ratifications by states parties.[49]

In addition, the Minority Rights Committee is set up and funded to meet only twice a year, in the spring and summer. It is hard to imagine how a committee that meets for only three weeks twice a year can effectively monitor the practices of the 161 parties to the convention. This problem is widely acknowledged at the Office of the High Commissioner for Human Rights (OHCHR). Yet, due to the tangible reality of a small staff and a small budget, there is no serious effort to expand the work of the committee.

In fact, there is a large degree of complacency about the weaknesses in the human rights reporting mechanisms. For example, staff members recognize that the only reason that the reporting system as a whole has not collapsed is because all states do not report. If these states did report, the small staff at the OHCHR could not cope. As a result, privately there is an acknowledged sense of relief that all states do not report, and there is no serious political push to get states to report on time. The result is that the reporting system remains ineffectual.[50]

These are serious issues. The Minority Rights Committee gives states the opportunity to say that they are not only concerned with discrimination and racial injustice, but are doing something about it. Yet, the structures and mechanisms theses states have established to address minority rights are underfunded and understaffed, and thus, ineffective.

Strengthening the UN's Approach to Minority Rights

The Development of Accurate Social Indicators

The Minority Rights Committee could benefit by incorporating the reports from the Economic Rights Committee into its standard operating procedures. The Commission on Human Rights urged treaty bodies to consider ways of reducing the reporting burden on states, including "considering the utility of single comprehensive reports and of replacing periodic reports with specifically tailored reports and thematic reports."[51] Economic and social rights are primarily the domain of the Economic Rights Treaty, and its treaty body, the Economic Rights Committee. States' reports to the Economic Rights Committee address the social and economic concerns of the Minority Rights Committee. In terms of economic and social rights, a single report to both of these treaty bodies ought to suffice.

The Economic Rights Committee has effectively specified and defined the content of economic and social human rights and established reporting guidelines that pay attention to issues of racial discrimination. The data from the Economic Rights Committee can provide the Minority Rights Committee with the information needed to formulate effective policy options responsive to the economic and social rights claims of racial and ethnic minorities. States parties would not have to report twice, but merely refer to the relevant sections in their report to the Economic Rights Committee. The current reporting guidelines allow for such practices to avoid duplication of effort.

The Economic Rights Committee has focused on issues of race and discrimination in the fulfillment of all the articles of the Economic Rights Treaty. For example, the Economic Rights Treaty article 6 recognizes the right to work "which includes the right of everyone to the opportunity to gain his [or her] living by work which he [or she] freely chooses or accepts."[52] In its reporting guidelines to states parties, the Economic Rights Committee requests the following:

> Please indicate whether there exist in your country any distinction, exclusions, restrictions or preferences, be it in law or in administrative practices or in practical relationships between persons or groups of persons, made on the basis of race, color, sex, religion, political opinion, nationality or social origin, which have the effect of nullifying or impairing the recognition, enjoyment or exercise of equality of opportunity or treatment in employment or occupation. What steps are taken to eliminate such discrimination?[53]

Similar data requests are made by the Economic Rights Committee for all articles, including: article 7, the right to just and favorable conditions of work; article 9, the right to social security; and article 11, the right to an adequate standard of living, including adequate food, clothing, and housing. Detailed information, for example, is requested on the right to adequate food. States parties must report on the extent to which hunger and/or malnutrition exists in their country. This information should include the situation for especially vulnerable or disadvantaged groups, including landless peasants, marginalized peasants, rural workers, rural unemployed, urban unemployed, urban poor, migrant workers, indigenous peoples, children, elderly people, and other especially affected groups.[54]

These state party reports combined with information provided by NGOs should give the Minority Rights Committee an accessible picture of racial discrimination in the fulfillment of economic and social human rights.

Professionalizing the Minority Rights Committee

Scholars and activists have noted the "splendid isolation" of the human rights convention treaty bodies from the rest of the UN system.[55] Unfortunately, the Minority Rights Committee has been marginalized and is seen as peripheral to the main work of the UN. Although all Minority Rights Committee reports (including concluding observations) receive general distribution within the UN and are posted on the OHCHR's website, they are read by few and have minimal impact. The Minority Rights Committee submits an extensive yearly report on its meetings and decisions to the UN General Assembly. Yet again, this report does not provoke extensive discussion nor serious actions to address the plight of racial and ethnic minorities.

There are a number of steps that can be taken to strengthen this system. First, the reports from the Minority Rights Committee should go not just to the General Assembly, but to the new UN Economic Security Council recommended in the Global New Deal (see chapter 8). This body will have the administrative staff and technical expertise to help states meet their obligations under the Minority Rights Treaty. This should not only cause the reports themselves to be taken more seriously, but also nudge states to implement policy to ameliorate racial and ethnic bias. States will know that these reports are not simply a bureaucratic assignment to get out of the way as quickly as possible. Rather, the reports will be evaluated and acted on by the main body within the UN system concerned with issues of economic equality—the UN Economic Security Council.

Some reform proposals call for consolidation of the six active treaty bodies into one permanent professional treaty body. In addition to the two already mentioned (Minority Rights Committee and Economic Rights Committee), the other treaty bodies are: the Women's Rights Committee, established under the Convention on the Elimination of All Forms of Discrimination against Women; Committee against Torture, established under the Convention against Torture and Other Cruel, Inhuman or Degrading Treatment or Punishment; the Committee on the Rights of the Child, established under the Convention on the Rights of the Child; and the Human Rights Committee, established under the Covenant on Civil and Political Rights. With a consolidation of these committees, states could harmonize and streamline reports to one body instead of six. There are clear advantages in terms of staff, money, administration, and so on.

However, the danger in such an approach is that the current focus on a single issue will become lost. Discrimination against racial minorities or against women, for example, could get buried in an overall report on state compliance to all international human rights law. Some consolidation of reporting is clearly essential, as demonstrated earlier in the proposal to eliminate the duplication in reporting to the Economic Rights Committee and the Minority Rights Committee. But it is important for the Minority Rights Committee to continue to highlight issues of racism and discrimination, and the Women's Rights Committee to address issues of women's rights. The specific mandates and concentrations of each of the six treaty bodies ought to be maintained. These six areas deserve the distinctive specialized attention the individual committees can provide.

There are two measures that can further the professionalization of the committee structure and significantly help the committees achieve their objectives. Rather than starting over, these proposals are intended to enhance and refine the current system. They build on the accomplishments of the committees to date. They also recognize the financial and political constraints facing the UN. They are realistic and doable. These proposals are designed to strengthen the UN treaty body system as a whole and, as a consequence, the functioning of the Minority Rights Committee.

The first proposal is to professionalize the operations of the experts on the committees. States parties elect the experts to sit on a treaty body committee at biannual meetings. Often, experts are elected who do not have the time to conscientiously evaluate government reports and NGO information. Nearly all have full-time employment elsewhere, and thus have difficulty even preparing for meetings. Sometimes political appointments are made and the nominee lacks true expertise in either international law or the subjects of concern to the committee. These problems can be easily overcome. To guarantee that the persons nominated for election to the committee are qualified to serve, a screening process can be established. The OHCHR, in consultation with relevant NGOs, could review the curriculum vitae of candidates and expose those who are unqualified to serve. Since the individual is to serve with impartiality and "in a personal capacity," this should not involve embarrassing any particular state party. Individual nominees from all countries would have to be experts in the field. And, perhaps more importantly, the experts elected to the committee should be paid to support their hard work. Currently, the members of the Minority Rights Committee work on a pro bono basis.[56] With human rights now a central focus of all UN activities, and with a rising number of states relating to the treaty bodies, it is totally unrealistic to expect members of the committee to be able to fulfill their responsibilities on a volunteer basis. With this structure, membership on the committees is limited to retirees, government officials, or academics subsidized by their governments. With such strong governmental support, the "independence" of the experts becomes questionable. A solution is to pay each committee member a half-time professional salary out of the UN budget for their committee work. This would allow these experts to take a leave of absence for half the year from their full-time jobs. Most professions would allow their employees to take an unpaid leave for six months in order to serve on such a distinguished committee. By funding these salaries for half a year, the UN would be giving the committee members time not only to attend the committee meetings, but also time for adequate preparation and follow-up. Committee members, for example, could then participate in additional working groups, including thematic working groups with members of other treaty bodies. Greater contact with members of other treaty bodies could help lead to joint efforts at eliminating duplication and streamlining operations. In addition, committee members could potentially make visits to states parties for follow-up activities in connection with reports and communications. It is reasonable to expect the UN to fund these part-time salaries to give committee members the time to fulfill their obligations. If the UN is serious about human rights, this minimal financial commitment should be forthcoming.

The second proposal is to professionalize the staff operations in the OHCHR to support the work of the committees. Additional professional staff is needed at the OHCHR to respond to the growing needs of the Minority Rights Committee and the other treaty bodies. For example, staff is needed to conduct a preliminary examination of a state report to the Minority Rights Committee, examine the human rights situation in the particular country, and prepare a working document for the committee. Coordination between treaty bodies can be facilitated with additional staff at the OHCHR. Additional staff is needed to streamline reporting mechanisms to avoid duplication resulting from overlapping instruments, to follow up on reports and communications, to provide technical advice and assistance to states, to draft general comments with one or more members of the committee, and so on. Minimal financial resources could address these concerns.[57]

When Mary Robinson announced that she would not seek an additional term as high commissioner for human rights, she expressed frustration with the UN's lack of financial support for the OHCHR. The OHCHR receives a minute part of the overall UN budget (approximately less than 2 percent), and even this is threatened.[58] This is unacceptable. The minimal funding needs necessary to make the human rights treaty body system work effectively must be forthcoming.

In its contribution to the preparatory process for the 2001 UN World Conference against Racism, Racial Discrimination, Xenophobia and Related Intolerance, the Economic Rights Committee notes: "The full realization of the substantive rights enumerated in the Covenant [on Economic, Social and Cultural Rights]—the rights to education, housing, food, employment, and so on—will go a long way towards the elimination of racism, racial discrimination, xenophobia and related intolerance."[59] Working in conjunction with the Economic Rights Committee, a Minority Rights Committee focus on education and health care for all could significantly contribute toward ending the marginalization and social exclusion of disadvantaged and vulnerable groups.

The Global New Deal and Race

Summary Observations

The work of the Minority Rights Committee can be enhanced with a focus on Sen's capabilities approach (outlined in chapter 2). This strategy can both clarify and simplify the reporting process on economic and

Global New Deal Proposals

The Minority Rights Committee needs to break out of the cumbersome traditions that now plague its functioning. Bold and progressive thinking and action can revitalize its work and increase its relevance. The

social rights and provide policy direction and focus. This approach provides the committee with the tools to help states formulate clear policies to achieve economic and social human rights for all.

Previous chapters have reviewed the policies and programs that states can follow to protect, respect, and fulfill economic and social human rights. The economic and social rights of racial minorities can be achieved through a focus on improving individual capabilities. These economic policies of social development include expanding basic education and basic health care, including access to clean water, sanitation, and adequate nutrition. The "success stories" of the 1980s and 1990s were those low-income countries (including Sri Lanka, Karala [India], Botswana, Barbados, and Costa Rica) that achieved levels of health and education comparable to the industrialized states. These recommendations of the Global New Deal are based on the progress of these nations in confronting poverty and suffering.[60]

proposal outlined in chapter 8 greatly simplifies the work of the committee in the area of economic and social human rights. The Global New Deal calls for prioritizing the rights of racial and ethnic minorities by focusing on investments in health care and education. Each state should be required to report on how it is addressing these two areas. These priorities are essential to the capabilities approach to human development and indispensable to effective public policy designed to end suffering and protect the vulnerable. With this approach, the Minority Rights Committee will be doing more than merely calling for states parties to "redouble [their] efforts," take "additional measures," "give more attention" to the issue, "intensify [their] efforts," "take steps to address" economic discrimination, and so on. Instead, the Minority Rights Committee will be recommending specific policies to end racial discrimination in the areas of health and education.

This proposal is also based on the current limitations in staff and funding confronting the Minority Rights Committee. With only limited resources, the committee must focus its attention on where it can be effective. The Minority Rights Committee can have a significant impact if it calls the states parties' attention to these indisputable priorities.

6

Gender and Economic and Social Human Rights

Do socially constructed international human rights advance the economic and social well-being of women? Or do these norms reflect a gender bias that hinders the betterment of women? How are women's economic and social human rights protected in this era of rapid economic globalization? Do particular approaches to international political economy provide a clear guide toward economic and social rights fulfillment for the world's women? How has the UN Committee on the Elimination of Discrimination against Women (Women's Rights Committee) dealt with the economic and social rights of women?

"Men do not want solely the obedience of women, they want their sentiments," wrote John Stuart Mill in 1869 in *The Subjection of Women*. Mill wrote that men desire to have in women "not a forced slave but a willing one. . . . They therefore put everything in practice to enslave their minds . . . turn[ing] the whole force of education to effect their purpose . . . [to show that] it is the duty of women . . . it is their nature, to live for others; to make complete abnegation of themselves, and to have no life but in their affections." Women are taught that "meekness, submissiveness, and resignation of all individual will into the hands of a man is an essential part of sexual attractiveness." Mill contended that "woman" was a social construct and ridiculed the idea that women's then current behavior revealed their "nature." He wrote that this is like planting a tree half in a vapor bath and half in the snow, and then, seeing that one part is flourishing and the other part shriveling, saying that it is the nature of the tree to be that way.[1]

Ideas of the social construction of consciousness have an intellectual lineage going back to at least the nineteenth century. Karl Marx labeled this process of manufacturing identity, and the fabrication of male and female human nature, the creation of false consciousness. Marx and Frederick Engels wrote that "consciousness is . . . from the beginning a social product."[2] While postmodernists reject the term "false," since most people believe in the "truth" of their identity, there is agreement among critical scholars on the potent role of culture and power in the social creation of individual understandings of one's identity as a woman or man. For centuries, patriarchal power has depended on a social construction of the idea of a nonthreatening "women's nature" to support an aggressive "natural male." Philip Gourevitch notes that "power largely consists in the ability to make others inhabit your story of their reality."[3] Male power is often contingent on women accepting and inhabiting man's story of their reality.

To a large extent, the international movement to claim women's human rights is an attempt to challenge this oppressive history by forcing men to accept and inhabit women's reality. Working through the UN system, the international women's movement has attempted to articulate the unique claims specific to women. For example, the UN Fourth World Conference on Women held in Beijing adopted a final declaration on 15 September 1995 embracing the collective human rights of women. The broad declaration called on world governments to raise the economic circumstances of women and protect them from increasing levels of violence. At Beijing, governments pledged to act against domestic violence, empower poor women by giving them access to bank services and credit, and give women the right to decide freely all matters relating to their sexuality and childbearing.[4]

But these pledges and norms are also socially constructed, and feminists are divided over the gendered nature of international human rights law. Examine the opposing positions of Hilary Charlesworth and Barbara Stark concerning women's economic and social human rights:

On one hand, Charlesworth states that "the current international human rights structure itself and the substance of many norms of human rights law create obstacles to the advancement of women." She argues that the Economic Rights Treaty[5] is of little help to women because it "does not touch on the economic, social, and cultural contexts in which most women live, since the crucial economic, social, and cultural power relationship for most women is not one directly with the state but with men—fathers, husbands, or brothers—whose authority is supported by patriarchal state structures."[6]

On the other hand, Stark writes that the Economic Rights Treaty is a "postmodern feminist text" that privileges women over men and focuses on the substantive problems traditionally left to women. Stark's argument is that the Economic Rights Treaty recognizes the rights of every human being to be nurtured: "[T]o be cared for, housed, fed, clothed, healed, educated, and made to feel part of a community. These 'nurturing rights' are descriptions of women's work." The Economic Rights Treaty privileges concrete rights over abstract ones in its focus on food, shelter, and health care rather than on abstractions like liberty and equality. These economic and social rights are found in the private arena and can be considered "women's rights."[7]

Human rights are moral claims to a certain standard of treatment that derive solely from the very fact of being human. Women's economic and social human rights strive to prohibit de facto and de jure discrimination through the enactment of measures to provide job training for women, child care, paid leave for childbirth, and so on. All women in all societies can make these claims. However, as Charlesworth points out, unless issues of power are addressed at the same time, these normative pronouncements will be meaningless. Progress does not occur through good will alone, nor simply from good intentions. Women's economic and social human rights will occur when there is structural and economic change for women.

So where does this leave us? There are clear differences in interpretation of the importance and impact of international women's rights as they have been defined in international bodies. However, even accepting Stark's argument that the Economic Rights Treaty privileges women's rights, it is hard to make the case that these rights have been implemented internationally in a conscientious fashion. In fact, there is clear evidence that, as these documents were being drafted, the position of women's economic and social rights deteriorated with deepening economic globalization.[8]

It is therefore imperative to link feminist theories of human rights with feminist theories of international political economy (IPE). Economists, political scientists, and policy makers have struggled for decades to understand the relationship between women/sex/gender and economic development. Neither human rights theories nor positivist legal human rights action alone can fundamentally address global and national inequities in power based on patriarchy and class. Combined with theories of IPE—which examine these power relations—strategies for the promotion and protection of the economic and social human rights of women can be formulated.

Utilizing Amartya Sen's analysis of freedom and capabilities—the capabilities approach—the Global New Deal articulates a proposal for achieving women's economic and social human rights. Such a strategy involves collapsing the conceptual boundaries between international human rights law and international economic policy and those between state sovereignty and transnational law. Central to such a policy is the enactment of gender planning and gender analysis on all levels (local, national, and international) to determine how trading and economic systems, and international and national law, impact women. Or, to use Sen's framework, gender planning involves the enactment of public policy to guarantee women the freedom to achieve well-being.

On the one hand, it is true that human beings construct their social worlds and identities and thus can change them. But on the other hand, it is also true that enduring patterns and institutions make change very difficult. To be effective, a strategy for the protection and promotion of women's international economic and social human rights must therefore address both the social construction of identities/norms and the structural constraints that block change.[9] The capabilities approach, which allows for the integration of IPE (with its focus on structures) to human rights (with its focus on socially constructed norms), provides a way forward.

This chapter analyzes central aspects to these issues in the following sections:

- Women's economic and social human rights
- Feminist approaches in IPE and development economics
- Linking IPE to women's economic and social human rights fulfillment

---

Women's Economic and Social Human Rights

Stark argues that the Economic Rights Treaty is the "marginalized half of international human rights law." The privileged half, the Political Rights Treaty, replicates familiar hierarchies like "male over female" and "abstract over concrete practice." But despite its marginalization, she believes that the Economic Rights Treaty does recognize the specific needs and rights of women. Stark argues that the Economic Rights Treaty "privileges a postmodern proliferation of contextualized options over a modern quest for universal, abstract solutions."[10] In other words, as opposed to documents that call for abstract principles (like "justice" and "equality"), the Economic Rights Treaty specifies a number of clear rights found in both the private and the public arenas.
Examine articles 2.2 , 3, and 10.2:

Article 2.2: "The States Parties to the present Covenant undertake to guarantee that the rights enunciated in the present Covenant will be exercised without discrimination of any kind as to race, color, sex, language, religion, political or other opinion, national or social origin, property, birth or other status."[11]

Article 3: "The States Parties to the present Covenant undertake to ensure the equal rights of men and women to the enjoyment of all economic, social and cultural rights set forth in the present Covenant."[12]

Article 10.2: "Special protection should be accorded to mothers during a reasonable period before and after childbirth. During such period working mothers should be accorded paid leave or leave with adequate social security benefits."[13]

These statements on banning gender discrimination can be interpreted to prohibit de facto as well as de jure discrimination. The state is then legally required to enact measures to remedy existing gender discrimination, for example, by providing job training for women, child care, or paid leave for childbirth and after.

In other words, the Economic Rights Treaty attempts to move the dialogue away from legal formal equality to actual substantive (or de facto) equality. Too often the extension of legal formal rights and protections against gender discrimination does not create the same equal opportunities for men and women. Unfortunately, all societies suffer structural inequalities, economic disparities, and the marginalization of some groups. Standards that appear to be neutral may in reality reinforce a dominant patriarchal power structure that does not reflect the needs of the marginalized sex. Thus, de jure or formal equality may in fact reinforce inequality. Those arguing for de facto or substantive equality are concerned with outcomes and results. The starting point is the actual living conditions experienced by individuals and groups and the barriers to gender equality. This approach demands positive action to eliminate these structural obstacles blocking substantive equality.[14]

Stark's argument is that the Economic Rights Treaty requires states parties to take these positive actions. As noted, this covenant recognizes the rights of every human being to be nurtured: "[T]o be cared for, housed, fed, clothed, healed, educated, and made to feel part of a community."[15] The covenant implies state responsibility in all these areas, which if assumed would imply a corresponding decrease of the burden on women.[16]

The public–private dichotomy has been "central to almost two centuries of feminist writing and political struggle."[17] Women are relegated to the private sphere of home and family while men operate in the public arena of the workplace, politics, law, intellectual life, and so on. In general terms, civil and political rights exist in the public arena—the administration of justice and the conduct of public political life—and historically have been considered "men's rights." Economic and social rights are found in the private arena—the family, health care, food, shelter, clothing, and education—and can be considered "women's rights." There is thus a substantial overlap between women's work and the rights enunciated in the Economic Rights Treaty. Paul Hunt notes that the resistance to incorporating norms and programs to address the private sphere is demonstrated in the well-developed procedures and institutions associated with civil and political rights compared to the weak (and often nonexistent) policies and customs in the social realm. "The juridical marginalization of social rights reflects the public–private dichotomy and the gendered nature of law."[18]

The Economic Rights Treaty is not the only international human rights instrument concerned with women's economic and social rights. The UN approach has been to treat women's rights as a separate issue rather than as part of human rights in general. From the establishment of the Commission on the Status of Women (CSW) in 1947 to the Fourth World Conference on Women in Beijing in 1995, women's rights have been treated as a specialized subset of human rights to be dealt with by distinct bodies. The Women's Rights Treaty (International Convention on the Elimination of All Forms of Discrimination against Women), which came into force in 1981, is of particular importance. As of March 2002, 168 states had ratified the Women's Rights Treaty, making it the second most widely accepted international human rights treaty after the Convention on the Rights of the Child.[19] The Women's Rights Treaty obligates states parties to eliminate discrimination against women. States parties are required to take measures, including legislation, to overcome discrimination in economic and social areas such as employment (article 11), education (article 10), and health care (articles 12 and 14).[20]

As with the Economic Rights Treaty, the Women's Rights Treaty also actively goes beyond formal equality and encompasses substantive equality. Examine articles 1, 4(1), and 4(2):

Article 1: "[T]he term 'discrimination against women' shall mean any distinction, exclusion or restriction made on the basis of sex which has the effect or purpose of impairing or nullifying the recognition, enjoyment or exercise by women, irrespective of their marital status, on a basis of equality of men and women, of human rights and fundamental freedoms in the political, economic, social, cultural, civil or any other field."[21]

Article 4(1): "[Advocates the adoption] by States Parties of temporary special measures aimed at accelerating *de facto* equality between men and women."[22]

Article 4(2): "[Advocates the adoption] by States Parties of special measures . . . aimed at protecting maternity."[23]

These articles clearly call for equality of result or substantive equality through special measures like affirmative action programs and protection against indirect discrimination. This is the model of equality in international law. Men and women are to be treated equally. This standard is repeated throughout the convention with the phrase "on a basis of equality of men and women." For example, article 11, concerning employment, reads: "State Parties shall take all appropriate measures to eliminate discrimination against women in the field of employment in order to ensure, on a basis of equality of men and women, the same rights."[24]

This phrase "on a basis of equality of men and women" is repeated in all the economic and social areas discussed in the Women's Rights Treaty, including education (article 10), employment (article 11), health care (article 12), economic and social life (article 13), women in rural areas (article 14), and marriage and family relations (article 16).[25]

Charlesworth, Christine Chinkin, and Shelley Wright argue that the underlying assumption of the Women's Rights Treaty's definition of discrimination is that women and men are the same. "But the notion of both equality of opportunity and equality of result accept the general applicability of a male standard (except in special circumstances such as pregnancy) and promise a very limited form of equality: equality is defined as being like a man."[26]

Feminists argue that this approach negates real differences and inequities and, furthermore, ignores real issues of power. "Thus, equality is not freedom to be treated without regard to sex but freedom from systematic subordination because of sex."[27] Thus, the Women's Rights Treaty, while recognizing discrimination as a legal issue, "is premised on the notion of progress through good will, education and changing attitudes and does not promise any form of structural, social or economic change for women."[28]

The Women's Rights Treaty establishes the Women's Rights Committee (Committee on the Elimination of Discrimination against Women). The Women's Rights Committee consists of twenty-three members, elected by the states parties for four-year terms, who act in their individual capacities and do not represent particular states. The secretary general is to provide the necessary facilities and staff to service the meetings of the Women's Rights Committee. Unlike other treaty committees, the Women's Rights Committee is not serviced by the Office of the High Commissioner for Human Rights (OHCHR), but by the UN's Division for the Advancement of Women. This has meant that the sessions of the Women's Rights Committee have never been held at the OHCHR in Geneva. Until 1993, the Women's Rights Committee met alternatively between Vienna, the headquarters of the Division for the Advancement of Women, and New York. Many observers felt that the separation of the Women's Rights Committee from the other main UN human rights bodies contributed to the marginalization of women's rights issues. In 1993, the Division for the Advancement of Women was relocated to UN Headquarters in New York. As a result, the Women's Rights Committee since its thirteenth session in 1994 has always held its meetings in New York. This has assisted the work of the committee and has increased its visibility within the UN system.[29]

The Women's Rights Committee was initially limited by Women's Rights Treaty article 20 to a single two-week annual meeting. However, in 1996 the General Assembly approved an increase in meeting time for the Women's Rights Committee, allowing it to meet for two three-week sessions annually, each preceded by a one-week working group session.[30]

As opposed to every other major institution of the international legal order, the Women's Rights Committee is staffed by women and not men. With a single exception, the Women's Rights Committee has always been an all-female committee dealing with women's issues.[31] The state representatives reporting to the committee have, for the most part, been male. Some observers argue that this has resulted in the proceedings becoming adversarial in nature, with the representative feeling victimized and responding defensively.[32] In response to these concerns, the UN Economic and Social Council (ECOSOC) called on the states parties to nominate both female and male experts for election to the Women's Rights Committee. It is instructive to note that ECOSOC did not call on states to correct the much more common dominance of men in all the other human rights supervisory bodies. The Women's Rights Committee rejected ECOSOC's recommendation on the grounds that it could potentially undermine the committee's effectiveness. The committee further called on ECOSOC to attend to equality of representation elsewhere before interfering with its membership.[33]

As with the Minority Rights Committee, the primary responsibility of the Women's Rights Committee is the consideration of states parties' reports. The reporting guidelines are found in article 18 of Women's Rights Treaty, which, after the initial report, requires periodic reports to be submitted at least every four years and whenever the Women's Rights Committee requests them. On the basis of these reports, the Women's Rights Committee adopts suggestions and recommendations concerning the matters reported to it.

As with the other treaty bodies, the Women's Rights Committee also faces a serious problem of states ignoring their legal obligations and refusing to report. As of March 2002, there were 257 overdue state reports to the Women's Rights Committee.[34] If all of these delinquent states were to report, the current system could not handle it; in fact, the committee can not even keep up with the reports it does receive. It has been estimated that just to deal with the backlog, if the Women's Rights Committee were to consider ten reports per session, on the basis of two sessions per year it would take the committee roughly ten years to work through these late reports.[35] The Women's Rights Committee is not set up to handle the volume of reports required by the binding treaty.

However, since 1982, when the Women's Rights Committee started its work, hundreds of state reports have been submitted. These reports vary in quality and suffer from the inherent problems of subjectivity intrinsic to self-reporting. Yet, often these reports help focus a government on issues of women's rights and stimulate action. For example, in the initial report Guatemala submitted to the Women's Rights Committee, the government noted the difficulty of assembling the report, stating that "studies of this type are only a recent innovation." The task of preparing the report "has also been a positive exercise in thought, analysis and self-appraisal with respect to the position of women in Guatemala . . . [stimulating action to design] strategies and targets . . . to improve the situation encountered in the short and medium term." The report notes that the work of Guatemalan women "is poorly paid or not paid at all and is generally of low productivity owing to lack of access to capital. It is falsely assumed that the man is the one who makes the principal economic contributions to the family, for which reason he is the owner and beneficiary of all payments and services. . . . In the paid work that she does, her salary is inferior to a man's and her instability in the sense of a job is greater." The reporting requirements of the Women's Rights Committee clearly helped the Guatemalan government focus on these issues of gender discrimination and the economic and social well-being of women.[36]

An Optional Protocol to Women's Rights Treaty was adopted by the CSW on 12 March 1999 and by the General Assembly on 6 October 1999. After receiving ten ratifications, the optional protocol entered into force on 22 December 2000. As of March 2002, seventy-five states had signed and thirty states had ratified the optional protocol.[37] This amendment allows for the submission of individual complaints to the Women's Rights Committee and establishes a procedure under which serious and systematic violations of the convention can be investigated. The optional protocol opens the door for women (individuals or groups) to have their voices heard in the UN system. The Women's Rights Committee can now initiate inquiries where there are grave or systematic violations of women's rights. These new procedures enhance the ability of the Women's Rights Committee to serve as an international forum for women and recommend remedies for violations of women's rights. Individual complaint procedures on other treaty bodies have spurred governments to evaluate means of redress available at the national level (see the discussion of the complaint procedure to the Minority Rights Committee in chapter 5). The Optional Protocol to Women's Rights Treaty should now provide an incentive for governments to evaluate the protection of women's rights at the national level.[38]

The Women's Rights Committee also issues general recommendations to states parties that interpret and clarify the legal duties and obligations in the Women's Rights Treaty. The Women's Rights Committee's general recommendations thus serve a similar purpose as the Economic Rights Committee's general comments (reviewed in chapter 3) in the progressive development of international human rights law. A number of the general recommendations have dealt with the economic and social rights of women:[39]

General Recommendation no. 5 calls on states parties to "make more use of temporary special measures such as positive action, preferential treatment or quota systems to advance women's integration into education, the economy, politics and employment."[40]

General Recommendation no. 13 urges states parties to ratify International Labor Organization Convention no. 100 concerning equal remuneration for men and women workers for work of equal value.[41]

General Recommendation no. 16 calls on states parties to include "in their reports to the Committee information on the legal and social situation of unpaid women working in family enterprises . . . [and t]ake the necessary steps to guarantee payment, social security and social benefits for women who work without such benefits in enterprises owned by a family member."[42]

General Recommendation no. 17 encourages states parties to measure and value the unremunerated domestic activities of women, for example, "by conducting time-use surveys as part of their national household survey programmes and by collecting statistics disaggregated by gender on time spent on activities both in the household and on the labour market." States parties are asked to quantify and include the unremunerated domestic activities of women in the gross national product.[43]

General Recommendation no. 18 addresses the human rights of disabled women and asks states parties to take "special measures to ensure that they have equal access to education and employment, health services and social security, and to ensure that they can participate in all areas of social and cultural life."[44]

General Recommendation no. 24 addresses state responsibilities in regard to article 12 of Women's Rights Treaty, which affirms that access to health care, including reproductive health, is a basic human right. This very detailed recommendation calls on states parties to implement a comprehensive national strategy to promote women's health. It is noteworthy that in this general recommendation the Women's Rights Committee explicitly addresses the public–private dichotomy and acknowledges the negative impact on women's nutrition and health resulting from the unequal power relationships between women and men in the home and workplace.[45] This analysis reinforced the 1992 General Recommendation no. 19 on violence against women, which directly confronts discrimination and violations of human rights in public and private acts. "Private" activity includes family violence and abuse, forced marriage, dowry deaths, and female circumcision.[46] Andrew Clapham argues that this recommendation represents "a giant leap forward in the conceptual thinking surrounding human rights theories and illustrates the crucial importance of collapsing the public/private boundary in the human rights field."[47]

It is impossible for the Women's Rights Committee in two three-week meetings a year to address the numerous patriarchal practices that globally subordinate women. In addition, the numerous reservations made by states parties to the Women's Rights Treaty suggest that discrimination against women is still regarded as more acceptable than other practices. Furthermore, the Women's Rights Committee is underfunded and understaffed and has not been given effective "power" to correct women's rights violations.

Upendra Baxi writes: "The near-universality of ratification of [Women's Rights Treaty] . . . betokens no human liberation of women. Rather, it endows the state with the power to tell more Nietzschean lies. . . . 'State is the name of the coldest of all cold monsters. Coldly, it tells lies, too; and this lie grows out of its mouth: "I, the state, am the people."'"[48] States can use their ratification of Women's Rights Treaty to claim "progress" in meeting women's rights while simultaneously implementing gendered policies that undermine women's economic and social security. Until the Women's Rights Committee is adequately funded and staffed, and international human rights claims are linked to the threats to women posed by economic globalization and economic liberalization, these norms and laws in the name of women's rights will not only remain weak, but continue to provide the state with "the power to tell more Nietschean lies." Thus, the earlier recommendations to professionalize the operations of the Minority Rights Committee apply equally to the Women's Rights Committee as well.

First, the reports from the Women's Rights Committee are presently submitted through ECOSOC to the General Assembly and transmitted to the CSW for information. These reports should go, not just to the General Assembly, but to the new UN Economic Security Council recommended in the Global New Deal (see chapter 8). This should cause not only the reports themselves to be taken more seriously, but it should also nudge states to implement policy to protect women's rights. The reports will then be evaluated and acted on by the main body within the UN system concerned with issues of economic equality—the UN Economic Security Council.

And second, the experts elected to the Women's Rights Committee should be paid to support their hard work. Currently, the members of the Women's Rights Committee receive only $3,000 per year (apart from their daily allowance). As a result, members must keep full-time employment elsewhere and somehow find the time to attend to the committees affairs.

A solution (as noted with the Minority Rights Committee) is to pay committee members a half-time professional salary out of the UN budget for their committee work. This would allow these experts to take a leave of absence for half the year from their full-time jobs to serve on the Women's Rights Committee. The member states of the UN can show their commitment to women's rights by approving this minimal funding request to make the Women's Rights Committee functional.

Unfortunately, the economic and social rights of women are threatened by global forces that the current UN system of rights protection seems unable to address. Women are too often the first to experience the negative consequences of the globalization process. The Women's Environment and Development Organization (WEDO) has traced the progress of national implementation of the Beijing Platform for Action since the UN's 1995 Fourth World Conference on Women in Beijing (see the information box on WEDO in chapter 3). WEDO finds that since the Beijing Conference: "Women's access to equal opportunity and equal pay in work, labor and organizing rights have been severely eroded in the global economy." WEDO documents how women's economic and social rights are undermined in developed and underdeveloped countries.[49]

In the developed world, public-sector employment has been one of the few areas where women have had access to full-time and unionized jobs with decent pay and benefits. "Women in public sectors have suffered massive layoffs and/or loss of benefits in Canada and the U.S., with women from ethnic and aboriginal minorities hit the worst."[50]

In the underdeveloped world, export-processing zones have mushroomed with a preponderance of female workers. "This feminization of employment, often interpreted as a positive outcome of structural adjustment, is in fact a result of international and local demand for cheap and docile labor that can be used in low-skill, repetitive jobs in unsafe and insecure conditions without minimum guarantees."[51] National reports from Malaysia, the Republic of South Korea, the Philippines, India, Sri Lanka, Egypt, and Mexico dramatically illustrate the gendered nature of economic globalization. Egypt, for example, adopted an Economic Reform and Structural Adjustment Program in 1991 on the basis of agreements with the International Monetary Fund (IMF) and the World Bank. According to the WEDO report, these programs have accentuated poverty and reduced access to basic social services such as health care and education. Women's overall unemployment in Egypt is now estimated to be around 60 percent, which will increase with further privatization. Scarce public and private employment opportunities make these women prime candidates for exploitative working conditions and low wages.[52] The protection of women's human rights law is thus fundamentally linked to national and international economic policy.

IPE and Women's Human Rights

It seems that everyone currently talks of including the voice of women in their development approach. Conservative, liberal, and radical perspectives on political economy all now stress the need for including women and/or gender in their analysis. Some of the key feminist IPE theories and approaches to economic and social human rights fulfillment include Women in Development (WID), Women and Development (WAD), Gender and Development (GAD), Development Alternatives with Women for a New Era (DAWN), and ecofeminism.

Women in Development

WID represents a liberal feminist approach to development. The assumptions of liberal modernization theory are for the most part accepted. While "traditional" societies are often seen as patriarchal, modern society is regarded as potentially democratic and liberating. The fulfillment of women's rights is envisioned through the integration of women's issues into modernization and development programs. WID brings visibility to women's issues in development thinking. Furthermore, it calls for the integration of women into economic planning and production. WID does not advocate fundamental change in economic structures. According to Nalini Visvanathan, WID has been central to the mainstreaming of gender issues into development agencies.[53]

The aim of WID, following the path-breaking work of Ester Boserup in 1970, was to integrate women into development. Since the fruits of development were not trickling down to women, women should be factored into development programs. Boserup documents the ways in which development programs in the less developed countries (LDCs) not only do not benefit women, but actually have led to the deterioration of women's economic status. While men were drawn into the "modernized" economic sectors, women remained in subsistence agriculture, which was suddenly viewed as "backward." Only men had access to new technology, credit, and educational opportunities. As men became engaged in commodity production, women continued to produce food for household consumption. Boserup's concern was with equality and integrating women into development models. She brought the issue of gender and development out in the open, and her thinking was essential to the development of WID. She addressed issues of intrahousehold dynamics and demonstrated the ways in which family income is not equally available to all members of the household.[54]

By the mid-1970s, WID programs had become institutionalized around the world in a variety of sections, departments, and projects within donor countries' development bureaucracy. In the 1980s, women's bureaus and

---

MEASURING GENDER INEQUALITIES IN HUMAN DEVELOPMENT

In its yearly *Human Development Report,* the UN Development Program (UNDP) publishes the following two indispensable indices that measure gender inequality around the world:

The Gender Development Index

The Gender Development Index (GDI) takes account of inequality of achievement between men and women in longevity, knowledge, and decent standard of living. The "longevity" category compares female and male life expectancy at birth. The "knowledge" category examines two areas: (1) female and male adult literacy rates and (2) female and male combined enrollment ratios. The "decent standard of living" category compares female and male earned income. Gender disparity in basic human development is captured by this index.

In 2001, the UNDP estimated the GDI for 146 countries and found gender inequality everywhere. In forty-three countries—including India, Mozambique and Yemen—male literacy rates are at least fifteen percentage points higher than female rates. In twenty-seven countries,

---

ministries were established in the countries of the South. WID became a respectable field of study. Lobbying by WID specialists led to a wider interest in women's role in the development process. The first UN conference on Women and Development was held in 1975 in Mexico City. The years 1976–1985 were declared the Women's Decade, which ended with the Nairobi Women and Development Conference in 1985. The Forward Looking Strategies that emerged from Nairobi called for the full integration of women into mainstream economic development. By the mid-1980s, WID had become thoroughly integrated into the development programs of the leading development international organizations and major government bureaucracies. Women demanded equality: equal access to land and capital, education, and training.[55]

Women and Development

WAD emerged as a critique of WID's acceptance of traditional development economics. Proponents of WAD argue that women were always

girls' net enrollment declined at the secondary level between the mid-1980s and 1997.

The Gender Empowerment Measure

The Gender Empowerment Measure (GEM) focuses on whether women can participate in economic and political life. It measures gender inequality in areas of economic and political decision making and participation. It calculates the percentage of women in parliament and the legislature and among senior officials and managers and professional and technical workers. It also reflects the gender disparity in earned income, an indication of economic independence. GEM helps to assess gender inequality in economic and political opportunities.

In 2001, the UNDP estimated GEM for sixty-four countries. In only eight countries did women hold 30 percent or more of the seats in parliament. Women working in industry and the service sector were typically paid 78 percent of what men earned. The statistics also reveal that high income is not a prerequisite to equal opportunity for women. The UNDP notes that some developing countries outperformed much richer industrial countries. The Bahamas and Trinidad and Tobago, for example, are ahead of Italy and Japan.[a]

a. UNDP, *Human Development Report 2001* (New York: Oxford University Press, 2001), 14–16, 210–217.

part of the development process, so the issue is not the integration of women into development. In fact, women's work in the public and private arenas is absolutely critical to the maintenance of modern capitalism. WAD calls for an examination of the nature of the integration of women in development, which has the effect of sustaining existing international structures of inequality.[56]

According to WAD scholars, the WID perspective fails to challenge the capitalist model of development. Gender hierarchies intensified as capitalist systems spread. The public–private cleavage became central. In the public sphere, male labor brought economic rewards, while in the private sphere, female labor was channeled into nonexchange activities, reproduction, and the well-being of the family. Female labor was thus hidden and uncompensated. WAD draws attention to these issues of women's unpaid domestic work and the need for reproductive services.

WAD highlights the gender inequalities that are embedded within current economic and political structures. Gendered market failure occurs when markets fail to invest in and reward women's productive and reproductive work. Gendered public-sector failure occurs when public institutions fail to include women equitably in their services and operations. These are structural failures and not the product of an irrational sexist individual decision maker. WAD focuses on the institutional level of gender bias.[57]

Cynthia Enloe eloquently describes the gendered nature of economic structures—that is, banking policies, transnational corporate investments, structural adjustment policies, and so on. Writing about export processing zones, Enloe explains:

> The centerpiece of the bankers' export strategy has been the "Export Processing Zone." Indebted governments set aside territory specifically for factories producing goods for the international market. Governments lure overseas companies to move their plants to the EPZs by offering them sewers, electricity, ports, runways, tax holidays and police protection. Most attractive of all is the governments' offer of cheap labor. Women's labor has been the easiest to cheapen, so it shouldn't be surprising that in most Export Processing Zones at least 70 per cent of the workers are women, especially young women. The eighteen-year-old woman at the sewing machine—or electronics assembly line or food-processing plant—in Panama's Colon Export Processing Zone has become the essential though unequal partner of the banker in his glass and chrome office in London or Chicago. The risk-taking banker needs the conscientious seamstress to hold his world together. The politician and his technocratic advisor need the seamstress to keep the banker and his home government pacified. If the seamstress rebels, if she rethinks what it means to be a woman who sews for a living, her country may turn up on the list of "unstable regimes" now kept by politically sensitive bankers.[58]

WAD thus draws our attention to the impact of the global economy on the lives of women and structural violence impacting working women. WAD demonstrates how sexual inequality comes hand in hand with capitalist expansion. WAD proponents argue that radical structural reform could be the first step toward addressing women's economic and social human rights. WAD's structuralist focus is a distinct alternative to WID's liberal orientation.

Gender and Development

Why the word "gender" instead of "women"? Feminists in GAD reject an essentialist and universal definition of the category of women. The use of "gender" as opposed to "women" in the late 1970s and 1980s was to eliminate the biological determinism often underlying feminist analysis.

Critical theory called for the deconstruction of not only key identities (e.g., men/women and homosexual/heterosexual) but the gendered nature of social institutions as well. As R. Pearson, A. Whitehead, and K. Young wrote in 1984: "[O]ur point of departure was that the relations between men and women are social and therefore not immutable and fixed. The form that gender relations take in any historical situation is specific to that situation and has to be constructed inductively; it cannot be read off from other social relations nor from the gender relations of other societies."[59]

This approach signifies not just a change in language but an understanding that it is gender relations that subordinate women and should be the focus of analysis (as opposed to women per se). GAD calls our attention to this centrality of gender relations in all development activities. This means expanding the focus beyond a concern for "women's issues" (family planning, women's health, women's employment, and so on) to broader issues of macroeconomic planning (structural adjustment programs, debt, environmental degradation, and so on).[60] Adopting the GAD perspective, agencies shift their approach from a consideration of women's roles only to the socially constructed roles of both women and men. Projects are no longer limited to women, but to gender issues in general development programs.[61]

GAD recognizes the importance of redistributing power and challenges male social and economic privileges in order to enable women to equally profit from these same resources. Changing institutional rules is seen as key to this challenge. Advocates of GAD produce training packages, guidelines, and "tool kits" for development policy makers. The hope is that this "training approach" will change sexist attitudes.[62]

Development agencies, including the World Bank and the UN Food and Agriculture Organization, adopted GAD approaches and began training their experts in "gender literacy" and accounting for women's concerns at all levels in their organizations. This involves "screening policy documents, employment policies, planning of projects, sex segregated data collection, monitoring and evaluation procedures, and so on. All development agency staff pass through compulsory training in gender analysis and gender planning."[63]

For example, at the Beijing women's conference, the World Bank made the case for gender on efficiency grounds, linking the interests of women with economic liberalization: "Sound economic policies and well functioning markets are essential for growth, employment and the creation of an environment in which the returns to investing in women and girls can be fully realized."[64]

Critics charge that it is fundamentally problematic and counterproductive when women appear to be just added on to existing programs. As with WID, GAD also does not challenge the prevailing development theory of modernization and economic growth. For example, there is not enough attention paid to the sexual division of labor. Thus, when employment and income-generating activities are introduced for women, they are in addition to women's work in the home. When the fullness of women's lives is ignored, the result is often the deepening of female oppression.

A further problem that GAD feminists face is how to define what women have in common (without embracing essentialism) while being clear about differences of culture, ethnicity, and class (without negating commonality). Sex and gender may be socially constructed ideas that contain different meanings in different societies. The challenge to GAD feminists is to construct an analysis of gender that addresses common oppression women face globally while being sensitive to cultural (and other) differences. The problems of essentialism/universalism versus relativism/difference remain.

If "women" is a socially constructed product strongly influenced by male preferences, then what remains of "women's issues" and "women's rights"? At the nongovernmental organization forum at the Beijing Conference in 1995, speakers asserted that this shift from women to gender had become counterproductive "in that it had allowed the discussion to shift from a focus on women, to women and men and, finally, back to men."[65]

Development Alternatives with Women for a New Era

In the mid-1980s, women from the LDCs organized DAWN, a critique of development's impact on poor women. DAWN's focus on race, class, and nation leads to a vision of a world where basic needs become basic rights. Key in this outlook is the empowerment of women through political consciousness-raising and popular education in the workplace, the community, and the home.

The feminism of DAWN has its own independent history and was not imposed by Northern, white, middle-class women. DAWN women from the South believe that all women's work should be accounted for in national accounting systems. They question an economic model based on economic growth and call for "equitable development based on the values of co-operation, resistance to hierarchies, sharing, accountability and commitment to peace." They are aware of the multiple nature of the subordination of women in the South—sex, race, class, and their position in the international economic order. Strategies for women's empowerment can only come about by simultaneously examining all of these domains.[66]

DAWN questions whether women in the South want to be integrated into mainstream development models, thereby challenging the WID approach. WID affirms the primacy of the economic growth model. DAWN sees such an approach as deeply exploitative of women's time, labor (paid and unpaid), and sexuality.

Feminists associated with DAWN took the lead in the 1980s and 1990s in opposing the structural adjustment programs (SAPs) of the IMF from a gender perspective. SAPs negatively impact gender equality by forcing governments to cut social-sector investments, especially in education and health, which hit women the hardest. For example, the Nairobi Women's Conference called for the elimination of illiteracy and an increase in the life expectancy of all women to at least sixty-five years by the year 2000. In a number of countries, the inability to meet this goal can be partially attributed to misguided IMF SAP directives.[67]

Ecofeminism

Ecofeminists draw parallels between male control over nature and over women. Feminist models of sustainable development are put forward as alternatives to the current development models that assault the ecological health of the planet. The global market's destruction of forests and farming systems is contrasted with traditional practices of indigenous peoples.

Vandana Shiva's work in this area has had a tremendous impact in the academy and in civil society. Shiva's 1989 book *Staying Alive* was influential in the development of ecofeminism. In this work, she draws on Hindu religion and philosophy to describe the "feminine principle" (prakriti) as the source of all life. The relationship that rural women in India have with nature is the reality and embodiment of the feminine principle. For the phrase "sustainable development" to have meaning, it must recover this relationship. Colonialism, "development," and the "green revolution" destroyed small-scale agriculture, created unsustainable export oriented agriculture, and marginalized poor women.[68]

Shiva's powerful argument links the violation of nature with the violation of women. Through their role as providers of sustenance, food, and water, women are usually linked to life and nature. Maria Mies calls women's work in producing sustenance the production of life; they make things grow.[69] But women's special relationship with nature is destroyed under capitalist development. "'Productive' man, producing commodities, using some of nature's wealth and women's work as raw material and dispensing with the rest as waste, becomes the only legitimate category of work, wealth and production. Nature and women working to produce and reproduce life are declared 'unproductive.'"[70]

The UN Development Fund for Women (UNIFEM) articulated a new paradigm linking gender and sustainable development, and created a global Women, Environment and Development Program "designed to help women in the developing world establish sustainable relationships with the environment and to promote the integration of women and development concerns into global environmental policy." The program hopes to provide women with:

1. the means to farm more productively,
2. the knowledge and technologies to use and manage resources more efficiently,
3. the financial support necessary for women to act in their own self-interest and in the interest of environmental sustainability, and
4. a larger voice in environmental decision making.[71]

The term "ecofeminism" refers to a range of theoretical positions that draw critical connections between the domination of nature and of women, between feminist and ecological concerns. Two positions found within ecofeminism have been labeled "cultural ecofeminism" and "social ecofeminism." Cultural ecofeminists, located within the essentialist tradition, include contributions by Mary Daly and Susan Griffin. Male culture is seen as aggressive, individualistic, and hierarchical. Women and nature are victims of patriarchal power structures. Women's essential features, such as empathy, caring, and connectedness, are seen as indispensable to the creation of a less violent and more sustainable way of life.[72]

Social ecofeminism is based on the recognition of the social construction of gender. This approach links itself to the socialist-feminist tradition stressing the development of conceptual tools to bring about social and ecological change. Proponents criticize cultural ecofeminists for reversing hierarchies (putting women on top), which, they believe, in the end is self-defeating. Social ecofeminists stress the connections between gender and class—the relationship between gender roles and the organization of production, which structures the interface between women and the environment.[73]

Linking Feminist IPE and Feminist Human Rights Theory

Advocates of these differing perspectives of feminist IPE can find support for their positions within the current international human rights framework.

WID proponents could point to the Women's Rights Treaty's call for states to pledge to embody "the principle of equality of men and women" in their constitutions and other legislation as support for their demand for equality and the equal integration of women into development. The Women's Rights Treaty also calls for legislation against discrimination against women; legal protections of the rights of women on an equal basis with men; measures to eliminate existing discrimination "by any person, organization or enterprise"; and the repeal of all provisions of the penal law that are discriminatory.[74] All of these measures support WID's program of integration.

FEMINIST PERSPECTIVES ON INTERNATIONAL POLITICAL ECONOMY (IPE)

There are many voices speaking through the various feminist perspectives on IPE. Clarifying common elements within each perspective might help us understand their relationship to women's economic and social human rights. At the risk of oversimplification, some common elements can be summarized in the following manner:

- Women in Development (WID) seeks to reform current economic and political structures through the integration of women into development programs and institutions
- Women and Development (WAD) and Development Alternatives with Women for a New Era (DAWN) seek to humble and transform the constraining influence of international economic structures that perpetuate patriarchy and deny women power
- Gender and Development (GAD) and ecofeminism seek positive change for women through an understanding of the human construction of gender roles and the exposure of the male basis to current (mal)development models that undermine environmental sustainability.

The radical structural reform called for by WAD mirrors the demand found in the 1986 General Assembly Declaration on the Right to Development: [T]he right of "every human person and all peoples . . . to participate in, contribute to and enjoy economic, social, cultural and political development, in which all human rights and fundamental freedoms can be fully realized."[75] WAD advocates could also point to article 28 of the Universal Declaration of Human Rights, which states that "[e]veryone is entitled to a social and international order in which the rights and freedoms set forth in this Declaration can be fully realized."[76]

The GAD assault on the socially constructed nature of women's and men's public and private roles in society is supported by the challenge to social and cultural patterns of behavior found in the Women's Rights Treaty article 5, in which states parties agree to take appropriate measures to "modify the social and cultural patterns of conduct of men and women, with a view to achieving the elimination of prejudices and customary and all other practices which are based on the idea of the inferiority or the superiority of either of the sexes or on stereotyped roles for men and women."[77]

DAWN's focus on the multiple nature of the subordination of women (sex, race, and class) and, in particular, on the attention to both poverty and gender subordination is echoed in both the Women's Rights Treaty and the Minority Rights Treaty. The Minority Rights Treaty calls for "special and concrete measures to ensure the adequate development and protection of certain racial groups or individuals belonging to them for the purpose of guaranteeing them the full and equal enjoyment of human rights and fundamental freedoms."[78] The Women's Rights Treaty, as we have seen, calls for "special measures aimed at accelerating *de facto* equality between men and women."[79] DAWN's attention to poverty and basic rights is found in the UN's Right to Development, which requires that national development policies aim for the constant improvement of the well-being of the entire population.[80] The UN's Copenhagen Summit on Social Development also addressed these concerns.

Ecofeminists could point to principle 20 of the "Rio de Janeiro Declaration on Environment and Development": "Women have a vital role in environmental management and development. Their full participation is therefore essential to achieve sustainable development."[81] The ecofeminist focus on sustainability could draw support from the "Stockholm Declaration of the United Nations Conference on the Human Environment"[82] and the UN General Assembly Resolution 37/7 on a World Charter for Nature.[83]

It thus appears that supporters of these different feminist IPE theories can all vindicate their approaches with references to the existing human rights framework and positivist international law. What does it mean that human rights law can validate and support incompatible and conflicting economic policies and programs? What is the utility of women's human rights to policy makers at the local, corporate, state, and international levels if these norms can be used to justify opposing policies? Is this human rights framework at all helpful in the real world to those charged with developing economic policy?

Women and the Capabilities Approach

Feminist approaches to IPE and human rights should not be seen as mutually exclusive and contradictory. Since valuable insights are found in all of them, perhaps a more eclectic policy approach is the most fruitful road toward the achievement of women's economic and social human rights. Issues of structure and power can be incorporated into understandings of the social construction of gender and visa versa. These theories can address the ongoing structural dimensions of injustice with an analysis of the social construction of patriarchy. Structural constraints historically block change and perpetuate mechanisms of exploitation. But understanding the social construction of identities and/or norms that accept these constraints may provide a vehicle to challenge these very structures.

Liberal WID scholars are correct in pointing to the importance of equal treatment. But for equality to be meaningful, issues of class and power must be confronted, as pointed out by proponents of WAD and DAWN. Equal treatment often leads to affirmative action (national and international) and reverse discrimination (national and international) and other programs to support the poor. Liberal schemes of "justice" often fall flat when they refuse to articulate principles of international distributive justice. Gender justice hinges on global attention to basic health care, child care, income support, adequate nutrition, and unemployment insurance. This means challenging the social and economic structures that confine women to the private sphere, as articulated by scholars from WED and ecofeminists. Women's economic and social human rights depend on attention to all of these dimensions.

Caroline O. N. Moser points to such a multidimensional approach to gender justice in her call for policy makers to incorporate "gender planning" into development schemes. Gender planning takes into account the fact that women and men play different societal roles in the formulation of practical and strategic economic policy. Economic planning must disaggregate households and families within communities on the basis of gender. She points to the "triple role of women" in low-income households in LDCs: reproductive work (the childbearing and rearing responsibilities), productive work (often as secondary earners), and community managing work (the struggle to manage their neighborhoods). If developers are blind to this triple role of poor women, policies will fail to meet women's specific requirements. Moser therefore calls for a more integrative approach in which planning accounts for both income and gender difference. Policy makers will need to identify both strategic and practical gender needs.[84]

Maxine Molyneux identifies strategic gender needs as some of the following:

- the abolition of the sexual division of labour;
- the alleviation of the burden of domestic labour and childcare;
- the removal of institutionalized forms of discrimination such as rights to own land or property, or access to credit;
- the establishment of political equality;
- freedom of choice over childbearing; and
- the adoption of adequate measures against male violence and control over women.[85]

Moser defines "practical gender needs" as those needs "which are formulated from the concrete conditions women experience, in their engendered position within the sexual division of labour. . . . Therefore in planning terms, policies for meeting practical gender needs have to focus on the domestic arena, on income earning activities and also on community-level requirements of housing and basic services."[86] These proposals link rights claims with economic policy options to overcome structural obstacles.

There are obviously great disparities in knowledge and vulnerability between the rich and the poor. A poor woman may not have the option to refuse the economic arrangements presented to her. The weak suffer from those who take advantage of their vulnerable position and ignorance, and nothing shields them from the consequences of international economic forces. These international economic forces are not regulated, yet they can have a devastating impact on the lives of poor women. Poor women cannot alter or change economic structures that hurt them. Low wages, dependence on those who provide credit, patriarchal patterns, and customs of male entitlement within the family all exacerbate the vulnerability of poor women.

Feminist IPE theories attempt to bring into sharp relief the importance of economic power on women's lives. Liberal human rights theories often ignore these powerful forces with proclamations of equality that have no basis in real women's lives. The integration of these perspectives is essential to formulate effective policy for women. Institutional power, international economic structures, and family entitlement customs can be changed and modified to address issues of women's human rights. Only with an incorporation of these issues of power and wealth into the human rights framework can poor women's claims be understood.

A promising incorporation of these issues is found in Sen's capabilities approach (described in chapter 2). What are the actual capacities and opportunities for women to act? This approach acknowledges that people have varying needs for resources: a pregnant woman needs more calories than a nonpregnant woman, a breast cancer patient has unique medical needs, and an unemployed mother in all cultures needs more resources to become productively employed than those not in this situation. The issue is the amount of resources necessary for this person to achieve adequate functioning. As Martha C. Nussbaum writes: "This approach to quality-of-life measurement and the goals of public policy holds that we should focus on the questions: What are the people of the group or country in question actually able to do and to be? Unlike a focus on opulence (say GNP per capita), this approach asks about the distribution of resources and opportunities. In principle, it asks how each and every individual is doing with respect to all the functions deemed important."[87]

Sen's research shows that gender inequality cannot be understood solely in terms of income differences, but should be analyzed in relation to "the extent of relative deprivation of women to the existing inequalities of opportunities (in earning outside income, in being enrolled in schools and so on). Thus, both descriptive and policy issues can be addressed through this broader perspective on inequality and poverty in terms of capability deprivation."[88]

Nussbaum develops the capabilities approach as a vehicle for overcoming the oppression and exploitation of women. She argues that "international political and economic thought should be feminist, attentive [among other things] to the special problems women face because of sex . . . problems without an understanding of which general issues of poverty and development cannot be well confronted." The denial of basic human needs and basic rights is "frequently caused by their being women."[89]

Nussbaum develops a list of "Central Human Functional Capabilities" that marks the most significant difference between her approach and Sen's: Sen never made such a list. This list of capabilities includes ten broad areas: life; bodily health; bodily integrity; senses, imagination, and thought; emotions; practical reason; affiliation; other species; play; and control over one's political and material environment. Nussbaum's goal is to determine a "decent social minimum" in these areas, contending that "the structure of social and political institutions should be chosen, at least in part, with a view to promoting at least a threshold level of these human capabilities." She argues for protecting a minimum threshold in each of the ten areas of central human functional capabilities as well as for according each of them equal value. The minimum threshold is central to her argument as it trumps culture, family, and religion.[90]

With her Central Human Functional Capabilities list, Nussbaum elaborates a universal set of liberal values to judge and scrutinize all cultures. For example, feminism in India runs up against long-standing cultural practices and religious beliefs. Those who "challenge entrenched satisfactions are frequently charged with being totalitarian and antidemocratic for just this way of proceeding. Who are they to tell real women what is good for them, or to march into an area shaped by tradition and custom with universal standards of what one should demand and what one should desire?" Yet, preferences can be manipulated by tradition and intimidation and "clash with universal norms even at the level of basic nutrition and health." In one desert area in India, women had no feelings of anger or protest about their own severe malnourishment or the lack of a reliable clean water supply: "They knew no other way. They did not consider their conditions unhealthful or unsanitary, and they did not consider themselves to be malnourished." How does a feminist get outside of this box?[91]

A consciousness-raising program changed the situation by challenging entrenched preferences. These same women now fight for clean water, electricity, and a health visitor, all of which enhances their basic capabilities. The power of this story lies in the interface between universal norms and local culture. Despite poverty and suffering, these women seemed to prefer their traditional way of life. Yet, Nussbaum argues, this local preference should not be respected until these women have been given other options. The capabilities approach demands that a woman have a real opportunity to surmount economic deprivations and low expectations. Nussbaum believes that, given the choice, women's preferences in India will shift to universal goods, rather than those preferences that were mere reflections of women's restricted situations. It is the failure of a person to have various basic human capabilities that is important in itself, and not just because the person minds it or complains about it.

Nussbaum's Central Human Functional Capabilities list reinforces existing women's human rights claims. The corpus of international human rights law clarifies the economic, social, cultural, political, and civil rights claims to which all individuals are entitled. It has taken decades of struggle for the international women's movement to achieve clarity and unity around these basic human rights for women. Nussbaum's interpretation of the capabilities approach should be linked directly to these efforts in international law. The capabilities approach is not an alternative to the well-established framework of human rights.[92] Rather, the capabilities approach provides a means to articulate and measure public policy to achieve women's human rights. The capabilities approach gives us the tools to analyze what is preventing women from realizing basic rights to security, subsistence, and freedom, or, to use Sen's phrase, the "freedom to achieve adequate functioning." The capabilities approach helps direct public policy (in education, health care, and so on) to create an environment for women to realize their basic human rights.

The Global New Deal and Gender

Summary Observations

Policies to support economic equality (as defined in chapter 2) are central to the realization of the rights of women enunciated in Women's Rights Treaty. There is not one feminist theory of IPE (WID, DAWN, and so on) that in itself is adequate in addressing policies for economic equality. Rather, aspects of each theory can be woven together to create policy to respect, protect, and fulfill women's economic and social human rights.

Global New Deal Proposals

Central to the Global New Deal is the realization of the economic and social human rights of women through the implementation of the capabilities approach. The Global New Deal in chapter 8 calls for national and international public policy to focus on the education and health of women. The Women's Rights Committee should concentrate on helping states craft policy to meet the education and health care needs of women. The enhancement

Human rights law has historically been "defined by the criterion of what men fear will happen to them."[93] In the 1980s and 1990s, the women's movement articulated a new conception of human rights that began to take into account what women fear will happen to them. Included in these demands were the ways in which women are denied basic economic and social human rights as a result of both socially constructed gender roles and structural economic forces. Women pushed the human rights framework beyond the public sphere and into the private sphere, which meant holding state and nonstate actors accountable to these norms. Merging this analysis with an eclectic approach to feminist IPE theories can help formulate public policy in the real world to help women realize their rights.

of women's capabilities in these two areas is key to economic and social rights protection overall. By addressing human capabilities, we expand the real freedoms that women enjoy and create an environment in which women's human rights can be realized.

Through a focus on the health care and education of women, two of the priority areas from the Beijing Platform of Action, the Women's Rights Committee can help states formulate national policy to respect, protect, and fulfill economic and social human rights. The Women's Rights Committee could focus like a laser on these issues of women's education and health. Governments would be put on notice: when they come before the Women's Rights Committee they will be particularly questioned on policies to achieve equity in women's education and women's health.

7

Military Spending and Economic and Social Human Rights

What is the economic impact of high levels of military spending on economic well-being? Do such expenditures create real security? Why do the citizens in the most militarized societies feel the least secure? How does a society provide a "basic right to physical security" without compromising other basic human rights? Are there trade-offs between rights to physical security and rights to subsistence? Do recent proposals from the UN point to a means of achieving a better balance between conflicting sets of human rights claims? How are these concerns incorporated into a coherent foreign policy agenda?

The global community has exerted an extraordinary amount of energy articulating human rights norms and codifying human rights principles into international law. International lawyers now consider the Universal Declaration of Human Rights to have the status of customary international law, establishing a common standard to judge states' actions. Earlier chapters have reviewed the impact of other key legal human rights documents including the Economic Rights Treaty, Minority Rights Treaty, and Women's Rights Treaty. This is true progress: a yardstick has been developed to measure the degree to which nations uphold or violate the most basic human dignities. Yet, despite global progress in defining normative goals and rights, there has not been similar success in pushing states to implement a human rights agenda. This has led to cynicism about the UN and other intergovernmental organizations. Human rights proclamations and declarations are not followed by significant action to alleviate suffering. As a result, human rights treaties and resolutions are often greeted with scorn and derision, as though, to recall Jean-Paul Sartre, principles like liberty, equality, and fraternity are little more than "chatter, chatter."[1]

Part of the problem lies in the fact that there are often direct conflicts between different claimed rights. Western political systems often prioritize civil and political liberties claiming that these rights "trump" other claims. Freedom and liberty are frequently manipulated by governing elites and ruling majorities to deny other collective human rights, including subsistence rights. Few actions are taken to meet the entire spectrum of rights articulated in the International Bill of Human Rights.[2] To make human rights the cornerstone of domestic and foreign policy means determining the often difficult trade-offs between rights that must be made in order to build a just society. There are conflicts between rights, and resolution of such conflicts might require the accommodation of different values. The metaphor of rights as trumps that override all competing considerations is only partially useful. Real life is more complex. The UN, for example, has affirmed both a people's right to self-determination and a people's right to development. In the name of self-defense and liberty, an astounding quantity of military weapons have been purchased around the world. Yet, these military expenditures consistently impede economic development. These nations appear to be denying their people basic economic rights in the name of military preparedness to protect the right to self-determination and freedom.

This chapter explores these issues in the following sections:

- The economic impact of military spending
- Rethinking security
- The enduring tension between military spending and human rights
- Inhibiting militarism

The Economic Impact of Military Spending

Boutros Boutros-Ghali, the former UN secretary general, asserts that "development cannot proceed easily in societies where military concerns are at or near the center of life. Societies whose economic effort is given in substantial part to military production inevitably diminish the prospects of their people for development. . . . Preparation for war absorbs inordinate resources and impedes the development of social institutions."[3] Jack Matlock, a former U.S. ambassador to Moscow, makes a similar point in relation to the required weapons spending for new members joining NATO: "It's extraordinarily unwise for these countries to shoulder these costs when they must pay the costs of meeting their social needs."[4]

Webster's New World Dictionary defines "militarism" as a "policy of maintaining a strong military organization in aggressive preparedness for war."[5] Militarism thus includes the disposition to maintain national power by means of strong military forces projecting menacing arms potency capable of deterring or compelling enemy nations. The secretary general and the ambassador argue that militarism represents a structural choice that accords military priorities and arms spending a higher priority than meeting basic human needs. Are these distinguished diplomats right? Are there dire economic consequences to high levels of military spending? And if so, what are the human rights implications of militarization?

The negative effects of militarism on society overall are often dramatically shown through analysis of the policies of repressive governments in the less developed world—from Myanmar to Iraq to Syria. These dictatorial regimes clearly choose militarism over human rights. But the detrimental impact of military spending goes far beyond these imperious regimes. There is a global trade-off between militarism and economic growth that affects the protection of rights in all countries. High levels of military spending in developed and less developed countries prevents all governments from fulfilling the basic economic and social rights articulated in the International Bill of Human Rights.

Military Spending in the United States

A useful beginning may be made by examining the effect of military spending on the United States, given its pivotal role in the U.S. economy. If significant military expenditures have a positive impact on the U.S. economy, it will be difficult to argue that less developed countries (LDCs) should not pursue such policies. This analysis is particularly important given the publicity in the global media about the "growth" and "success" of the U.S. economy at the end of the twentieth century and the current concerns about a potential recession. What is the relationship between military expenditure and the state of the U.S. economy? Does such spending accelerate or impede the government's ability to respect, protect, and fulfill economic and social human rights?

The heinous and horrifying terrorism of 11 September 2001 in New York City, Washington, D.C., and Pennsylvania shocked the world and altered the security framework. Terrorist threats from individuals and transnational organizations are now elevated above the traditional security issues, such as nuclear arms control and missile defense. President George W. Bush pledged in his 2002 State of the Union address to spend "whatever it costs to defend our country."[6] While the United States—and even the whole world—experienced seemingly unendurable grief for the thousands of innocents murdered by fanatical terrorists, such calls for increased defense spending got cheers from both Democrats and Republicans. The United States clearly must act to prevent further terrorism and another 11 September. Unfortunately, given its history of waste and its bloated bureaucracy, spending billions more at the Pentagon is probably not an efficient way to fight terrorism. Furthermore, as will be demonstrated, such a squandering of our precious national wealth results in a lack of resources for economic reforms and social programs. As a result, neither the physical nor the economic security of the American people is protected through such an indefensible military budget.

The United States consumes a significant amount of its overall national wealth on weapons systems and standing armies. The 2001 defense budget was around $311 billion for the year. The 2002 budget submitted by President Bush and Defense Secretary Donald Rumsfeld added a further $18 billion, increasing the Pentagon budget to a stunning $329 billion. For 2003, Pentagon spending under the Bush plan will surpass $379 billion. The Bush budget also calls for spending $16.8 billion on Department of Energy programs, which include maintaining the nuclear stockpile, bringing total military spending in 2003 to $396 billion. Few hard choices have been made in the 2003 budget, which instead calls for an additional $48 billion, the largest increase in military spending in twenty years. Overall, the Bush administration calls for increasing the Pentagon's yearly budget by approximately $120 billion over the next five years to over $451 billion in 2007.[7]

During the 1990s, the Clinton Pentagon spent on average at least $720 million a day, about $30 million an hour.[8] The United States spends more on defense than all of its NATO allies combined and five to six times more than its rivals. Both the Russian military budget of $40 to $64 billion and the Chinese of $37 billion pale in comparison to the $329 billion spent in 2002 by the United States. There is no historical parallel: Historians note that no nation in history has ever outspent its rivals to this degree.[9] Over 42 percent of the entire world's military expenditures are made by the United States. The federal government spends four times as much on the military as on education, job training, housing, economic development, and environmental protection combined. Nearly half of every federal tax dollar pays for current and past military expenses.[10]

The U.S. government has relied on the military budget above all to stimulate the economy. The Keynesian "logic" that military spending can prevent a recession or depression has not been challenged by any administration since World War II. The economic prosperity of the United States during that war left a deep impression. In the 1930s, the country experienced the Great Depression, with unemployment rates hovering around 25 percent. In 1944, the unemployment rate dropped to 1.2 percent. The public's willingness to finance a large military establishment is linked to the perception that these expenditures perform a positive overall economic function in the national economy.

With defense spending consuming such a huge percentage of the federal budget, scholars in the 1980s and 1990s documented the effect of such expenditures on the federal budget deficit.[11] During the Reagan years, the United States spent $2 trillion on defense while cutting taxes. The resulting budget deficit, combined with high interest rates and large trade deficits, sent the economy spinning. Furthermore, while the United States in the 1980s devoted around 5 to 6.5 percent of its gross national product (GNP) to defense, its major economic competitors, Japan and Germany, allocated a smaller proportion (approximately 1 and 3 percent, respectively).[12] As a result, the United States consistently had less capital to invest in civilian industries. Scholars attribute the relative decline of the U.S. global economic position vis-à-vis Japan and Germany from the 1970s to the 1990s to this draining of scarce capital from civilian industries. It has been estimated that for every 1 percent of GNP devoted to military spending, overall economic growth is reduced by about 0.5 percent. Ron Smith, for example, uses regression analysis to calculate the ratio of investment to GNP against the GNP growth rate, unemployment, and military expenditure as a percentage of GNP. He discovers a powerful correlation between increases in defense spending and decreases in investment spending, supporting the argument of a trade-off between defense and economic growth.[13]

Fortuitously for the United States, events in Germany and Japan at the close of the twentieth century undercut the competitiveness of these economic adversaries. German reunification—in particular the fixation of too high a par value for the East German currency in terms of the West German one—proved extremely costly. Scholars estimated a seemingly perpetual transfer of about 5 percent of gross domestic product (GDP) to pay for reunification, which had the impact of reducing German competitiveness. Japan was criticized for irresponsible macroeconomic policy and suffered from an inability to reinvest its surpluses productively. As a result, the U.S. economic model was seen by pundits and laissez-faire economists as dramatically superior to welfare state economic models.[14]

Yet, the actual performance of the European and Japanese economies over the last thirty to forty years is still much stronger than that of the U.S. economy. According to economist William K. Tabb: "Over the shorter period since the second half of the 1990s, real GNP growth slowed but still increased as much over the decade in the European Union and Japan as in the United States. Taking the longer view, capital stock increased more, as did the productivity of capital employed per worker, and real wages grew faster in these economies than in the United States." Furthermore, the unemployed in Japan and western Europe received much better benefits than their counterparts in the United States. In fact, most workers in the United States saw their standard of living decline in the 1980s and 1990s, despite economic "growth."[15]

Due to the overall growth of the U.S. economy, by the mid-1990s there was a decline in the proportion of GDP that the United States devoted to defense. Defense spending increased in the 1990s, but the U.S. GDP increased even more. By 2001, the United States devoted about 3.3 percent of its GDP to defense, the smallest share since 1940. The Clinton and Bush administrations made this fact central to their arguments for increasing the Pentagon's budget. Both the White House and Congress contend that this decline in the ratio of military spending to GDP justifies huge increases in the military budget. As Michael O'Hanlon, a senior fellow at the Brookings Institution, writes: "Besides, American defense spending—at 3 percent of our gross domestic product—is not unreasonably high. As a percentage of GDP, it was twice as high in the Reagan years and three times as high during the 1950s and 1960s."[16]

The logic of this argument is most peculiar. Its singular focus on this sole yardstick—U.S. defense spending as a percent of the U.S. GDP—misleads and misdirects policy makers and the public. First, it ignores current comparisons between the United States and its military competitors. Some competitors spend a greater percentage of their national wealth on defense than does the United States, but the absolute level of spending is much lower than that of the United States (as the budget figures on China and Russia quoted earlier demonstrate). Second, this argument dismisses current comparisons between the United States and its economic competitors. The United States spends a considerably higher percentage (3.3) of its GDP on defense than any of its key economic rivals. The United Kingdom, for example, spends 2.7 percent, China 2.2 percent, Brazil 1.8 percent, Germany 1.6 percent, Canada 1.3 percent, Japan 1.0 percent, and so on.[17] The United States spends much more than the world average. To stay economically competitive, the United States must pay attention to infrastructure, debt reduction, health care reform, and technology research. Military investments compete for scarce resources with these and other key economic areas. Many scholars and diplomats believe that the critical strategic competition in the world today is in the economic realm and not the military arena. If so, the United States should be pursuing a strategy of reducing its defense GDP share as far as military security obligations will allow. From a political realist position, this also makes sense, since the long-term military strength of the United States depends on a healthy economy.[18]

The absurdity of this GDP ratio argument for increasing military spending becomes obvious in an examination of the actual numbers. In 1987, at the height of the Cold War, defense spending was $287.4 billion or 6.2 percent of the GDP, which was $4.605 trillion. In 2000, the GDP equaled approximately $9.106 trillion; thus, 6.2 percent of the 2000 GDP would thus equal $573 billion, almost double the 2001 defense budget![19]

Since 1985, the United States' share of world military spending has increased 20 percent. In 1985, the United States spent only 65 percent as much on defense as did potential enemy "threat" states (Iran, Iraq, Syria, Libya, North Korea, and so on). In 2001, it spent twice as much as this group. U.S. standing relative to threat states has thus improved by a factor of more than three—from 65 percent of their total in 1989 to more than 200 percent in 2001.[20]

There are two key points here: the enormity of the military budget and the economic difference between expenditure and investment.[21] Mainstream economic thought has long viewed military expenditures as an impediment to economic progress because they are merely outlays for goods and services and not investments. Adam Smith in *The Wealth of Nations* probably said it best: "The whole army and navy, are unproductive labourers. They are the servants of the public, and are maintained by a part of the annual produce of the industry of other people. Their service, how honourable, how useful, or how necessary soever, produces nothing for which an equal quantity of service can afterwards be procured."[22] Military expenditures are designed to meet an immediate goal. Investments, on the other hand, are designed to increase future resources. Military research and development has created well-publicized inventions and technological innovations of benefit to the civilian economy. But overall, massive military spending has drained the national wealth.

The diversion of significant amounts of national resources toward nonproductive military expenditures results in the long-term decline in productive capacity and efficiency. This has occurred in the United States. Since the mid-1970s, the U.S. government has documented the decline in the U.S. standard of living. Despite current "growth" indicators in the national economy, it has in fact become harder to climb out of poverty in the United States in the last two decades. The U.S. economy has become less and less hospitable to the young, the unskilled, and the less educated. This lack of equal opportunity limits the viability of liberal rights.[23] The Census Bureau, for example, reported that the percentage of full-time workers with low earnings grew sharply in the 1980s, despite the economic expansion that brought increased prosperity to the affluent. The bureau defined low earnings as $12,195 a year, expressed in 1990 dollars and adjusted for inflation. At the end of the 1970s, 12.1 percent of all full-time employees earned below the equivalent of $12,195. By 1990, that figure had risen to 18 percent.[24] The number of American children living in poverty grew by more than 1 million during the 1980s, and in 1989 about 18 percent of children in the United States lived in families with incomes below the federal poverty line, including 39.8 percent of all black children, 38.8 percent of American Indian children, 32.2 percent of Hispanic children, 17.1 percent of Asian-American children, and 12.5 percent of white children.[25]

These trends are continuing. The Census Bureau reported in 1994 that the typical American household saw its income decline in 1993, and more than a million Americans fell into poverty that year. In 1994, Labor Secretary Robert Reich declared, "America is in danger of splitting into a two-tiered society. This is not anyone's idea of progress."[26] Inflation-adjusted wage rates for the median worker fell in the 1980s and continued to decline sharply in the 1990s. From 1989 to 1997, real wages for the majority of workers in the middle—the vast American middle class—continued to erode, with the median worker's wage falling 5 percent since 1989.[27]

As the United States entered the twenty-first century, the social health of the nation was deteriorating. Sterile economic figures should not hide the human tragedy represented by these economic conditions. Indicators of worsening performance include rising rates of child poverty and child abuse, alarming numbers of teenagers committing suicide, escalating numbers of citizens without health care insurance coverage, declining average weekly wages, and soaring inequality. For example, child poverty continued to worsen in the United States in the 1990s. Among children under eighteen, poverty increased from 14.9 percent in 1970 to 19.8 percent in 1996, a 33 percent increase.[28] The performance of the United States in preventing child abuse and youth suicide has been worsening over the last twenty years. In 1976, official reported cases of child abuse reached a rate of 10.1 for every 1,000 children. By 1996, an estimated 3.1 million children were reported to have been abused—a rate of 47 cases for every 1,000 children, a 300 percent increase from 1976.[29] In 1996, the suicide rate among youth aged fifteen to twenty-four was 12.0 deaths per 100,000, up from 8.8 in 1970.[30] The proportion of the U.S. population lacking health insurance increased over the same time: 15.6 percent, a total of 41.7 million Americans, had no health insurance in 1996, up from 10.9 percent in 1976.[31] Average weekly earnings fell sharply: in constant dollars, earnings went from $315 in 1973 to $256 in 1996, a decline of 19 percent.[32] The proportion of the nation's income received by the poorest fifth of American families declined dramatically, while the proportion held by the richest increased. The respected Gini Index calculates that this form of inequality has worsened by 20 percent since 1970.[33] In September 2000, the U.S. Agriculture Department revealed the depths of hunger in America: 31 million Americans were hungry and face food insecurity.[34]

A key factor in the absolute decline in the living standards of most Americans since the 1970s is the amount of capital spent for nonproductive military purposes. U.S. military spending contributed to a decline in competitiveness. For much of the Cold War, manufacturing productivity growth in most European nations averaged twice the U.S. rate, and in Japan was often three times that of the United States. The Europeans and the Japanese could drop the prices of their goods more quickly than U.S. firms. Investment was a key factor in productivity growth. U.S. arms production diverted engineers and scientists from civilian projects. Some of the brightest, most highly skilled people no longer worked directly to increase the productivity and competitiveness of the nation's manufacturing sector.[35]

Academic studies from the 1980s through the 1990s confirm the negative relationships between militarism and economic growth. Steve Chan, for example, concludes that the evidence is clear for advanced Western economies: military spending does not encourage or facilitate sustained economic growth. In the long run, "these expenditures are more apt to have a negative than a positive impact on investment, inflation, employment, balance of payments, industrial productivity, and economic growth. The evidence on the United States . . . indicates especially significant costs in these regards." Heavy defense spending "seems to have a particularly important impact in dampening capital formation and investment, which in turn reduces economic growth in the long run." Chan also notes the "customary preference of officials to finance defense and war by running budget deficits rather than by cutting other programs or raising taxes, [with] much of the cost of this spending shifted to future generations."[36] These conclusions were confirmed in a 1995 study by Alex Mintz and Randolph T. Stevenson that was grounded solidly in neoclassical economic theory. Using longitudinal data from 103 countries, they demonstrated that increases in nonmilitary spending contribute to growth significantly more than increases in military expenditures. Military expenditures had either a negative effect or no effect on growth in about 90 percent of the cases. Mintz and Stevenson demonstrated that a shift away from military spending significantly contributes to economic growth in the long run.[37]

The central purpose of economic activity is to create material well-being. A healthy economy produces and distributes consumer goods and services to satisfy material needs (e.g., refrigerators) and producer goods (e.g., machinery and transport equipment). Goods or services that do not contribute to material well-being are opportunities lost and therefore represent economic costs. The production of military goods and services is a noncontributing activity. An economy that is persistently dominated by military production will divert critical economic resources to noncontributive activities and experience a long-term decline in productivity. Investment to improve efficiency in the civilian sector will have been stifled.[38] This tendency for defense activities to divert resources away from public and private investments more able to promote growth leads Todd Sandler and Keith Hartley to conclude that the net impact of defense spending on growth is negative.[39] When defense activities take scarce resources, including research and development funds, from private investment, long-term growth is impeded.

Many argue that high levels of military spending create jobs. However, according to Robert W. DeGrasse Jr., "most industries selling to the Pentagon create fewer jobs per dollar spent than the average industry in the

American economy."[40] DeGrasse documents how seven of eleven manu-facturing industries selling the greatest volume of goods to the military—including the three largest, which together account for over 40 percent of the Pentagon's purchases from the private sector—create fewer jobs per dollar than the median manufacturing industry. Three simulations demonstrate that transferring military expenditures to either civilian gov-ernment spending or tax cuts creates higher employment. For example, shifting $62.9 billion from military purchases to personal consumption expenditures created some 1.5 million jobs.[41] Moreover, the Congressional Budget Office of the U.S. Congress, using two different models of the U.S. economy, concluded in 1992 that the use of the peace dividend to reduce the federal deficit would benefit the economy in the long run.[42] There is also an indirect negative effect of military spending. Mintz and Chi Huang, for example, analyze the indirect impact of arms expenditures on education spending. Their empirical study indicates no negative short-term effects but demonstrates a significant indirect long-term trade-off between spending on defense and on education. The negative effect on education was felt to be attributable to the impact of military policies on investment and growth. Over a "longer time period, military spending crowds out investment, which reduces growth, thereby affecting the amount the government spends on education programs."[43]

And then there is the extensively documented and widely reported issue of Pentagon waste. Pentagon graft, fraud, incompetence, and waste is a disgrace and harmful to the security of the United States. The Penta-gon's own inspector general reported in March 2000 that only $2.6 trillion of a total of $6.9 trillion in accounting entries could be fully documented. Furthermore, $2.3 trillion worth of entries were "not supported by ade-quate audit trails or sufficient evidence to determine their validity."[44] The U.S. General Accounting Office (GAO) found that the Defense Depart-ment cannot "account for billions of dollars of inventory and national defense assets, primarily weapons systems and support equipment." In addition, the GAO determined that the Pentagon already had $37 billion worth of paraphernalia it does not need.[45] Experts estimate that an astounding 70 percent of the defense budget is spent on overhead and infrastructure, with only 30 percent reaching the combat forces in the field. No city in America would allow 7 out of 10 police officers to sit at their desks pushing paper. While the private sector can replace parts in two days, it takes the Pentagon up to three weeks. The list of waste and inefficiency goes on and on.[46]

This outrageous squandering of the country's wealth is reminiscent of the extravagant and unrestrained practices of the top-down bureaucracies of the former Soviet Union. Such unchecked, unaccountable, and waste-ful actions finally exhausted the Soviet economy. On a daily basis, Penta-gon waste pulls down and dampens the U.S. economy.

In summary, there are at least three different ways that military spending restricts economic growth in the United States: first, it leads to a decrease in investment and thus retards the expansion of civilian industry; second, it leads to lower employment and an inefficient use of labor resources; and third, it takes resources away from civilian research and development, impeding nonmilitary innovation and growth and siphoning off highly qualified engineers and labor from the civilian sector. The result is a diversion of resources away from the human rights of education, health care, and subsistence. The implementation of basic economic and social rights depends on a shift in scarce resources away from militarism and toward these areas of human need.

Military Spending in the Developing World

Militarization, of course, is a global phenomenon. Expensive and sophisticated weapons are sought and purchased everywhere in the name of security and self-determination. World military spending of $815 billion in 1992 equaled the income of nearly half the world's people. Military expenditures in developing countries rose three times as fast as those of the industrial countries between 1960 and 1987; from $24 billion to $145 billion, an increase of 7.5 percent a year, compared with 2.8 percent for the industrial countries. In 1990–1991, the ratio of military to social spending (calculated as military expenditures as a percentage of the combined education and health expenditures) was an astounding 373 percent in Syria, 222 percent in Myanmar, and 190 percent in Ethiopia. Some of the poorest countries are among those that spend more on their military than on education and health: Angola, Mozambique, Pakistan, Somalia, and Yemen, as well as Ethiopia and Myanmar.[47]

According to the World Bank, military spending continues to drain the economies of the poorest countries in the twenty-first century. Currently, sixteen developing countries spend between 5 and 20.5 percent of their GDP on defense. While military spending remains high in these poor countries, investments in areas of human security—economic and social human rights—remain low. Examine, for example, the following 1997 expenditures (the latest figures available): Pakistan spent 5.7 percent of its GDP on its military and only 2.7 percent on education; the Syrian Arab Republic spent 5.6 percent of its GDP on its military and only 3.1 percent on education; and Myanmar spent 7.6 percent of its GDP on its military and only 1.2 percent on education.[48]

Did these expenditures provide security? Unfortunately not. In developing countries, the chances of dying from social neglect (from malnutrition and preventable diseases) are thirty-three times greater than the chances of dying in a war from external aggression.[49] Yet, U.S. arms and military aid continue to flow to countries that face no significant external enemy. As a consequence, the function of the military in these countries often becomes internal repression (as was heinously demonstrated in Guatemala throughout the 1980s).

The human cost of military spending in developing countries is enormous. The statistics are numbing. Twelve percent of military spending in developing countries could provide funds for primary health care for all, including immunization of all children, elimination of severe malnutrition, and reduction of moderate malnutrition by half, and provision of safe drinking water for all. Four percent could reduce adult illiteracy by half by providing universal primary education and educating women to the same level as men. Eight percent could provide basic family planning to all and stabilize the world population by 2015.[50]

Military spending and war preparation in poor countries has led to insecurity and actual conflict. Since World War II, the wars of the world have occurred overwhelmingly in the poor countries, and the devastation of war has been felt by the world's poorest people. The World Bank reports that during 1987–1997 more than 85 percent of all world conflicts were fought within national borders—fourteen were in Africa, fourteen in Asia, and one in Europe. Ninety percent of the war deaths were civilians. For example, 1.7 million people died in Cambodia during twenty years of fighting and political violence. In Rwanda, approximately 800,000 Tutsis and moderate Hutus were killed by Hutu extremists in 1994. These wars cripple national economies; public spending is diverted from productive activities and investments often cease. Skilled workers emigrate abroad. Economists estimate that in a civil war a country's per capita output falls an average of more than 2 percent a year relative to what it would have been without the conflict. The human costs are even greater, especially on the children.[51]

The impact of militarism on the poorest countries thus has the most profound of consequences. As with the United States, militarism in the poor countries diverts scarce resources away from productive investment, lowers employment, and takes resources away from civilian research and development. This results in a diversion of resources away from sanitation, education, health care, and so on. But the repercussions of militarism in these poorest countries goes much further. The violence and bloodshed spawned by militarist policies ravage and overwhelm. In a society of militarism and violence, human rights become inane and preposterous.

Costa Rica provides an alternative approach. Costa Rica's success in human development stems from its refusal to accept and embrace militarism. Despite its lower-middle-income status, Costa Rica has been able to attain social indicators close to that of an industrialized country. Table 7.1 compares Costa Rica to Latin America and the Caribbean in key dimensions of social development.[52]

Costa Rica's success is directly linked to its spending priorities. Public

Table 7.1. Costa Rica and Human Development

	Costa Rica (percent of total pop.)	Latin America (percent of total pop.)
People Not Expected to Survive to Age Forty (1998)	3.9	9.7
Adult Illiteracy Rate (1998)	4.7	12.3
Population without Access to Safe Water (1990–1998)	4	22
Population without Access to Sanitation (1990–1998)	16	29
Underweight Children under Age Five (1990–1998)	2	10

spending for social programs, including health, education, water and sewerage, and so on, averaged from 20 to almost 24 percent of its GDP throughout the 1980s and 1990s.[53] Costa Rica has the resources to address the economic and social needs of its people because it refuses to militarize its society. While spending over 20 percent on social programs, Costa Rica spends only 0.6 percent of its GDP on its military![54]

Rethinking "Security"

The attitudes that sustain large and deadly military machines did not fall with the Berlin Wall. The logic is mesmerizing: The world is a dangerous place divided into sovereign nation-states, each seeking to improve its position in an anarchic international system. There are few opportunities for cooperation. Each state maintains the right to be free from the scrutiny and intervention of other states in its internal affairs. Each nation is surrounded by danger and must protect itself to survive, which gives rise to a preoccupation with power, particularly military power. Internalizing this acute sense of danger makes it easier to accept high taxation to pay for militarization at the expense of social development. Yet, such militarization in the name of security and peace often backfires and creates conditions of insecurity and conflict. Furthermore, such expenditures consistently undermine the ability of nations to fulfill other international human rights, in particular economic and social rights. "Security" defined solely as the heavily armed defense of one's borders can subvert the secure lives of the people living within those borders. How does a nation provide a basic right to physical security without compromising other human rights? What types of military and other expenses should be budgeted to attain physical security?

Feminist peace researchers and other scholars in peace studies distinguish between negative peace and positive peace. Negative peace and negative security stem from a desire to inhibit the existence of a destructive entity. Deterrence and the conventional "realist" power-politics paradigm are examples of negative peace. Here, security is the result of canceling one threat by another: threats and counterthreats cancel out the actual use of force and create "negative" peace. The goal is to be able to threaten someone else, as in a householder's purchase of a gun for protection from crime. A secure state is therefore one that is able to counter any military threat it may face. Negative peace refers to the absence of war and other direct violence.[55]

Positive peace and positive security, on the other hand, reflect the desire to eliminate the threat by addressing its cause. The objective is not to counter the threat but to end all threats by addressing the source of the problem. The goal is to cure the disease rather than to simply address its symptoms. Central to positive peace is not just the absence of war and violence, but also the protection of human rights and social justice. The elimination of underdevelopment and institutionalized poverty are considered signs of peace.[56] Positive security, for example, would embrace serious arms control negotiations and agreements. The proliferation of all types of arms (conventional, biological, and nuclear) makes conflict more volatile and escalation more likely. When the U.S., French, British, and German governments subsidize arms exporters and fail to take the lead in disarmament measures, they exacerbate the threat and undercut their own security.

In the pursuit of positive security, scholars have argued that territorial security is less important than peoples' security; they urge a reconceptualization from security through armaments to security through sustainable human development. The 1994 *Human Development Report,* for example, outlines seven main categories of threats to human security: economic, food, health, environmental, personal, community, and political. The critical threats are poverty and malnutrition, inadequate education, environmental degradation, population pressures, and inadequate health care.[57] Proponents of positive peace describe conditions of insecurity in pollution, war, sickness, oppression, and poverty. Transformation toward positive peace must involve the participation and support of the world's peoples; it cannot be attained by a few leaders alone. Peace is not merely the resolution of isolated conflicts, a return to a prewar condition. Rather, peace involves attention to conditions of cultural destruction, malnutrition, disease, poverty, and discrimination based on race, gender, and sexual orientation. Peace studies thus include economic well-being, self-determination, human rights, and ecological issues.

The Enduring Tension between Military Spending and Human Rights

Militarism describes one type of society and world vision; international human rights describe a very different world. The two visions are incompatible. To implement a human rights agenda means sacrificing the fixation with military growth and military spending.

Human rights claims evolve over time. There is a strong link between the growth of new human rights and social development. As modern global society has matured, accompanied by deep ecological interdependence, new threats to the individual and the group have surfaced. To combat these threats, governments and nongovernmental organizations (NGOs) have raised issues of environmental balance, economic growth, social equality, refugee relocation, drug interdiction, and disease eradication. Global cooperation between state and nonstate actors is seen as critical to address this perplexing new agenda of world politics. Accordingly, the list of human rights claims keeps growing. Complex social relations give rise to these demands as new claims are made to alleviate suffering. What appears fundamental in one historical era may not be in another. Human rights claims today have no relation to a primitive state of nature where people lived with a few essential needs. As Norberto Bobbio points out, there are no current charters of rights that do not recognize the right to education, which broadens as society develops to include secondary and university as well as primary education. Yet, none of the better-known descriptions of the state of nature mention such a right.[58] International human rights today are a product of this particular historical period.

The International Bill of Human Rights incorporates civil, political, economic, social, and cultural rights. It acknowledges human needs of survival, well-being, identity, and freedom. In the twenty-first century, collective human rights of gender, class, sexuality, and ethnicity/race have been added to this framework. The goal is to create political, civil, and socioeconomic rights that enable all individuals through group membership to develop a valuable, independent life in civil society. We now have the ability to create a world of humane governance informed by these normative priorities. Perhaps in other times such an ambitious agenda was not possible, but there is no question that today with new economic developments, technological breakthroughs, and innovations in communications, we have the ability to protect basic human dignity.

It is now commonly accepted that it is not possible to achieve significant progress on human rights without subsistence needs (food, sanitation, education, and so on) being met. It is also impossible to achieve human rights progress and development in societies controlled by repressive and corrupt regimes. The government can be the main obstacle to achieving either economic or political rights. Most UN scholars and human rights activists promote an interdependence between the two sets of rights (civil/political and economic/social/cultural) and criticize those who make too sharp a distinction between them. Economic and social rights are complimentary to libertarian principles found within civil and political rights. They are both symbiotic and mutually dependent. Civil and political rights can be enacted only if everyone has a minimum of economic security.

This human rights agenda can also only be implemented within a framework of peace. Militarism has neither created a world of peace and stability, nor has it protected the human right to physical security. Overemphasis on military superiority undermines the ability to build regimes of trust and harmony. Large militaries and extensive arms programs are usually symptoms of deep conflict. The underlying causes of these conflicts are not addressed through further military spending. Arms control and disarmament and the demobilization of armed forces are often prerequisites to providing a cooperative framework within which nations may pursue the implementation of the corpus of international human rights law.

International security and stability are dependent on domestic security and stability. The roots of conflict within domestic societies are often the result of economic, social, and environmental pressures that cause poverty and unemployment and pit one community, class, sex, or ethnic group against another. Human rights as the core of domestic and foreign public policy can provide a route for the achievement of peace and stability. Preoccupations with "balance of power" and military prowess can only continue to produce a world of insecurity and war. Policies based on outmoded notions of realpolitik exacerbate insecurities. The irony is that human rights policies provide the clearest road to achieve the "realist" objectives of security and stability. Long-term interests in international stability should compel governments to explore human security and positive peace.

It is commonly accepted that totalitarianism and human rights are incompatible. The negative impact of militarism on basic human rights must also be understood. A militarized society exists in contradiction to basic human rights and negates the opportunities for human freedom.

Inhibiting Militarism

The collective human right to self-determination and the individual human right to personal security are fundamental needs of every human community. For this reason, proposals for immediate and unilateral disarmament consistently fail. As long as societies and individuals feel threatened, the need will be felt to possess armaments to keep aggressors at bay. But could security be achieved without militarism?

There are three clear areas in which a beginning could be made in inhibiting militarism while protecting personal security rights: curbing arms sales, initiating steps toward common security and basic deterrence, and launching institutions of war prevention and preventive diplomacy. Building on the following brief discussion of limiting arms sales and creating common security, the Global New Deal in chapter 8 calls for the creation of two new institutions of war prevention and demilitarization.

Limiting Arms Sales

Global military spending since World War II totals at least $30 to $35 trillion. Enormous resources are needed every year just to maintain superfluous military equipment. Converting military industries is the first step to the release of resources needed to implement international human rights.

In the United States, the lock that the military–industrial complex has on the government was again demonstrated in August 1997 when the Clinton administration decided to lift a nineteen-year-old ban on weapon sales to Latin America. Reversing the ban imposed by President Jimmy Carter in 1978, the administration announced that it would now consider allowing arms sales on a case-by-case basis. The reversal was a huge victory for military contractors like the Lockheed Martin Corporation and the McDonnel Douglas Corporation.[59] From Thucydides to present-day political scientists, it has been noted that the influx of new weapons into a region sets off arms races and rekindles traditional rivalries. Nations either acquire arms or form alliances with distant states to balance out the perceived military power of their neighbors. The Clinton administration, however, in an Orwellian twist, asserted the opposite: its spokesperson claimed that lifting the ban would stabilize the region and promote democracy. In all probability, selling F-16s and other high-powered weaponry to Latin America will have the opposite effect.[60]

For the United States, a program of positive peace would be based on converting a military-based economic system to a civilian-based system. The conversion process can begin with a restriction on arms exports. No longer can such weapon sales be justified as a means of preserving jobs and stemming economic decline. According to the annual arms survey of the Congressional Research Service (CRS), the U.S. share of the international weapons trade grew by nearly 23 percent in 1996, to $11.3 billion in orders, representing 35.5 percent of the global market.[61] In 2000, the CRS reported that the United States solidified its position as the world's biggest arms dealer. U.S. contractors sold nearly $11.8 billion in weapons in 1999—more than a third of the world's total and more than all European countries combined. Roughly two-thirds of all arms were sold to developing nations. Again, the United States led the way with $8.1 billion in sales to LDCs.[62]

U.S. taxpayer money currently supports this weapons trade. In 2001, the arms industry received approximately $7.5 billion in federal support including grants, subsidized loans, and marketing assistance. This represented the second largest subsidy program for business in the federal budget (after agricultural price supports). A first step toward limiting arms sales is to end this corporate welfare. This will not be easy. The weapons industry fights hard to keep its privileges and government largess. Over the past decade, these international arms dealers have poured more than $59 million into federal campaigns. Such investments continue to bring dividends. In November 2000, Congress quietly passed a bill that would give $300 million in new tax breaks to U.S. arms exporters—on top of the $7.5 billion federal support they already received.[63]

The consequences of these arms sales abroad are shameful. U.S. weapons transfers have supported brutal dictators from the Shah of Iran, to Ferdinand Marcos in the Philippines, to Mobutu in Zaire. U.S. weapons helped arm the Guatemalan death squads and the Somali warlords, including Siad Barre. Weapon sales to governments who abuse the human rights of their people are a moral disgrace. Taxpayer money to subsidize such sales is an outrage.

A legitimate use of taxpayer money, on the other hand, is to help the arms industry convert to production for peaceful ends. Conversion must begin by transforming these military industries to civilian enterprises. The government can play a key role in helping industries make this transformation. Clearly, cooperative security, positive peace, and Third World development are not enhanced by the sale of high tech weapons systems. The defense technologies developed during the Cold War can be redirected toward productive civilian ends.[64] A compulsory registration of arms sales and transfers should be established under UN auspices. An international code of conduct on arms transfers is being promoted by a commission of seventeen Nobel Peace Laureates to ensure that weapons are not sold to countries that violate human rights. World conflicts and the fires of war are exacerbated by these sales. The NGO community can plan a key role in publicizing illegal and surreptitious sales of arms.

Basic Deterrence and Common Security

Since the end of the Cold War, serious scholars and policy makers have argued that the U.S. military budget should be dramatically reduced. The implementation of international human rights depends on the execution of such proposals. Theories of common security and basic deterrence, as opposed to national security and extended deterrence, help frame the issues.

William Kaufmann and John Steinbruner from the Brookings Institution, for example, argue for a common approach to security in which the military establishments of various nations are all "on the same side, . . . defensively configured, and . . . primarily committed to providing mutual reassurance." This would require nations to "systematically limit offensive capabilities that might support ground invasions or might undertake long-range bombardment to achieve some political objective." Before joining the Brookings Institution, Kaufmann had been a top adviser to Democratic and Republican secretaries of defense from 1960 to 1980, and Steinbruner had spent fifteen years as director of foreign policy studies at Brookings.[65] Kaufmann and Steinbruner list key rules for cooperative defense strategies. Modern ground forces in any given area should be kept "low enough to signal defensive rather than offensive intent." Air forces should be altered to "favor defense over deep interdiction." Formerly secret information about "basic research activities, new weapons deployment plans, and major operational exercises" should be published. Only small nuclear forces should be maintained, exclusively for retaliation. And strict, joint controls on weapon exports and related technology should be imposed. The cooperative security budget proposed by Kaufmann and Steinbruner would save the United States approximately $424 billion over a ten-year period.[66]

Michael O'Hanlon, also of the Brookings Institution, argues that the United States could prudently cut defense spending by as much as 10 percent without risking its ability to respond to simultaneous regional crises or to maintain global commitments. His proposal would generate an additional $100 billion in cumulative savings beyond White House projections over seven years.[67] Randall Forsberg, the director of the Institute for Defense and Disarmament Studies, goes much further. She argues that if the United States adopted a "cooperative security" policy, annual military spending could be cut by 80 percent. Savings would come to $180 billion per year. She believes that such an approach to security is a prerequisite to stopping the global proliferation of armaments and arms industries. Her plan is based on reducing conventional forces to nonoffensive defenses, decoupling nuclear weapons from the deterrence of conventional war, and replacing unilateral military intervention with multilateral peacekeeping.[68]

Whether the scale of change is as modest as Kaufmann and Steinbruner's and O'Hanlon's, or as ambitious as Forsberg's, the resources released could then be used to meet the United States' human security needs: health and environmental security, rebuilding decaying infrastructure, and so on. For example, Business Leaders for Sensible Priorities is an organization committed to changing U.S. government spending priorities that are undermining economic security. This organization is made up of over 450 of the most successful business leaders in the country. These business professionals describe how reductions in Pentagon spending can protect our children. They propose the following measures:

- Eliminate 6,500 nuclear weapons (which still leaves the U.S. nuclear arsenal with the equivalent of 23,000 Hiroshima bombs). This will save $17 billion per year, enough money to hire 425,000 teachers to reduce class sizes in schools across the United States.
- Decommission 75,000 troops stationed overseas, saving $4 billion per year. This will pay for 971,000 eligible kids, who currently cannot take part due to inadequate funding, to participate in HeadStart.
- Cancel the 339 F-22 fighters designed to thwart Soviet air defenses that were never built. The $11 billion per year savings over five years will pay for health insurance for all 11 million American children who now have no health care protection.[69]

These proposals point in the right direction. To protect its economic security, the United States must scale back its arms factories and military industries. However, to avoid devastating layoffs, a comprehensive, proactive conversion policy for the United States would have to be in place. A great deal can be learned from the post-1945 experience when the United States reduced the defense component of its economy from about 40 percent of GNP to about 6 percent in just two years. Despite this huge shift, the level of employment and consumption were maintained through proactive public policies. Scholars have recently outlined a number of such policies that could be implemented today.[70]

The Global New Deal and Military Spending

Summary Observations

War and military spending are bad for the economy. Defense spending stunts, rather than stimulates, economic growth. Military spending utilizes economic resources that would otherwise be put to more productive use in civilian industries. Massive military spending leads to an inefficient use of labor resources and siphons off highly qualified engineers and labor from the civilian sector. Economic and social rights fulfillment in all nations depends on a shift in resources away from militarism and toward human development.

Global New Deal Proposals

To achieve a significant global cutback in military spending, it is necessary to develop new institutions specifically committed to demilitarization and human rights. Since the end of the Cold War, a plethora of proposals for the restructuring of the UN have been produced.[72] The Global New Deal embraces the construction of two new global institutions dedicated to overcoming militarism and establishing a framework of common security: an International Verification Agency and a Global Demilitarization Fund. These proposals described in chapter 8 pro-

For the vast majority of individuals on the planet, human rights remain a fantasy, a utopian dream, aspirations for some long-distant future. To these individuals, human rights just do not seem feasible in today's world of intractable geopolitical rivalries, massive arms races, and unspeakable human suffering. Human rights can also provide a fairy-tale façade that serves to disguise the often vicious nature of autocratic and/or highly inegalitarian societies. Acting "as if" certain rights were authentic often inhibits people's ability to recognize when they are, in reality, unrealizable.[71]

International human rights can, however, move beyond the realm of utopia and serve as the cornerstone of domestic and foreign public policy. Human rights are not utopian dreams, but tools to inform and guide policy. A human rights–based public policy can restrain excessive militarism.

vide an institutional framework for achieving positive peace. The International Verification Agency can ensure compliance with disarmament agreements, thereby creating a global framework for monitoring and verification. The Global Demilitarization Fund can help to finance not only disarmament efforts, but also other human security needs— such as famine relief and merciful responses to natural disasters (see chapter 8).

A human rights public policy agenda means moving toward positive peace and common security. If the global community is serious about this, bold and dramatic action is needed. It is no longer enough just to point out the interrelationships between peace, demilitarization, and human rights. Human rights strategies must direct public policy toward peace and development.

8

The Global New Deal

To overcome human suffering at the height of the Great Depression, Franklin Delano Roosevelt proposed a New Deal for America. Roosevelt's New Deal embraced a series of policy proposals to overcome market failure, to provide for public goods, and to protect the most vulnerable. Some of these policies succeeded while others failed. Yet, the premise behind his actions, that governments have a duty and responsibility to act for the public welfare, continues to inspire. The public institutions and economic reforms created out of the New Deal gave the government the ability to provide a basic level of economic security to its citizens. These institutions and reforms were designed to provide short-term relief and the eventual implementation of a long-term economic safety net for all Americans. It is true that Roosevelt's New Deal failed to adequately meet the needs of women, African Americans, and the very poor. But it is also true that these public policies, including social security, have literally prevented millions from falling into poverty and destitution.

Today, we need a Global New Deal. Suffering in every nation is linked not only to national economies, but also to the global economy. The denial of basic public goods and market failure are often the result of forces outside the control of an individual nation-state. Public policy at the international level is needed to correct these insufficiencies. To provide for the public welfare, governments must work through international law and international organizations to correct the maldevelopment currently accompanying globalization. Roosevelt gives us an

---

THE GLOBAL NEW DEAL

- Promote economic equality
    Establish a UN Economic Security Council
    Rivet on the twenty-twenty proposal
- Finance global public goods
    Launch a Global Public Goods Fund
    Implement the Tobin Tax
- Hear the victims' voices
    Adjudicate violations of economic and social human rights
    Enhance the power of the UN Economic Rights Committee
    Approve an expanded Optional Protocol to the Economic
       Rights Treaty
- Maintain ecological balance
    Set up a World Environment Organization
- Prioritize the rights of racial and ethnic minorities
    Focus policy on the health care and education of racial and
       ethnic minorities
- Prioritize women's rights
    Concentrate policy on the health care and education of women
- Inhibit militarism
    Found an International Verification Agency
    Institute a Global Demilitarization Fund

---

inspiring example of state mobilization at the national level. Today, mobilization is needed at the global level to implement international public policy to protect the innocent. This book is an attempt to take up this responsibility and to identify international public policy to safe-guard the general welfare.

The Global New Deal is formulated within the normative framework of human rights. Since World War II, the international community at the UN has successfully defined, articulated, and elaborated the content of international economic and social human rights. The Global New Deal is an attempt to develop policy to fulfill these basic economic and social human rights.

The Global New Deal

Promote Economic Equality: Establish a UN Economic Security Council

The existing UN Security Council is the most powerful organ in the UN system. It is charged with maintaining international peace and security and has the power to enforce collective security through economic sanctions and military force. The violent deaths of at least 50 million people in World War II forced the international community to try a new framework for peace. The UN Security Council is mandated to act with force to uphold international law and punish aggressors who commit interstate violence. Over the last fifty years, the UN's role in the area of peace and security has evolved to include peacekeeping, peacebuilding, and peacemaking. Although failures and setbacks have occurred, it is widely recognized that the active role of the UN Security Council in the area of peace and security has fundamentally altered the fabric of international relations.

Today, we need a new security council, a UN Economic Security Council (ESC), to alter the fabric of international economic relations. An ESC should replace the UN Economic and Social Council (ECOSOC), which has been widely recognized as ineffective.[1] The needless suffering of millions around the world demands nothing less. As previously noted, almost half of the world's people—2.8 billion—live on less than $2 a day, and 1.2 billion—a fifth—live on less than $1 a day. In poor countries, as many as 50 percent of all children are malnourished.[2] More than 30,000 children die every day from mainly preventable causes.[3]

Just as the startling violence of World War II compelled states to join together to try a new peace system, so today the astonishing brutality of our unregulated global economic system should lead us to a new framework for economic cooperation. This is not a utopian proposal. It is in every individual state's national interest to support the establishment of an ESC. Rich and poor states can all benefit from a cooperative international organization committed to the idea of promoting global economic equality.

Tinkering with existing international organizations that work on global economic affairs (from the UN Development Program [UNDP] to the International Monetary Fund [IMF]) is not adequate. Strong, bold action by the international community is necessary. As the late Mahbub ul Haq, the chief architect of the UNDP's annual *Human Development Report,* wrote: "Often, a courageous step helps focus the collective human mind, while minor adjustments in arrangements go unnoticed and have little impact."[4]

Bureaucratic malaise and political deadlock on these central issues can be overcome. The political courage that Roosevelt demonstrated at the height of the Great Depression should be our guide. Member states of the UN are constantly called on to demonstrate the "political will" necessary to effectively address daunting global challenges from global poverty to the destruction of the earth's biosphere. But in addition to political will, these nations must also show political courage. Responsible, caring leaders will show courage and take the political risks that always accompany proposals for fundamental change.

Haq and the UNDP were among the first to propose the formation of an ESC within the UN. Haq envisioned an expansive ESC that would implement a program based on security in its fullest sense: security for people, from food security to ecological security. Haq's ESC was conceived to provide leadership in resolving global economic crisis. This proposed ESC would also provide an "early warning system" to plan assistance in internal conflicts. The UNDP mentioned five quantitative indicators for an early warning system for human security: income and job security, food security, human rights violations, ethnic and other conflicts, and the ratio of military to social spending. The UNDP also hoped that this expansive ESC would work to strengthen the UN development system.[5] The Haq–UNDP proposal has considerable merit. However, perhaps we should begin with a more focused mandate for the ESC.

A streamlined and efficient ESC could focus primarily on the promotion of economic equality. Economic equality, as defined in chapter 2, refers to the equal provision of public goods, including nutrition, a clean environment, sanitation, shelter, clothing, primary and secondary education, and basic health care. We have seen the ways in which globalization and "market failure" threaten these public goods and contribute to global human misery (so clearly described by the World Bank and the UNDP). The ESC can center on measures to end this needless suffering through the promotion of economic equality. It could do this by concentrating on the twenty-twenty compact for human development.

ESC Mandate: Promote Economic Equality

The ESC can fulfill its mandate of promoting economic equality by riveting on the proposed twenty-twenty compact for human development developed by UN International Children's Emergency Fund (UNICEF) and the UNDP. The ESC could require yearly reports from all member states on individual progress toward achieving twenty-twenty. The ESC could hold states accountable to implement the twenty-twenty agreement.

The twenty-twenty compact calls for 20 percent of aid budgets and 20 percent of national budgets to be allocated to the provision of basic needs for all. Almost all the member states of the UN agreed to the final declaration from the World Summit for Social Development in Copenhagen in 1995, which adopted the UNICEF–UNDP proposed twenty-twenty compact for human development. These nations pledged to ensure the provision of at least the very basic human development levels for all their people. Most nations can achieve minimal levels of nutrition, safe drinking water, primary health care, population stabilization, and access to basic education by adjusting existing developmental priorities. However, some of the poorer countries will require international assistance in addition to their own domestic efforts. At Copenhagen, the UNDP estimated that these additional costs would be $30 to $40 billion a year over ten years.[6] Five years later, it was estimated that the global shortfall is between $70 to $80 billion a year. The fulfillment of these basic social services is now estimated at approximately $206 to $216 billion, while current funds channeled to these areas total about $136 billion. As a result, an increase of at least $70 to $80 billion is annually needed to provide full coverage.[7]

The twenty-twenty compact illustrates how most of these funds can be found within existing budgets. Currently, developing countries devote on average only 13 percent of their national budgets to these basic human development concerns. Raising this figure to 20 percent will produce additional billions. This money would be diverted primarily from wasteful military spending and prestigious development projects. This restructuring is doable; achieving the budgetary goal of 20 percent is feasible. Developed donor countries, on the other hand, currently allocate only 8.3 percent of their aid to these human priorities (health care, basic education, mass-coverage water supply systems, and so on). If these donors would readjust their aid allocation for these human priority goals, this would provide additional billions to these human rights priorities. Combined, the twenty-twenty compact could potentially produce most of the required $80 billion. It should be emphasized that these funds are already there, and no new taxes are envisioned. These needs can be met through a restructuring of existing budget priorities.[8]

In developing countries, average spending on these social services unfortunately remains very low. A recent study indicates that spending averaged between 12 to 14 percent in these critical areas for thirty developing countries. Defense spending and debt service continue to be given priority. Few developing countries currently allocate the minimum 20 percent to basic social services. Some are astonishingly low: 4 percent in Cameroon, 7.7 percent in the Philippines, and 8.5 percent in Brazil.[9]

The ESC could focus primarily on twenty-twenty. It would be responsible for pressuring states to implement twenty-twenty. Some developing states are now living up to their side of twenty-twenty and allocating 20 percent of public spending to basic social services. But currently, no donor state is living up to its commitment to allocate 20 percent of its aid budget to basic social services.[10] Historically, the UN has often been successful in the mobilization of shame against violators of international norms. The ESC could help to mobilize public pressure to get states to fulfill their obligations under twenty-twenty. As mentioned, states would be required to report yearly on their progress toward achieving twenty-twenty. The ESC could pressure international financial institutions (IFIs; e.g., the World Bank, IMF, the World Trade Organization [WTO], and so on) to moderate their policies to help states achieve twenty-twenty. The ESC could goad nations to cut back on senseless and wasteful military spending and invest in the protection of public goods. Twenty-twenty shows that it is possible to readjust priorities and develop policies to meet basic needs and promote economic equality. With this clear and straightforward mandate, the ESC could play a principal leadership role in global economic governance.

The composition of the new ESC should reflect the new balance of economic and political power in the world today with all important geographical regions or political constituencies represented. Permanent members of the ESC could be the most populous and those with the largest economies. This would include the United States, Japan, China, Germany, France, Russia, India, Italy, United Kingdom, Brazil, Indonesia, Pakistan, Bangladesh, and Nigeria. Other nations and regions could be represented on a rotating basis. For example, rotating members of the UN Security Council are elected from the following regions: three from Africa; two from Asia; three from Europe; and two from Latin America. The ESC could establish a similar scheme to ensure global representation. It would be important to keep the membership relatively small and manageable—thirty members or less would be ideal. Decisions should be made only in a way that reassures both the developed and underdeveloped countries. Thus, a majority of the representatives of both areas would be required to agree. And finally, the ESC would need a competent professional secretariat. The final composition of the ESC will have to be carefully negotiated. But the establishment of a balanced and functional ESC dedicated to the principles of economic equality is clearly feasible, practical, and necessary.[11]

Finance Global Public Goods: Launch a Global Public Goods Fund

Economic and social human rights depend on the protection and provision of public goods. I have defined public goods to include adequate nutrition, safe drinking water, primary health care, population stabilization, and access to basic education. In addition, global public goods include international peace and the prevention of deadly conflict, health and the eradication of disease, equitable development and poverty alleviation, and environmental sustainability and the preservation of the global commons. As previously noted in chapter 2, these goods are all nonexcludable and nonrivalrous in consumption and are frighteningly undersupplied. Individual nations can provide these public goods for each of their citizens only through multilateral action in international law and international organization.

The twenty-twenty proposal is a clear beginning, but it will not raise sufficient funds for the protection and fulfillment of all global public goods. The second proposal of the Global New Deal is to establish a Global Public Goods Fund. This fund would raise the capital necessary for the provision of these public goods. The fund could also be used to finance international responses to earthquakes, hurricanes, resource depletion, famines, and other natural disasters and human emergencies.

To create conditions for true economic equality, funding is needed to respond adequately to the crisis conditions confronting millions. The list is extensive and involves the rebuilding of war-torn societies (from Haiti to Nicaragua to Rwanda to the Congo) and resettling the millions of refugees whose lives have been disrupted by wars; this funding has often been funded and directed by the major powers. The UN Conference on the Environment and Development in Rio de Janeiro in 1992 produced an action plan called "Agenda 21." Implementation of this global program of environmental protection and renewal is estimated to cost about $125 billion per year in external financing alone. The Copenhagen World Summit for Social Development estimated that a poverty eradication program would cost an additional $40 billion per year. The twenty-twenty proposal is a start. But clearly as these costs continue to rise, more funding is necessary. The Global Public Goods Fund is intended to fill this financing gap in the provision of public goods. The fund could be administered by the ESC.[12]

The Tobin Tax

The most widely debated proposal for raising the capital to support global public goods is called the "Tobin Tax." James Tobin, winner of the Nobel Prize for Economics in 1981, first suggested a small tax on the international movement of speculative capital over a quarter of a century ago. In his Janeway Lectures at Princeton in 1972, Tobin viewed the tax as a means to enhance the efficacy of macroeconomic policy. This idea, as Tobin said, "sank like a rock" and was anathema to central bankers. Yet, the proposal received a strong boost at the World Social Summit in Copenhagen in 1995 where it was endorsed and promoted by a number of distinguished economists and politicians, including President François Mitterrand of France. (Conservatives and bankers would like the Tobin Tax to go away. One central banker commented, "Oh, that again. It's the Loch Ness Monster, popping up once more!")[13]

Estimates at the Copenhagen Summit were that a tax rate of only .05 percent on the international movement of speculative capital from 1995–2000 could raise over $150 billion a year. The volume of foreign exchange transactions worldwide reached $1.3 trillion a day in 1995, a total of $312 trillion in a year of 240 business days. Thus, a small tax of .10 percent would yield approximately $312 billion, and a tax of .05 percent well over $150 billion.[14]

Tobin cautions, however, that these figures should be scaled back with more modest expectations predicted. First, the tax itself will reduce the overall volume of such international transactions and thus reduce revenues. And second, the job of tax collection would fall to member states themselves. It would be desirable to allow small, underdeveloped countries to retain shares of the collected revenues, sometimes up to 100 percent. These countries clearly need these funds to provide for public goods. Furthermore, it might "sweeten the pill if each nation were allowed to retain at least 50 percent of the proceeds and to choose—among internationally agreed alternatives—where the tax revenues would go."[15]

Accepting these conditions on splitting the revenue from the Tobin Tax, Inge Kaul and John Langmore forecast that most of the revenue would be retained nationally—up to 100 percent for low-income countries. Even if this is the case, a tax of just .10 percent minus these conditionalities would still raise $27 billion a year for international purposes.[16]

It should be noted that Tobin's main motivation was never to raise revenue. In his mind, the central benefit of this tax on the movement of speculative capital was to reduce short-term speculation and increase national policy autonomy. The volatilities and financial crisis of the last fifteen years have led many to agree with the need for some control on financial markets. The Mexican crisis, in particular, convinced many of the need for some regulation of speculative capital. And this is the beauty of the Tobin Tax. For not only does it potentially raise the funds needed to provide for global public goods, it also pushes, as Tobin writes, "exchange rates [to] reflect to a larger degree long-run fundamentals relative to short-range expectations and risks." Tobin estimates that 80 percent of foreign exchange transactions involve "round trips of seven days or less. Most occur within one day." As seen in Mexico, Indonesia, and elsewhere, the human suffering caused by such rapid capital flight is horrifying. The Tobin Tax would lessen the incentive for such irresponsible action.[17]

Hear the Victims' Voices: Adjudicate Violations of Economic and Social Human Rights

One of the central dilemmas in the development of a workable system of global governance in the area of human rights is the concept of sovereignty. In international law, states have certain sovereign rights and peoples have rights to self-determination. Attempts at the enforcement of human rights from above, a top-down approach, often appear in conflict with principles of nonintervention and the prerogatives of a local community. UN attempts to "mobilize shame" and enforce sanctions against violating states often provoke a local backlash. Who is the UN to come in and tell a native people what to do? And furthermore, international organizations are often out of touch with the reality of forces on the ground. This has led to misjudgments and secondary effects of actions (like sanctions) hurting the vulnerable population the action was intended to help.

However, the successes in international action in support of human rights provide a direction for future action. One such success was the international campaign against apartheid in South Africa. The international "mobilization of shame" and global economic sanctions did contribute to the successful effort of the African National Congress to end this racist system of governance. The fundamental reason these international actions were effective is because they were done in conjunction with a local movement for national liberation. The international community was following the lead of the people of South Africa and responding to their requests. The UN was not imposing sanctions against the will of the people. The people organizing and fighting for human rights in South Africa requested the UN support and asked for the economic sanctions. NGOs, intergovernmental organizations (IGOs), and individual states responded and imposed harsh sanctions to help force the government of South Africa to adhere to the basic standards of human dignity found within international human rights law.

The third part of the Global New Deal draws on these lessons and attempts to create a system responsive to the voices of the victims and those struggling for social justice. Under this proposal, UN actions of rights enforcement and monitoring would be in response to the voices of the victims and coordinated with efforts for change being conducted at the local level. This approach is responsive to the criticisms of the proposed social clause to the WTO (reviewed in chapter 3), which is often perceived as a top-down effort that could potentially undermine local reform efforts. Instead of a social clause, the Global New Deal calls for the enhancement of the power of the Economic Rights Committee to be able to hear and respond to the voices of the oppressed.

The relevant organs of the UN should approve an expanded Optional Protocol to the Economic Rights Treaty. The idea is to link the Economic Rights Committee directly to individuals and groups in civil society who are denied economic and social rights protection. The purpose of the optional protocol is to give legal standing to victims of abuse and those organizing for social change. The voices of those individuals who are denied economic and social human rights deserve to be heard. Their legal cases deserve to be adjudicated.

The current draft optional protocol approved and forwarded by the Economic Rights Committee to the Human Rights Commission provides the basic framework for a workable system.[18] The Economic Rights Committee has formulated clear procedures for the submission of complaints from individuals and groups. The draft spells out how the Economic Rights

Committee is to process and adjudicate these complaints. As noted in chapter 3, the Economic Rights Committee already reviews the self-reporting by states parties on their compliance with the terms of the Economic Rights Treaty. But self-reporting is obviously inadequate, as most states will want to present the best case possible. The optional protocol is a means for the Economic Rights Committee to obtain more reliable and objective information. It will allow individuals and affected groups to present to the Economic Rights Committee evidence on state policies that fail to uphold their obligation to respect, protect, and fulfill economic and social human rights. Victims will be able to appeal to the Economic Rights Committee for redress under international law.

However, in this era of globalization, individuals and groups should be able to raise violations of international law by IFIs and transnational corporations (TNCs) as well as states. The often negative impact of economic globalization on the poor has been documented and discussed. These IFIs and TNCs should be held accountable to international human rights law and global workers rights standards. Citizens from both developed and underdeveloped countries need an avenue to voice their complaints against IFIs and TNCs. The Economic Rights Committee should provide the means for the victims to speak and the legal support for their case to be heard. The idea of an expanded optional protocol is to allow the Economic Rights Committee to examine the work of IFIs and TNCs as well as states. Currently, the Economic Rights Committee has no legal basis on which to assess the impact of IFIs and TNCs on economic and social human rights. An expanded optional protocol can change this and give the Economic Rights Committee this authority.

Under international trade law (WTO, NAFTA, and so on), only states may file complaints of unfair protectionist trading practices. There should also be a mechanism in international society for individuals and groups to file complaints of unjust and inequitable trading practices that harm the economic and social rights of a nation's citizens. The Economic Rights Committee is the logical body to hear and resolve such complaints. Citizens and organizations within the developed and underdeveloped states would have the authority to register such complaints. The impetus for these actions would thus come from the local community, the citizens themselves. There would be no imposition of norms from outside, but rather a cooperative movement to protect social justice. This proposal, in effect, consolidates the social clause idea into an expanded Optional Protocol to the Economic Rights Treaty. The Economic Rights Committee would be empowered to hear complaints against all economic actors, including states, TNCs, and IFIs.

The current Optional Protocol to the Political Rights Treaty has not led to an overwhelming and unworkable magnitude of individual complaints. The Human Rights Committee procedures weed out frivolous complaints.

Individuals must first exhaust all local remedies. These same procedures would be in place with the new expanded Optional Protocol to the Economic Rights Treaty. The hope is that the mere existence of these procedures will cause states, IFIs, and TNCs to show more respect for economic and social human rights. In addition, NGOs and individuals in civil society can use the judgments and rulings of the Economic Rights Committee in their work to help mold public opinion. All of this is key to global governance and central to the creation of a new international environment that protects, respects, and fulfills economic and social human rights.

The dispute settlement procedures of the WTO and NAFTA give sovereign power to these organizations above the states. Member states must adhere to the decisions of the dispute settlement bodies of these intergovernmental organizations or face penalties, including economic sanctions. We are not yet at the point in global governance to set up similar enforcement measures in the area of economic and social rights. In an ideal world, states, IFIs, and TNCs that violated the economic and social rights of individuals and groups would also face scrutiny by international organizations and be subject to sanctions for noncompliance. If states can now be punished for violating liberal principles of free trade, why should they also not be subject to sanctions for violating the economic rights of their citizens? Eventually, such a system may evolve. But in the current international environment, it is hard to envision states giving this much power to the UN or other international organizations committed to social justice.

However, it is realistic to think that states would approve an avenue for the voices of the victims to be heard. It is realistic to believe that an expanded Optional Protocol to the Economic Rights Treaty could be ratified. The people of the developed and underdeveloped worlds have a joint interest in correcting injustices in the global economy. Enhancing the powers of the Economic Rights Committee provides a way to shine a bright light on these human adversities and mobilize political support for change within affected states.

Maintain Ecological Balance: Set up a World Environment Organization

A myriad of proposals have been drafted to strengthen international environmental governance. Some suggest upgrading the UN Environment Program's (UNEP) status from a program to an organ of the UN General Assembly, such as the UNDP. Others assert that a new functional commission of ECOSOC or standing committee on the environment should be established. Additional ideas call for transforming the UN Trusteeship Council into an environmental security council or remodeling the UN Security Council to allow global environmental issues to be integrated more fully into the UN's functioning.[19] The Global New Deal calls for the creation of a new World Environment Organization (WEO) as a specialized agency of the UN to replace UNEP as the lead environmental IGO.

In 1994, Daniel C. Esty proposed such a WEO to provide the comprehensive international coordination needed to respond to environmental threats. He called for the creation of a single organization with a mandate and resources to coordinate worldwide efforts to protect the environment. Such an organization could provide a counterweight to the WTO. Esty believes that free traders and environmentalists would both benefit from the creation of an international institution committed to the development of collective-action responses to ameliorate long-term environmental harms. Esty writes:

> Like the GATT [WTO], a [WEO] . . . would provide a bulwark against domestic pressures that undermine long-term thinking and make sensible policies hard to achieve. Such a body could serve as an honest broker in transnational environmental disputes, assessing risks and benefits from environmental threats and allocating costs and cleanup responsibilities. Just as the GATT built on the core concept of nondiscrimination as a means to trade liberalization, a [WEO]. . . would establish guidelines, centered on the polluter pays principle, to promote international cooperation in addressing environmental matters and the integration of economic and environmental policy goals.[20]

Michael W. Doyle and Rachel I. Massey believe that Esty's hypothetical WEO is optimistic. Given the underfunding of current international environmental organizations, they find it hard to imagine the political commitment to establish WEO. Doyle and Massey argue instead that any new international environmental organization should have clear but limited goals and relatively little funding. Their idea is to begin with a pragmatic mandate, achieve measurable success, and then grow over time. They argue that this is a more realistic approach than to expect backing for a robust WEO set up with large amounts of capital.[21]

A further argument against a strong, centralized WEO is that the establishment of a chief environment agency could take pressure off other UN agencies to integrate environmental protection into their programs. To address these concerns, some advocate strengthening international environmental organizations through the creation of a high commissioner for environmental protection within the UN system. Rather than creating a new institution (like WEO), the high commissioner could coordinate international environmental policy and force long-range planning. The prestige and clout of the Office of the High Commissioner—the highest rank in the UN system under the secretary general—would hopefully bring more credibility and thus more action on environmental priorities.

The high commissioner would be appointed by the UN General Assembly and would receive and assess communications from states, private organizations, and private individuals concerning compliance with or violation of international environmental law. When appropriate, the high commissioner could request further action from the Commission on Sustainable Development (CSD) or UNEP. The high commissioner could help the CSD determine state violations of international obligations related to environmental protection.[22]

Hilary French, however, notes that debates over form should not distract us from the more critical questions of function. There is a pressing need for centralizing global environmental governance. A WEO, for example, could serve an important monitoring and implementing role in international environmental law. The current dispersed collection of treaty bodies could be brought under one roof. WEO would need to be given sufficient financial resources to monitor treaty compliance and stimulate innovative programs. French points to the precedent set by the International Labor Organization (ILO), which has successfully strengthened hundreds of labor standards such as workplace safety and child labor. The ILO also reviews members' compliance with its standards and provides technical assistance to help them with this task. Through its investigations alone, the ILO often generates enough pressure to bring an errant country into line. The tripartite governing structure of the ILO of labor, business, and government may also be a model for a WEO to emulate.[23]

A strong WEO with the authority of a UN specialized agency and enhanced funding would address the fear expressed by P. M. Haas, R. O. Keohane, and M. A. Levy of "institutional overload."[24] They note that there are so many organizations and treaties in existence relating to the environment that governments are spread too thin and have difficulty complying with them all. International environmental protection thus suffers from institutional overload. An effective and well-funded WEO could resolve this conundrum. Rather than multiple organizations to relate to, governments would be able to work with WEO on environmental matters. WEO could consolidate the reporting procedures of international environmental treaties and work with developing states to ease their reporting and compliance burdens.

In addition to UNEP, the CSD, and the Global Environment Facility (GEF), there are now an overwhelming number of environmental IGOs. The Food and Agriculture Organization, UNDP, UN Industrial Development Organization, World Bank, and World Meteorological Organization all have significantly expanded activities related to monitoring or protecting the environment. There are also issue-specific treaty secretariats for biodiversity, climate, and the ozone. All bureaucracies fight for higher budgets, bigger projects, and a central role. The result is that these environmental organizations compete with each other for management responsibility and limited international financing. A strong WEO could resolve disputes, streamline reporting and monitoring, and establish efficient management systems. The less developed countries, in particular, would benefit from the central coordination of these reporting, monitoring, and managing functions. WEO would not be replacing these other environmental IGOs. Rather, it would be ending redundancy, simplifying reporting, and establishing efficiency.

WEO should be given powers equal to the WTO. Trade measures should be evaluated by the WTO for efficiency and by WEO for environmental protection. Currently, WTO rules are enforced through binding dispute resolution procedures. If a national law is found in violation of WTO rules, a dispute resolution panel has the power to require the offending country to either pay a financial penalty (equal to the foregone trade) or amend its legislation. WEO should be given the same binding and compulsory power to enforce international environmental law as the WTO has to enforce international trade law.

Furthermore, when trade liberalization and environmental protection collide, the two organizations should be required to resolve the dispute collectively before any action could be taken. Both WEO and the WTO, for example, would evaluate and determine whether a national environmental law was really a "nontariff barrier to trade" or a legitimate tool to protect the environment. A trade organization, like the WTO, should not be able to trump an environmental organization, like the proposed WEO. Global ecological balance should be in the hands of a WEO, not the WTO. WEO should be made up of international civil servants, individuals highly skilled in the technical areas challenging our biosphere. The arguments in favor of a WEO to match the influence and visibility of the WTO are compelling and persuasive.

As a specialized agency of the UN, WEO could not only maintain and expand UNEP's current programs, but also coordinate the work of the other environmental IGOs, including the CSD and GEF. This coordination function is critical to prevent overlap and redundancy. WEO should not try to gather all these organizations under one roof. As outlined earlier, these organizations serve clear purposes and functions and their existing capabilities and usefulness should not be undermined. By clarifying responsibilities and facilitating communication, WEO should help these other environmental organizations do their jobs well.

A beginning point for WEO is to learn from the experience of the General Agreement on Tariffs and Trade (GATT). GATT was organized around a few basic principles of liberal economics, such as nondiscrimination, reciprocity, and liberalization. Esty argues that a WEO should begin the same way, by organizing its work around a few basic environmental principles, including the following: the polluter pays principle, thereby creating powerful incentives for pollution prevention and environment care; pollution prevention rather than end-of-pipe treatments; and the precautionary principle.[25]

The precautionary principle, in particular, could provide a clear and viable focus to launch the new WEO. First promoted by Greenpeace, the precautionary principle is now a fundamental principle of international environmental law. The precautionary principle shifts the burden of proof to the institution or individual engaged in a potentially dangerous activity. Such activity could not be undertaken until the public is guaranteed that it is harmless. This idea is found in principle 15 of the "Rio de Janeiro Declaration on Environment and Development," which declares that "[i]n order to protect the environment, the precautionary approach shall be widely applied by States according to their capabilities. Where there are threats of serious or irreversible damage, lack of full scientific certainty should not be used as a reason for postponing cost-effective measures to prevent environmental degradation."[26] A World Bank paper on global warming states: "When confronted with risks which could be menacing and irreversible, uncertainty argues strongly in favor of prudent action and against complacency."[27] The Kyoto Protocol on climate change in 1997 also adopted the precautionary perspective.[28]

WEO could begin with a focus on these environmental principles and help nations integrate these standards into their development plans. WEO would play a significant role in the strengthening and enforcement of international environmental law and could help make international environmental law work.

States have a legal obligation under current international law not to degrade the environment and a responsibility for environmental damage. Other duties of states in international environmental law include: "the duty to notify and consult, the need to obtain prior consent of other states for given activities, state responsibility for given activities of private operators, and development of early-warning mechanisms and environmental-impact assessments."[29] The fundamental principle embodied in the maxim *sic utere tuo ut alienum non laedas* (use your own property so as not to injure the property of another) is central to the work of the International Law Commission, international regimes to protect the environment, and the settlement of international environmental disputes.[30]

Effective enforcement of international environmental law, however, is often difficult. There is no central authority to administer and execute either criminal sanctions and fines, or disincentives and incentives. A WEO could be a critical step in the enhancement of the effectiveness of international environmental standards and regulations. States have voluntarily signed significant global legislation to protect the environment. Their ratification indicates that these states see these treaties in their individual national interest. Individual self-interest should further dictate that the national interest is served through the enforcement of these measures. It is not unrealistic to expect governments to understand the need for a strong and effective WEO. Each state on our planet deserves nothing less.

The protection and renewal of natural capital is central to the Global New Deal and would be a dominant focus of the proposed WEO. WEO would be dedicated to the protection and renewal of natural capital. WEO would be committed to investing in the sustainment, restoration, and expansion of natural capital. It would not be promoting a particular belief system or political party, rather, it would be interested in protecting the biosphere on which all ideologies and economic models depend. It would recognize and act on the shared goal of all of humanity of species preservation.

With adequate financial backing, WEO could reinvigorate and put some teeth into "Agenda 21." Despite its weaknesses, "Agenda 21" still represents the most ambitious and comprehensive framework ever devised by governments for global environmental policy making. The intent of "Agenda 21" was to stimulate cooperation on 120 separate initiatives for environmental and economic improvement. However, every chapter's finance and implementation sections were weak, and promising environmentally needed measures were sacrificed. Political support for implementing the measures waned, and financing was not forthcoming. Rather than starting over, WEO could begin from the framework or understanding reached at the Rio Conference and develop a financing and implementation program to turn those promises into reality.

WEO could help subsidize research and development into energy efficiency, renewable energy, and zero-emission cars. Many believe, for example, that the only feasible alternative to our environmentally destructive fossil fuel or carbon–based energy economy is a solar/hydrogen-based economy. Solar/hydrogen-based energy sources include wind power, solar photovoltaics, geothermal power, and direct sunlight. Wind and solar cells are thought to be the cornerstones of a new energy economy. WEO could help nations make the transition to a solar/hydrogen-based economy.

WEO could focus on the disturbing trends in our natural capital— falling water tables, shrinking cropland area per person, the leveling off of the oceanic fish catch, the radical shrinking of the world's forests, and the accelerated extinction of plant and animal species. The statistics are alarming: 11 percent of the world's 8,615 bird species, 25 percent of the world's 4,355 mammal species, and an estimated 34 percent of all fish species are vulnerable or in immediate danger of extinction.[31] The earth's ecosystems are no longer working well. The well-funded WEO would be charged with reversing this horrible trend.

WEO must have the financial clout needed to fight for the world's environmental security. Many commentators have noted the social consequences of ecological decay. Millions of people in the 1980s and 1990s were displaced from their homes due to "natural" disasters greatly inten-sified by deforestation and climate change. Hurricane Mitch, for example, was the deadliest Atlantic storm in two centuries. As the per capita avail-ability of water, fish, and land continues to decline, regional instabilities are bound to produce conflict. Ecological devastation often leads to mas-sive homelessness by creating thousands of "environmental refugees" around the world. WEO gives humanity a chance to create real economic and environmental security.

Funding for WEO could come from the Global Public Goods Fund (already described) and the proposed Global Demilitarization Fund defined later in this chapter.

Prioritize the Rights of Racial and Ethnic Minorities: Focus Policy on the Health Care and Education of Racial and Ethnic Minorities

Health Care

The Minority Rights Committee could monitor the degree to which states parties ensure basic medical care to their entire populations, includ-ing all racial minorities.

The plight of the aboriginal people in Canada is illustrative. Aboriginal people have seven years less life expectancy than the overall Canadian population and almost twice as many infant deaths. The link here between social conditions and health could not be more stark. The poor health of indigenous people in Canada is directly related to the social environment. Canada as a nation is proud of its top ranking on the UNDP Human Devel-opment Index (HDI). Yet, if on-reserve native peoples of Canada were a nation ranked on the HDI, they would place a shocking sixty-third. Abo-riginal people are among the poorest of Canadians.[32]

The less developed and least developed countries have the ability to address basic medical needs. It is estimated, for example, that almost half of the preventable deaths of infants under five years old in poor countries are the result of diarrheal and respiratory illness, exacerbated by malnu-trition. These conditions can be most effectively dealt with through pre-ventive measures at local facilities. The Minority Rights Committee can examine if a nation is implementing cost-effective strategies for serving the entire population, rather than only the well off, or only a particular racial group. In some countries, for example, a single teaching hospital can take 20 percent or more of the government's health budget. Almost all developing countries can point to examples of major hospitals whose operational costs resulted in the curtailment of health clinics and preven-tive services. The right to health involves access to standard or primary medical care that must be taken to be more basic than the "freedom" to receive costly surgical procedures. Vulnerable populations in poor countries have the right to insist on access to basic medical care. The Minority Rights Committee should examine the distribution of health benefits and the provision of health services for all racial and ethnic groups.[33]

The policies of nonstate actors, however, will also have to be examined by the Minority Rights Committee. In Brazil, for example, IMF-mandated cuts of 40.5 percent in social expenditures led to reductions of 12.3 percent in education, 6.6 percent in health, 83.1 percent in the Social Action Sanitation Program, and 50 percent in the retraining programs for unemployed workers. These forced cuts make it difficult for Brazil to meet its economic and social obligations under international law. It becomes difficult for Brazil to achieve universal and equitable access by all people to primary health care. The poorest sectors of the population do not have access to the expensive, technologically complex health care in the urban areas. Inequality and social exclusion are the result as a double network of social services is created—one for the rich and the other for the poor. The solution to these dilemmas will only come about with an understanding of the causes. Therefore, the role of the IMF in the creation of these conditions must also be addressed.[34]

Education

The Minority Rights Committee could monitor the degree to which states parties ensure basic education to their entire populations, including all racial minorities.

International human rights law requires states to ensure basic education for its citizens. Poverty again is not an excuse for failing to implement policies and practices toward these ends. UNICEF has documented the ways in which poor countries can achieve remarkable results with commitment and farsightedness. In Asia, for example, the Indian state of Kerala (India) has achieved a 90 percent literacy rate. This is far in excess of the 58 percent rate in Punjab, which has more than double Kerala's per capita income. Or compare Vietnam and Pakistan. Pakistan, with a much greater per capita, has a 38 percent literacy rate compared to Vietnam's 94 percent. Pleas of poverty ring particularly false when military spending in South Asia continues unabated (approximately $13.6 billion a year for the region).[35]

It is within the Minority Rights Committee's charge to regulate states parties' compliance with the provisions of the Minority Rights Treaty requiring access to education without discrimination. Indigenous and racial minorities consistently face unequal educational opportunities around the world. In Peru, for example, the national average illiteracy rate is 13 percent, but among the indigenous population it reaches 33 percent, and in the case of indigenous women 44 percent. In Uruguay, the black population has a greater dropout rate at all levels of schooling, and overall average a year and a half less schooling than white people.[36] In 1984 in Slovakia, 80 percent of Roma children attended kindergarten, but only 15 percent did so in 2000. In the 1990s in India, the adult literacy rate among women of established tribes was 24 percent, compared with 39 percent for all Indian women.[37] The Minority Rights Committee can push Peru, Uruguay, Slovakia, and India to confront these issues and correct these inequities in educational opportunities.

National governments have far more resources to devote to education than are allocated. Governments need to be roused to recognize the priority of education. For many states, education just is not a priority. Only fourteen of the seventy African countries (20 percent) participating in the European Community's Lomé IV aid agreement ranked education and training a high priority. The overwhelming majority, forty-five countries, saw it as a low priority and six had no education or training programs at all.[38]

Yet, the value of investing in basic education is now almost universally acknowledged. The role of UN treaty bodies is to hold nations accountable to their words. The Minority Rights Committee can push states parties to practice what they preach.

Prioritize Women's Rights: Focus Policy on the Health Care and Education of Women

The UNDP's Gender Development Index (GDI) measures differences between men and women in life expectancy, educational attainment, and earned income. The *Human Development Report 2000* calculated the GDI for 143 countries and found gender inequality in every single society. In thirty countries, women suffered twice the deprivation of low overall achievement in human development compared to men. However, some very diverse countries did show an improvement in the GDI rankings, including Denmark, Estonia, and Sri Lanka. This demonstrates once again that human development and gender equality can be achieved at different income levels, stages of development, and cultures.[39]

The 1995 Beijing Platform of Action called on governments to prepare national plans of action outlining implementation strategies to achieve the goals of the women's conference. By January 2000, a total of 116 states had submitted national action plans to the UN Division for the Advancement of Women. NGOs and other actors in civil society contributed to the documentation and analysis of many of these national reports. The UN Development Fund for Women reports that the majority of these reports focused on four critical areas: education and training, women in power and decision making, women and health, and violence against women. Only a few of the reports established time-bound targets and indicators for monitoring progress. When asked to assess achievements, most stated that a shortage of resources was a major obstacle to progress in all areas. Resource scarcity was often felt to be the result of a combination of IMF-imposed structural adjustment programs, the impact of globalization, the devastation of natural disasters, and armed conflicts. A global shift in spending priorities from the public to the private sector also contributed to the lack of resources to address programs for women. In all regions of the world, except South Asia, the trend for public expenditures to rise as a proportion of national income ended in the mid-1980s.[40]

Through a focus on the health care and education of women, two of the priority areas from the Beijing Platform of Action, the Women's Rights Committee can help states formulate national policy to respect, protect, and fulfill economic and social human rights.

Health Care

Gender inequality in the provision of basic health care is devastating to the world's women. Globally, over half a million women die from pregnancy-related causes every year, while another 15 million suffer serious long-term complications. It is estimated that up to 200,000 women, including teenage girls, die every year as a result of unsafe, illegal abortions. And women now account for nearly half of all new cases of HIV infection. Basic health care is central to the capabilities approach—providing women with the opportunity and freedom to achieve well-being.[41]

The Women's Rights Committee's General Recommendation no. 24 on women and health is a valuable resource for states parties to utilize in the formulation of public policy for women. In this very detailed general recommendation, the Women's Rights Committee asks states parties to report on their understanding of (1) how policies and measures on health care address the health rights of women from the perspective of women's needs and interests and (2) how they address the distinctive features that differ for women in comparison to men, such as biological factors, socioeconomic factors, psychosocial factors, and confidentiality. The general recommendation outlines the states parties' obligations to respect, protect, and fulfill. The obligation to respect requires states to refrain from obstructing action taken by women in pursuit of their health goals. For example, women's access to health services should not be restricted on the ground that women do not have the authorization of husbands, partners, parents, or health authorities or because they are unmarried. The obligation to protect requires states to take action to prevent gender-based violence, a critical health issue for women. The obligation to fulfill imposes on states the duty to use the maximum of its available resources to ensure that women realize their rights to health care.

The committee then calls on states parties to

implement a comprehensive national strategy to promote women's health throughout their lifespan. This will include intervention aimed at both the prevention and treatment of diseases and conditions affecting women, as well as responding to violence against women, and will ensure universal access for all women to a full range of high-quality and affordable health care, including sexual and reproductive health services. States parties should allocate adequate budgetary, human and administrative resources to ensure that women's health receives a share of the overall health budget comparable with that for men's health, taking into account their different health needs.[42]

These reports, combined with the national action plans for implementing the programs from the Beijing Conference, provide the Women's Rights Committee and national governments the information needed to craft policy to meet the health needs of women. The Women's Rights Committee can goad states to change policy and/or follow up on promises.

Education

Gender inequity in the provision of education is also devastating to the world's women.

In all developing countries, there are still 80 percent more illiterate women than illiterate men.[43] Overall, of the estimated 960 million illiterate people in the world, about two-thirds are women. In some communities, more than half the female population aged fifteen and over can neither read nor write. Female literacy differs among regions. In Latin America and the Caribbean, overall female literacy is 85 percent, in sub-Saharan Africa 49 percent, in northern and western Africa 45 percent, and in South Asia 38 percent. There are also major differences within countries and regions. For example, in the Arab world female literacy is slightly over 50 percent, but it ranges from lows of 20 percent in Yemen and 22 percent in Morocco to highs of 89 percent in Lebanon and 73 percent in Jordan and Kuwait. Rural and urban differences are often stark. In rural India, female literacy is only 30 percent, compared with 64 percent in urban areas. It is imperative for the Women's Rights Committee to monitor the degree to which states parties ensure basic education to women.[44]

Enrollment rates are about equal between girls and boys in primary school, yet girls' dropout rates are higher. Girls account for two-thirds of the 100 million children who drop out of primary school in the first four years. Girls are still socialized into areas traditionally regarded as more suitable for women and are still enrolled mostly in courses like home economics, humanities, education, and the arts.[45]

World Bank statistics confirm that women deprived of education face serious constraints in rearing healthy productive children. These women tend to have more children than they wish, often compounding family difficulties. Better-educated women are able to use contraception more effectively and communicate better with their spouse and others about family-size decisions. Studies also consistently show that women's education improves child survival. And furthermore, longitudinal studies in the United States and the United Kingdom show that, controlling for other household-level factors, a mother's education is associated with better child cognitive development.[46]

There are further benefits to prioritizing women's education. Education makes it possible and easier for women to obtain medical care, comply with instructions, and follow up with health care providers. Low education makes it more difficult for women to obtain health care information, prevent illness, and care for the sick.[47]

Cross-country analysis by the World Bank indicates that countries that invest in girls' education have higher rates of economic growth. The results are remarkable across the board. Closing the gender gap in schooling is critical to successful human development. For example, analysis from Kenya suggests that giving women farmers the same education and inputs as men increases yields by as much as 22 percent. An analysis from Burkina Faso indicates that output could increase by 6 to 20 percent through a more equitable allocation of productive resources between men and women.[48]

The Women's Rights Committee could focus like a laser on these issues of women's education. The committee should draft a general recommendation on education, similar to the one on health care, to crystalize the committee's expectations in this important area. Governments would be put on notice that when they come before the Women's Rights Committee they will be particularly questioned on policies to achieve equity in women's education. Hopefully, since their reputation is on the line, these governments will enact policies to protect women's rights. The concluding observations and other reports from the Women's Rights Committee could be forwarded to the new ESC. The central role and prominence of the proposed ESC should result in abundant publicity to its proceedings. This attention should put additional pressure on states to prioritize public policy for the health and education of women.

Respecting, protecting, and fulfilling the economic and social rights of women is central to the success of the Global New Deal.

Inhibit Militarism: Found an International Verification Agency and a Global Demilitarization Fund

The creation of a new International Verification Agency, proposed by Michael Renner, could help create confidence that disarmament enhances rather than undermines security. Ronald Reagan's quip to Mikhail Gorbachev, "trust but verify," holds true internationally. Effective inspections and monitoring arrangements are essential to verify compliance with disarmament agreements. This new agency would be charged with inspection responsibilities for nuclear, chemical, and conventional disarmament. The new International Verification Agency would draw on the successful experience of existing disarmament agencies and agreements and expand the verification function to cover other armaments.[49]

For example, the Convention on the Prohibition of the Development, Production, Stockpiling and Use of Chemical Weapons and on Their Destruction (CWC) entered into force on 29 April 1997. The CWC is the first multilateral disarmament agreement to provide for the elimination of an entire category of weapons of mass destruction within a fixed time frame and under a universal verification mechanism. By February 2001, 143 states parties had ratified or acceded to the CWC out of 174 signatories.[50] The CWC established the Organization for the Prohibition of Chemical Weapons (OPCW) to verify global adherence to the treaty. In its first 22 months of operation, the OPCW conducted 500 inspections, totaling 28,000 inspection days, at nearly 260 sites on the territories of 29 states parties. By the end of March 1999, the OPCW had also conducted a total of 170 inspections at 63 former chemical weapon production facilities and 33 chemical weapon storage sites. This record of the OPCW demonstrates that it is possible for the international community to successfully monitor the spread of weapons of mass destruction and verify their elimination.[51]

The 1997 Ottawa Convention on the Prohibition of the Use, Stockpiling, Production and Transfer of Anti-personnel Land Mines entered into force on 1 March 1999. The treaty has been signed by 138 governments and ratified by 101. This global treaty banning the use of land mines has achieved remarkable levels of success, despite the nonparticipation of the United States and China. A year and a half after the treaty went into effect, 10 million stockpiled antipersonnel mines had been destroyed, trade in these weapons had almost completely halted, and no shipments of land mines were recorded. In addition, marked decreases in deaths and injuries from land mines were noted in Afghanistan, Bosnia, Cambodia, and Mozambique.[52]

Similar verification measures are established in the Comprehensive Test Ban Treaty (CTBT) to halt nuclear weapons proliferation. As of 11 April 2001, 160 states had signed the treaty and 76 had ratified it. For the treaty to enter into force, all forty-four states listed in annex 2 to the treaty must deposit their ratifications with the UN secretary general. These annex 2 states are those that possess nuclear power or research reactors. As of 11 April 2001, of these forty-four states, forty-one had signed and thirty-one had ratified the treaty, including Russia. The treaty will only enter into force when the delinquent final 13 states in annex 2 submit their ratifications. Despite Russia's ratification of the CTBT, the United States, China,

Israel, Pakistan, and India refuse to participate in this international effort to make the world a safer place.

On 13 October 1999, after a brief debate and rushed vote, the U.S. Senate rejected ratification of the CTBT by a vote of 51 to 48. Senators voting against the treaty argued that it was unverifiable. Yet, the facts speak otherwise. The headquarters of the CBTB in Vienna has established an effective global verification regime. Ultimately, it will consist of a global network of 337 facilities: 170 seismic, 60 infrasound, 11 hydroacoustic, and 80 radionuclide stations supported by 16 radionuclide laboratories. These facilities will be located in some ninety countries around the world. By the end of 1999, 241 sites had been completed, including 15 stations of the primary seismic network as well as 31 auxiliary seismic stations, 8 infrasound stations, and 14 stations in the radionuclide network.[53] With this level of global monitoring and verification, it is very hard to imagine how a renegade state could successfully violate the CTBT and not get caught. Nuclear explosions are hard to hide. This strong and convincing case for a workable verification regime was not seriously studied or debated by the U.S. Senate. This U.S. body's blow against global disarmament makes it much more difficult to limit the spread of weapons of mass destruction. This action certainly made the world a more dangerous place.[54]

The CWC, Land Mines Convention, and the CTBT conclusively demonstrate that global monitoring and verification can be effective. A new International Verification Agency can build on these efforts and work to create a global framework for disarmament and peace. It is in every nation's interest to slow down and eventually halt weapons proliferation, particularly weapons of mass destruction. The most powerful nations, including the United States, can do little to halt the spread of these insidious weapons through unilateral action. It is only through international organization and multilateral action that true progress toward positive peace can be achieved.

The International Verification Agency could be funded through the creation of a Global Demilitarization Fund, as proposed by Nobel Peace Prize winner Oscar Arias. Arias calls on the nations of the world, both rich and poor, to commit themselves to at least a 3 percent a year reduction in their military spending levels. The rich would be asked to earmark only one-fifth of these savings toward the demilitarization fund, and the developing countries would contribute around one-tenth. The money raised could address not only disarmament efforts, but also other human security needs—such as famines, natural disasters, and resource depletion. The fund could be the key to adequate financing of WEO.[55]

In preparation for the UN Copenhagen Conference on Social Development in 1995, the UNDP estimated that a 3 percent reduction in global military spending would yield about $460 billion over five years, of which around $385 billion would be in the industrial world and around $75 billion in the developing world. If the rich nations were to allocate only 20 percent and the poor nations 10 percent of this "peace dividend" to the new Global Demilitarization Fund, this would generate at least $85 billion over five years, or about $14 billion a year.[56] This fund can be used to finance the verification sites and programs of the International Verification Agency. With adequate funding, international organizations can successfully monitor and control the spread of weapons of war.

As Nobel Laureate Arias writes: "Only global cooperation can foster the security we have sought for so long, but which has eluded us so frequently. Let us make a definitive effort to use the peace dividend for the construction of just, prosperous and demilitarized societies. And let us capitalize on the benefits of disarmament to promote and guarantee the rewards of peace."[57]

The Global New Deal in Action

Let me take a difficult example of the reality of global capitalism and see how economic and social human rights could be protected in the proposed Global New Deal. In 1995, garment workers in El Salvador earned fifty-five cents an hour sewing cotton tops and khaki pants for the GAP, a U.S. TNC. Workers were made to spend eighteen-hour days in unventilated factories with undrinkable water. Workers who complained were denied bathroom breaks and made to sweep outside all morning in the boiling sun. After an international outcry against sweatshops, including organizing by groups like the National Labor Committee (a union-backed, workers advocacy group based in New York), the GAP made some changes. By 2001, garment workers for the GAP received coffee and lunch breaks, bathrooms were unlocked, the factory cleaned up, and employees could complain to a group of independent monitors. The GAP clearly was embarrassed by its glaring abuse of employee dignity and rights. Yet, in 2001 these GAP garment workers in El Salvador earned only sixty cents an hour, merely five cents more an hour than six years earlier. GAP garment workers still endure long hours and must meet high production quotas. Their small earnings still do not provide enough compensation on which to live.[58]

Can anything be done? Not according to the *New York Times* reporters who wrote:

Yet the real alternative in this impoverished nation is no work. And government officials won't raise the minimum wage or even enforce labor laws too rigorously for fear that employers would simply move many jobs to another poor country. The lesson from the GAP's experience in El Salvador is that competing interests among factory owners, government officials, American managers and middle-class consumers—all with their eyes on the lowest possible cost—make it difficult to achieve even basic standards, and even harder to maintain them.[59]

In other words, there is no alternative! Without these exploitative, low-paying GAP jobs, there would be no jobs at all! The GAP's profits in 2000 were $877 million.[60] The GAP could pay liveable, decent wages to its workers and still reap profits for its shareholders. The GAP clearly benefits from the unwillingness of the government of El Salvador to raise the minimum wage. The government and the GAP are focused on investments and profits and not on the rights of the most vulnerable. The GAP can blame the government of El Salvador for not enforcing labor laws. The government can blame the forces of the global economy that cause it to keep wages low. The UN, afraid to challenge state "sovereignty," accepts the status quo. And consumers are left in the dark and buy products often created under conditions of inhumanity.

How could the Global New Deal address these issues of economic and social human rights in El Salvador? How would the Global New Deal hold governments, TNCs (like the GAP, Nike, and Reebok), IFIs, and other actors answerable to international human rights law?

First, the ESC would hold the government of El Salvador accountable to keep its part of the twenty-twenty proposal. The government would have to report on what actions it had taken to promote economic equality, that is, how much public investment was made in education, health care, nutrition, sanitation, and so on. Public policy to promote economic equality and protect public goods would be promoted by the council. The government would be called on to protect a minimal living wage for all workers, including TNC employees. The impact of the policies of the IMF, World Bank, and other IFIs on economic equality and the living standards of the people of El Salvador would also be assessed. In the past, IFI pressure for fiscal austerity has often led to government cuts in basic social services for the poor. The ESC could work with the IFIs to modify their austerity programs that have had such a devastating impact on the most vulnerable sectors.

Second, the ESC would hold aid donors responsible to keep their part of the twenty-twenty proposal. At least 20 percent of all existing aid to the country should go toward the provision of basic needs, including nutrition, sanitation, primary education, and so on. However, the Global Public Goods Fund (thanks to the Tobin Tax) could also help El Salvador fund such global public goods as the eradication of disease, poverty alleviation, refugee protection, and environmental sustainability. All of these public policies and programs would enhance the quality of life for all workers in El Salvador, including TNC employees.

Third, the UN Economic Rights Committee would accept complaints from TNC employees through its expanded optional protocol. These employees would have the opportunity to demonstrate the ways in which their economic and social human rights had been violated. Any UN actions of rights enforcement would then be in response to the voices of the victims. Through this mechanism, the TNC could be held accountable to pay a living wage and uphold the basic economic and social human rights affirmed in international law. A decision by the Economic Rights Committee in support of the requested changes by the TNC employees could help mobilize political support in El Salvador for such actions. TNCs, as well as states, are accountable to human rights law.

Fourth, WEO would work with the government of El Salvador to protect its natural capital and bring its national law into compliance with international environmental treaties. With managing and monitoring functions centralized in WEO, it will be easier for El Salvador to meet its reporting obligations under international environmental law. In addition, the environmental impact of trade agreements would be assessed. Thanks to capital from the Global Demilitarization Fund, WEO could help finance El Salvador's transition to a solar/hydrogen-based economy, the clear alternative to the environmentally destructive fossil fuel or carbon–based energy economy.

Fifth, the UN Minority Rights Committee would monitor the degree to which El Salvador ensures basic medical care and basic education to all of its citizens, including all racial minorities. The Minority Rights Committee would push for equal employment opportunities for all citizens, including access to jobs at TNCs. The Minority Rights Committee would work with the government of El Salvador to design public policy that guarantees economic and social rights for all without discrimination based on race or ethnicity.

Sixth, the UN Women's Rights Committee would look closely at the treatment of women in El Salvador, with a particular focus on education and health care. The Women's Rights Committee would work with El Salvador to develop time-bound targets and indicators for measuring progress in respecting, protecting, and fulfilling women's economic and social human rights. The impact of TNCs in El Salvador on women workers would be a particular concern. Policy designed to foster well-paying jobs for women would be promoted.

Seventh, the International Verification Agency, having established inspection and monitoring arrangements throughout Central America, would report to El Salvador on the level of compliance with disarmament treaties in the region. With this verified information, El Salvador could proceed with significant cuts in its military budget. Funds from this disarmament effort could be directed toward fulfilling the twenty-twenty priorities (outlined earlier). These programs of nutrition, basic education, health care, sanitation, and family planning benefit all workers in the country, including TNC employees.

It is only through this type of comprehensive approach that public policy for the protection of the economic and social human rights of the people of El Salvador or any country can be fulfilled. Human rights fulfillment depends on holding all economic actors to these ethical standards.

Globalization from Below: NGOs and the Global New Deal

A prominent component of Roosevelt's New Deal was the ubiquitous blue eagle indicating public participation in the National Recovery Act.[61] The Roosevelt administration understood the importance of widespread support and broad participation in its program of reform and recovery. Far-reaching popular collaboration is also indispensable for the success of the Global New Deal in this new century. Decisions that affect the quality of our lives and well-being cannot be left to remote global institutions that have historically suffered from a lack of transparency and accountability. Democratizing global governance is key to the success of the Global New Deal.

The sole mention of NGOs in the UN Charter is a single sentence in article 71 concerning the operations of the Economic and Social Council. The founders of the UN intended the organization to be a forum for sovereign states and never envisaged a central role for individuals from civil society operating through NGOs and transnational networks. Yet, through a focus on universal and timeless values combined with hard work and dedication, NGOs were able to overcome this statist bias and open up international organizations to new levels of public accountability. In addition, NGOs have developed alternative perspectives on global governance that often challenge the status quo and raise the concerns of the vulnerable and powerless.

By the 1990s, strong transnational organizations and movements for social justice, human rights, and ecological balance had emerged. It is thus impossible to really understand international relations today without analyzing the work and impact of these NGOs. According to the Brussels-based Union of International Organizations, there are now more than 24,000 NGOs operating across international borders.[62] NGO scholars estimate that half of all international social change NGOs work on three central issues: human rights, the environment, and women's rights.[63] These new global actors have fundamentally changed the fabric of international politics. They provide a vehicle for increasing public participation in global governance.

NGOs have joined together in powerful transnational networks and participated actively in all the major UN conferences in the last decade on the environment, human rights, population, women, cities, and racism. Individuals and NGOs were instrumental in the initiation, promotion, and adoption of the 1997 Ottawa treaty that banned antipersonnel land mines and the 1998 agreement in Rome to create a UN International Criminal Court. Working from the bottom up, national, transnational, and global NGOs can bring about fundamental change in international relations.

There are a myriad of initiatives in civil society relevant to the concerns of the Global New Deal (see Pivotal NGOs Working on Economic and Social Human Rights: Building Democratic Participation in chapter 3). Individual and transnational NGOs are already working for many of the proposals of the Global New Deal, such as the twenty-twenty proposal, the Tobin Tax, and a WEO.

This active popular support for these initiatives is central to their eventual adoption. In fact, the institutional and procedural changes at the global level proposed in the Global New Deal depend on broad widespread support among people in all nations, in all races, and in all classes. It is only with such support that these initiatives will be adopted. And it is only with the active involvement of global civil society that global institutions will be held accountable to implement and uphold the Global New Deal program of reform.

Final Thoughts

At the beginning of this book, I quoted a student of mine who wanted to believe in the possibility of a world based on human rights, peace, and ecological balance, but given current arrangements of economic and political power, he just didn't "honestly see how we can make the jump from here to there." *The Global New Deal* was written to articulate a first step on the path from here to there. I hope that the feasible alternatives for global humane governance are now clearer to my student and to all who are infected with "realist" pessimism. We no longer need to accept needless suffering. The public policy proposals of the Global New Deal illustrate that there are alternatives; the human community does have options. There is nothing preordained by either the structure of the international system of states or the economic system of the market that makes economic and social human rights a dream. They are not a utopian fantasy. They can be achieved. The question is: Do we have the courage to walk this path?

Notes

Chapter 1

1. World Bank, *World Development Report 2000/2001: Attacking Poverty* (New York: Oxford University Press, 2001), 3.

2. UN Development Program (UNDP), *Human Development Report 2000* (New York: Oxford University Press, 2000), 8.

3. The phrase "there is no alternative" has been attributed to Margaret Thatcher. See Douglas H. Boucher, *The Paradox of Plenty: Hunger in a Bountiful World* (Oakland, Calif.: Food First, 1999), 274. Pundits now refer to the phrase "there is no alternative" as "TINA."

4. Barbara Crossette, "What It Takes to Stop Slavery," *New York Times*, 22 April 2001, 5(4).

5. Barry Bearak, "Lives Held Cheap in Bangladesh Sweatshops," *New York Times*, 15 April 2001, 1(1). In an earlier era, such economic exploitation was called "imperialism," now it is called "globalization." Economist William K. Tabb provides a clear explanation of imperialism: "Imperialism is not simply about territorial acquisition, but more broadly involves gaining political and economic control over other peoples and lands, whether by military force or more subtle means. It is a matter of state policy and practice extending power and domination, often by economic means." See William K. Tabb, *The Amoral Elephant: Globalization and the Struggle for Social Justice in the Twenty-First Century* (New York: Monthly Review, 2001), 80.

6. Elisabeth Rosenthal, "Without 'Barefoot Doctors,' China's Rural Families Suffer," *New York Times*, 14 March 2001, 1(A).

7. Anthony DePalma, "Nafta's Powerful Little Secret," *New York Times*, 11 March 2001, 1(3).

8. Elizabeth Olson, "Nations Cutting Aid to the Jobless, Study Says," *New York Times*, 22 June 2000, 4(C).

9. Rachel Swarns, "Drug Makers Drop South Africa Suit over AIDS Medicine," *New York Times*, 20 April 2001, 1(A).

10. Melody Petersen, "Lifting the Curtain on the Real Costs of Making AIDS Drugs," *New York Times*, 24 April 2001, 1(C).

11. See Note to the Reader on Terminology and Acronyms in this book. Throughout the book, I will refer to each of the treaties and their relevant committees by subject matter. Thus, the International Covenant on Economic, Social and Cultural Rights becomes the Economic Rights Treaty and the committee established under it becomes the Economic Rights Committee. Hopefully, this language will be more accessible than the use of the standard UN acronyms to refer to the treaty and committee (CESCR and CESCR Committee). Thus, the International Convention on the Elimination of All Forms of Racial Discrimination becomes the Minority Rights Treaty and the committee established under it becomes the Minority Rights Committee, and so on.

12. UNDP, *Human Development Report 1996* (New York: Oxford University Press, 1996), 27.

13. Joel Cohen, *How Many People Can the Earth Support?* (New York: Norton, 1995), 54.

14. See Douglas Boucher, ed., *The Paradox of Plenty* (Oakland, Calif.: Food First, 1999); Partha Dasgupta, *An Inquiry into Well-Being and Destitution* (New York: Oxford University Press, 1993); *Poverty and Hunger: Issues and Options for Food Security in Developing Countries* (Washington, D.C.: World Bank, 1986); The Hunger Project, *Ending Hunger: An Idea Whose Time Has Come* (New York: Praeger, 1985).

15. For example, see the following suggestions: Richard Falk and Andrew Strauss's proposal for a "Global Parliament" in their "Toward a Global Parliament," *Foreign Affairs* 80, no. 1 (January–February 2001): 212–218; Richard Falk's outline for "Global Humane Governance" in his *On Humane Governance* (University Park: Pennsylvania State University Press, 1995); Al Gore's proposal for "A Global Marshall Plan" in his *Earth in the Balance: Ecology and the Human Spirit* (New York: Penguin, 1992); Mark Hertsgaard's plea for a "Global Green Deal" in his *Earth Odyssey: Around the World in Search of Our Environmental Future* (New York: Broadway, 1998).

16. See the chapter "The Morality of the Depths: The Right to Development As an Emerging Principle of International Law," in William F. Felice, *Taking Suffering Seriously: The Importance of Collective Human Rights* (Albany: SUNY Press, 1996), 69–90.

Chapter 2

1. Milton Friedman, *Capitalism and Freedom* (1962; reprint, Chicago: University of Chicago Press, 1982); James Caporaso and David Levine, *Theories of Political Economy* (New York: Cambridge University Press, 1992), 33–54; Dudley Dillard, "Capitalism," in *The Political Economy of Development and Underdevelopment,* ed. Charles Wilber and Kenneth Jameson (New York: McGraw-Hill, 1992), 85–93.

2. Dillard, "Capitalism," 88; see also P. T. Bauer, *Equality: The Third World and Economic Delusion* (Cambridge, Mass.: Harvard University Press, 1981).

3. Michael Joseph Smith, *Realist Thought from Weber to Kissinger* (Baton Rouge: Louisiana State University Press, 1986), 103.

4. Smith, *Realist Thought,* 99–133. Smith's chapter on Reinhold Niebuhr, "The Prophetic Realism of Reinhold Niebuhr," is exceptionally valuable.

5. See Jennifer L. Hochschild, *Facing up to the American Dream: Race, Class, and the Soul of the Nation* (Princeton, N.J.: Princeton University Press, 1996).

6. In a "perfect" market, a unique price for each good will arise out of all welfare-improving transactions. This price is a result of independent and voluntary actions of individuals pursuing the maximization of individual private satisfaction. If prices are free to respond to these independent actions, they will tend to settle at levels that allow for maximum welfare-improving transactions. The "free market" thus yields an optimum of social welfare. This type of group welfare has been termed "Pareto optimum" after its discoverer Vilfredo Pareto. See Caporaso and Levine, *Theories of Political Economy*, 82–83.

7. See Friedrich A. von Hayek, *The Road to Serfdom* (1944; reprint, Chicago: University of Chicago Press, 1994).

8. Robert Skidelsky, "Keynes's Middle Way," in *Readings in International Political Economy*, ed. David Balaam and Michael Veseth (Upper Saddle River, N.J.: Prentice Hall, 1996), 45–54.

9. Skidelsky, "Keynes's Middle Way," 49–50.

10. Mel Gurtov provides a useful and interesting comparison of realists and "corporate globalists." See Mel Gurtov, *Global Politics in the Human Interest*, 4th ed. (Boulder, Colo.: Rienner, 1999), 23.

11. Gurtov, *Global Politics*, 46–55.

12. Joel Cohen, *How Many People Can the Earth Support?* (New York: Norton, 1995), 272.

13. John Madeley, *Big Business, Poor Peoples: The Impact of Transnational Corporations on the World's Poor* (London: Zed, 1999), 72.

14. See Stanley Hoffmann, *World Disorders: Troubled Peace in the Post Cold War Era* (Lanham, Md.: Rowman and Littlefield, 1998), 108–122.

15. See Bertell Ollman, *Alienation: Marx's Conception of Man in Capitalist Society* (New York: Cambridge University Press, 1971), 73–84.

16. See William F. Felice, *Taking Suffering Seriously: The Importance of Collective Human Rights* (Albany: SUNY Press, 1996), 131–150.

17. André Gunder Frank, *Capitalism and Underdevelopment in Latin America* (New York: Monthly Review, 1967); André Gunder Frank, *Latin America: Underdevelopment or Revolution* (New York: Monthly Review, 1969).

18. Samir Amin, *Delinking: Towards a Polycentric World* (London: Zed, 1985); Samir Amin, *Maldevelopment: Anatomy of a Global Failure* (London: Zed, 1990).

19. Paul Samuelson, "The Pure Theory of Public Expenditure," *Review of Economics and Statistics* (November 1954): 387–389.

20. For a clear explanation of "nonexcludability" and "nonrivalrous consumption," see Inge Kaul, Isabelle Grunberg, and Marc A. Stern, eds., *Global Public Goods: International Cooperation in the 21st Century* (New York: Oxford University Press, 1999), 2–16.

21. Adam Smith, *The Wealth of Nations* (Indianapolis, Ind.: Liberty Classics, 1976), 723.

22. Kaul, Grunberg, and Stern, *Global Public Goods*, 509.

23. Kaul, Grunberg, and Stern, *Global Public Goods*, xx.

24. See Garrett Hardin, "The Tragedy of the Commons," *Science* 162 (13 December 1968).

25. Kaul, Grunberg, and Stern, *Global Public Goods*, 16.

26. Kaul, Grunberg, and Stern, *Global Public Goods,* 24–25, 454–455.

27. For example, see Robert Taylor, "Economics, Ecology, and Exchange: Free Market Environmentalism," *Humane Studies Review* 8, no. 1 (Fall 1992).

28. Partha Dasgupta, *An Inquiry into Well-Being and Destitution* (New York: Oxford University Press, 1993), 530, 540.

29. Dasgupta, *Inquiry into Well-Being,* 144.

30. Dasgupta, *Inquiry into Well-Being,* 149.

31. Dasgupta, *Inquiry into Well-Being,* 40, 54.

32. Robert O'Brien et al., *Contesting Global Governance: Multilateral Economic Institutions and Global Social Movements* (Cambridge: Cambridge University Press, 2000), 6–9.

33. For an astute analysis of the applicability of human rights law to international financial institutions, see Sigrun Skogly, *The Human Rights Obligations of the World Bank and the International Monetary Fund* (London: Cavendish, 2001).

34. James N. Rosenau, *Turbulence in World Politics* (Princeton, N.J.: Princeton University Press, 1990), 10.

35. James N. Rosenau, *Along the Domestic–Foreign Frontier: Exploring Governance in a Turbulent World* (Cambridge: Cambridge University Press, 1997), 38.

36. See Ed McCaughan, "Globalization, National Culture, and Left Discourse in Mexico" (unpublished manuscript, 1996), 4–5; see also Immanuel Wallerstein, "The Collapse of Liberalism," in *New World Order?: Socialist Register 1992,* ed. Ralph Miliband and Leo Panitich (London: Merlin, 1992), 96–110.

37. The terminology of IPE can be baffling, as the word "liberal" has many meanings. With their solid support of market principles of efficiency, both political conservatives and political liberals are classical economic "liberals." Political conservatives promote "laissez-faire liberalism," which champions minimal governmental interference in the market. Political liberals argue for "welfare-state liberalism," which implies more involvement by the government in the economy.

38. For example, UN Charter article 2(7): "Nothing contained in the present Charter shall authorize the United Nations to intervene in matters which are essentially within the domestic jurisdiction of any State or shall require the Members to submit such matters to settlement under the present Charter."

39. UN Development Program (UNDP), *Human Development Report 1997* (New York: Oxford University Press, 1997), 62.

40. UNDP, *Human Development Report 1997,* 9.

41. UNDP, *Human Development Report 1997,* 9.

42. UNDP, *Human Development Report 1997,* 9. "Commodity terms of trade" refers to the relationship between the prices a nation gets for its exports and the prices it pays for its imports. "An *improvement* in a nation's terms of trade requires that the price of its exports rise relative to the prices of its imports over the given time period. A smaller number of export goods sold abroad is required to obtain a given number of imports. Conversely, a *deterioration* in a nation's terms of trade is due to a rise in its import prices relative to its export prices over a time period. The purchase of a given number of imports would require the sacrifice of a greater number of exports." See Robert J. Carbaugh, *International Economics* (Cincinnati, Ohio: South-Western College Publishing, 1995), 63.

43. UNDP, *Human Development Report 1997,* 9.

44. Jose Bengoa, "The Silence of the Innocent: The Rights of the Poor and Excluded," *Social Development Review* 2, no. 3 (September 1998): 4–5.

45. Statement by the Committee on Economic, Social and Cultural Rights, "Globalization and Economic, Social and Cultural Rights" (May 1998), at www.unhchr.ch/html/menu2/6/cescrnote#note18b (accessed 14 July 2001).

46. Richard Jolly, "Profiles in Success: Reasons for Hope and Priorities for Action," in *Development with a Human Face: Experiences in Social Achievement and Economic Growth*, ed. Santosh Mehrotra and Richard Jolly (Oxford: Clarendon, 1997), 8.

47. See UNDP, *Human Development Report 2000* (New York: Oxford University Press, 2000), 147–155.

48. Paul Streeten et al., *First Things First: Meeting Basic Needs in Developing Countries* (New York: Oxford University Press, 1981).

49. Santosh Mehrotra, "Social Development in High-Achieving Countries: Common Elements and Diversities," in *Development with a Human Face*, ed. Santosh Mehrotra and Richard Jolly (Oxford: Clarendon, 1997), 29.

50. Mehrotra, "Social Development," 32.

51. Amartya Sen, "Agency and Well-Being: The Development Agenda," in *A Commitment to the World's Women: Perspectives on Development for Beijing and Beyond*, ed. Noeleen Heyzer with Sushma Kapoor and Joanne Sandler (New York: UN Development Fund for Women, 1995).

52. Mehrotra, "Social Development," 40.

53. Mehrotra, "Social Development," 41.

54. Mehrotra, "Social Development," 48; see also William F. Felice, "Militarism and Human Rights," *International Affairs* 74, no. 1 (January 1998).

55. Mehrotra, "Social Development," 49.

56. Instituto Del Tercer Mundo, *Social Watch Report No 2* (Montevideo, Uruguay: Instituto Del Tercer Mundo, 1998).

57. Instituto Del Tercer Mundo, *Social Watch*, 33.

58. Constanza Moreira, "Strategies in the Struggle against Poverty: A Comparative Approach," in *Social Watch Report No 2*, by Instituto Del Tercer Mundo (Montevideo, Uruguay: Instituto Del Tercer Mundo, 1998), 35.

59. See Amartya Sen, *Inequality Reexamined* (Cambridge, Mass.: Harvard University Press, 1992).

60. See Robert Nozick, "Distributive Justice," *Philosophy and Public Affairs* 3 (1973); Robert Nozick, *Anarchy, State and Utopia* (New York: Basic, 1974).

61. See John Rawls, *A Theory of Justice* (Cambridge, Mass.: Harvard University Press, 1971).

62. See Karl Marx, *Critique of the Gotha Program* (1891; reprint, New York: International, 1977).

63. For example, see conservative economist P. T. Bauer's rejection of the "unholy grail of equality" in Bauer, *Equality*.

64. Cohen, *How Many People*, 293.

65. Amartya Sen, *Development As Freedom* (New York: Knopf, 1999), 108.

66. John Arthur and William Shaw, "What Is Justice," in *Poverty Amidst Plenty: World Political Economy and Distributive Justice*, ed. Edward Weisband (Boulder, Colo.: Westview, 1989), 26–27.

67. David Beetham, "What Future for Economic and Social Rights," in *Politics and Human Rights*, ed. David Beetham (Oxford: Blackwell, 1995), 46.

68. Beetham, "What Future," 47.

69. Henry Shue, *Basic Rights: Subsistence, Affluence and US Foreign Policy* (Princeton, N.J.: Princeton University Press, 1980), 27.

70. Shue, *Basic Rights*, 32.

71. Rosa Luxemburg, *The National Question and Autonomy* (1909), reprinted in Micheline R. Ishay, ed., *The Human Rights Reader: Major Political Essays, Speeches, and Documents from the Bible to the Present* (New York: Routledge, 1997), 290–299.

72. Asbjørn Eide, "Realization of Social and Economic Rights and the Minimum Threshold Approach," in *Human Rights and the World Community*, ed. Richard Claude and Burns Weston (Philadelphia: University of Pennsylvania Press, 1992), 159–169. Eide argues that a state's obligation to fulfill the expectations of all for the enjoyment of the right to food may take two forms: "[A]ssistance in order to provide *opportunities* for those who have not; direct *provisions* of food or resources which can be used for food (direct food aid, or social security) when no other possibility exists, for example, (1) when unemployment sets in (such as under recession); (2) for the disadvantaged and the elderly; (3) during sudden situations of crisis or disaster . . . , and (4) for those who are marginalized (e.g., due to structural transformations in the economy and production)."

73. 1 Thess. 3:10, quoted in Sen, *Inequality Reexamined*, 77.

74. UNDP, *Human Development Report 1996* (New York: Oxford University Press, 1996), 52–54.

75. Sen states: "Egalitarian policies to undo the inequalities associated with human diversity are much less problematic from the point of view of incentives than policies to undo inequality arising from differences in effort and application, on which much of the incentive literature has tended to focus. Thus, the importance of human diversity in inequality evaluation . . . may also have some considerable bearing on the nature and force of the incentive problem in pursuing egalitarian policy (particularly in the context of moving towards less inequality of elementary capabilities). This is not a trivial issue, in so far as antecedent diversities (e.g. in gender, age, class) are among the central factors behind unequal freedoms that people have in the world in which we live." See Sen, *Inequality Reexamined*, 143.

76. See Eide, "Realization of Social and Economic Rights," 163.

77. "The Limburg Principles on the Implementation of the International Covenant on Economic, Social and Cultural Rights," UN Doc. E/CN.4/1987/17, Annex, comprising 1–103, which were agreed on by the twenty-nine participants of the symposium held from 2–6 June 1986 at the University of Limburg, Maastricht, Netherlands.

78. John Kenneth Galbraith, *Economic Development* (Cambridge, Mass.: Harvard University Press, 1964).

79. Mary Robinson, "Development and Rights: The Undeniable Nexus," UN Office of the High Commissioner for Human Rights, 26 June 2000.

80. UNDP, *Human Development Report 2000*, 20.

81. Sen, *Inequality Reexamined*, 4–5, 39.

82. Sen, *Inequality Reexamined*, 49, 81.

83. Sen, *Inequality Reexamined*, 81–82.

84. Sen, *Inequality Reexamined*, 33, 38.

85. Sen, *Inequality Reexamined*, 151.

86. Sen notes, for example, that the capability deprivation of African Americans cannot be explained solely through an examination of income figures. It is rather the result of a variety of factors, including problems of health care, education, and urban crime. Residents of Harlem have a higher income than the average Bangladeshi citizen. Yet, according to the *New England Journal of Medicine*, men in the Harlem region of rich New York City have less of a chance to reach the age of forty than Bangladeshi men. Information on incomes doesn't explain this phenomena. Nor does it explain for the country as a whole why African Americans in the age group thirty-five to fifty-five have 2.3 times the mortality rate as do whites in the United States. Low income is just one factor among many explaining these conditions. Sen points to other aspects of the social environment, including the inadequacy of health facilities, the violent modes of inner-city living, and the absence of social care. See Sen, *Inequality Reexamined*, 114–115.

87. Sen, *Development As Freedom*, 20–21.

88. Sen, *Development As Freedom*, 3.

Chapter 3

1. See the chapter "The Morality of the Depths: The Right to Development As an Emerging Principle of International Law," in William F. Felice, *Taking Suffering Seriously: The Importance of Collective Human Rights* (Albany: SUNY Press, 1996), 69–90.

2. The International Bill of Human Rights encompasses the Universal Declaration of Human Rights, the International Covenant on Civil and Political Rights (Political Rights Treaty), and the International Covenant on Economic, Social and Cultural Rights (Economic Rights Treaty).

3. Julia Hausermann, "The Realisation and Implementation of Economic, Social and Cultural Rights," in *Economic, Social and Cultural Rights: Progress and Achievement*, ed. Ralph Beddard and Dilys M. Hill (New York: St. Martin's, 1992), 49.

4. Kathryn S. Fuller, "Balancing Trade and Sea Turtles," *International Herald Tribune*, 16–17 May 1998.

5. The 1998 WTO Appellate Body ruling in the shrimp–turtle case, however, may have opened a door linking trade and environmental protection in the future. Article 20 of the General Agreement on Tariffs and Trade allows for certain environmental exceptions to trade rules. Traditionally, environmental laws that protected the environment outside the enacting country's borders had been ruled out. The 1998 ruling may have changed this by requiring merely a "sufficient nexus" between the law and the environment of the enacting state. Thus, transboundary impacts on air and water and on endangered and migratory species might provide such a nexus. See UN Environment Program, *Environment and Trade: A Handbook* (Winnipeg, Canada: International Institute for Sustainable Development, 2000), 30.

6. Address by President Bill Clinton to the World Trade Organization, Geneva, Switzerland, 18 May 1998.

7. As I mentioned in Note to the Reader on Terminology and Acronyms, throughout the book I will refer to each of the main treaties and their relevant committees discussed in the book by subject matter. Thus, the International Covenant on Economic, Social and Cultural Rights becomes the Economic Rights

Treaty and the committee established under it becomes the Economic Rights Committee.

8. For a comprehensive overview of the UN's approach to economic and social rights, see Scott Leckie, "Another Step towards Indivisibility: Identifying the Key Features of Violations of Economic, Social and Cultural Rights," *Human Rights Quarterly* 20, no. 1 (1998).

9. An emerging approach to international relations theory is called "constructivism." Constructivists examine how language is used to "construct" the social world. The social construction of legal rules and norms (like human rights laws and norms) are a particular focus due to their mediating role between people and society. See John Gerard Ruggie, *Constructing the World Polity: Essays on International Institutionalization* (New York: Routledge, 1998).

10. Virginia A. Leary, "The Paradox of Workers' Rights As Human Rights," in *Human Rights, Labor Rights, and International Trade,* ed. Lance A. Compa and Stephen F. Diamond (Philadelphia: University of Pennsylvania Press, 1996), 28. It is notable that the United States has ratified only one of the ILO's basic human rights conventions: Convention no. 105 on the Abolition of Forced Labor.

11. Paul Hunt, *Reclaiming Social Rights: International and Comparative Perspectives* (Hants, England: Dartmouth, 1996), 2.

12. Asbjørn Eide, "Economic, Social and Cultural Rights As Human Rights," in *Economic, Social and Cultural Rights: A Textbook,* ed. Asbjørn Eide, Catarina Krause, and Allan Rosas (Dordrecht, Netherlands: Kluwer Academic, 1995), 31.

13. See Center for Economic and Social Rights, "Economic, Social and Cultural Rights: A Guide to the Legal Framework" (January 2000): 6, at www.cesr.org/text%20files/escrguide.PDF (accessed 15 July 2001).

14. Eide, "Economic, Social and Cultural Rights."

15. "The Limburg Principles on the Implementation of the International Covenant on Economic, Social and Cultural Rights," UN ESCOR, Commission on Human Rights, 43rd sess., Agenda Item 8, UN Doc. E/CN.4/1987/17/Annex (1987), reprinted in "The Limburg Principles on the Implementation of the International Covenant on Economic, Social and Cultural Rights," *Human Rights Quarterly* 9, no. 2 (1987): 122–135.

16. "The Maastricht Guidelines on Violations of Economic, Social and Cultural Rights," *Human Rights Quarterly* 20, no. 3 (1998): 691–704.

17. See Danilo Turk, Special Rapporteur of the Sub-commission on Prevention of Discrimination and Protection of Minorities, "The Full Realization of Economic, Social and Cultural Rights (Final Report)," UN ESCOR, Commission on Human Rights, 48th sess., Agenda Item 8, UN Doc. E/CN.4/Sub.2/1992/16 (1992); Vienna Declaration and Programme of Action, UN GAOR, World Conference on Human Rights, 48th sess., 22d plenipotentiary meeting, UN Doc. A/CONF.157/24 (1993); "UN Seminar on Appropriate Indicators to Measure Achievements in the Progressive Realization of Economic, Social and Cultural Rights," UN GAOR, World Conference on Human Rights, 4th sess., Provisional Agenda Item 6, UN Doc. A/CONF.157/PC/73 (1993).

18. "Maastricht Guidelines," 692.

19. Henry Shue, *Basic Rights: Subsistence, Affluence, and U.S. Foreign Policy* (Princeton, N.J.: Princeton University Press, 1980).

20. "Center for Human Rights, Right to Adequate Food As a Human Right," UN Doc. E/CN.4/Sub.2/1987/23, UN Sales no. E.89.Xiv.2 (1989).

21. "Maastricht Guidelines," 693–694.

22. "Maastricht Guidelines," 694.

23. "Maastricht Guidelines," 697.

24. "Maastricht Guidelines," 696.

25. See Philip Alston, "The Committee on Economic, Social and Cultural Rights," in *The United Nations and Human Rights*, ed. Philip Alston (New York: Oxford University Press, 1992), 473–475.

26. See Matthew Craven, *The International Covenant on Economic, Social, and Cultural Rights: A Perspective on Its Development* (Oxford: Clarendon, 1995).

27. The United States has not ratified the First Optional Protocol to the Political Rights Treaty.

28. UN Educational, Scientific, and Cultural Organization (UNESCO), *Human Rights, Major International Instruments: Status As at 31 May 2001* (Paris: UN Educational, Scientific, and Cultural Organization, 2001), 20.

29. Office of the United Nations High Commissioner for Human Rights (OHCHR), *Human Rights*, no. 2 (Spring 1998): 13.

30. Mercedes Morales, Human Rights Officer, OHCHR, interview by author, Geneva, Switzerland, 22 May 1998.

31. OHCHR, *Human Rights*, 15–16.

32. OHCHR, *Human Rights*, 16.

33. UNESCO, *Human Rights, Major International Instruments*, 20.

34. Louis Henkin, *The Age of Rights* (New York: Columbia University Press, 1990), 33.

35. Henry J. Steiner and Philip Alston, *International Human Rights in Context* (Oxford: Clarendon, 1996), 316.

36. Craven, *International Covenant*, 104.

37. Philip Alston, "Out of the Abyss: The Challenges Confronting the New UN Committee on Economic, Social and Cultural Rights," *Human Rights Quarterly* 9 (1987): 352.

38. Vienna Declaration and Programme of Action, adopted by the UN World Conference on Human Rights, 25 June 1993, UN Doc. A/CONF.157/24; reprinted in 32 ILM 1661 (1993), see paragraph 5.

39. Abdullahi Ahmed An-Na'im, *Human Rights in Cross-cultural Perspectives: A Quest for Consensus* (Philadelphia: University of Pennsylvania Press, 1992), 5.

40. International Conference on Popular Participation in the Recovery and Development Process in Africa, *African Charter for Popular Participation in Development and Transformation* (Arusha, Tanzania, 1990) E/ECA/CM.16/11/Corr. 1.

41. UNDP, *Human Development Report 1997* (New York: Oxford University Press, 1997), 16.

42. UNDP, *Human Development Report 1996* (New York: Oxford University Press, 1996), 27.

43. UNDP, *Human Development Report 1996*, 27–28.

44. UNDP, *Human Development Report 1997*, 18.

45. UNDP, *Human Development Report 2000* (New York: Oxford University Press, 2000), 147.

46. UNDP, *Human Development Report 2000*, 147.

47. UNDP, *Human Development Report 2000*, 150–151.

48. UNDP, *Human Development Report 2000*, 151.

49. UNDP, *Human Development Report 2000*, 151, 157–158.

50. UNDP, *Human Development Report 2000*, 159–150, 170–171.

51. UNDP, *Human Development Report 2000*, 152.

52. UNDP, *Human Development Report 2000*, 153.

53. Virginia Dandan, Chairperson of the Committee on Economic, Social and Cultural Rights, interview by author, Geneva, Switzerland, 7 June 2000.

54. Dandan interview.

55. Dandan interview.

56. Dandan interview.

57. Dandan interview.

58. Scott Leckie, "The Committee on Economic, Social and Cultural Rights: Catalyst for Change in a System Needing Reform," in *The Future of UN Human Rights Treaty Monitoring*, ed. Philip Alston and James Crawford (Cambridge: Cambridge University Press, 2000), 134. Examples of NGO reports that have been strongly reflected in the concluding observations adopted by the Economic Rights Committee include: "A Report to the UN Committee on Economic, Social and Cultural Rights on Housing Rights Violations and the Poverty Problem in Hong Kong" (November 1994), prepared by the Society for Community Organisation and the Hong Kong Human Rights Commission; "Housing for All? Implementation of the Right to Adequate Housing for the Arab Palestinian Minority in Israel: A Report for the UN Committee on Economic, Social and Cultural Rights on the Implementation of Article 11(1) of the UN Covenant on Economic, Social and Cultural Rights" (April 1996), prepared by the Arab Coordinating Committee on Housing Rights, Israel (ACCHRI); and "El Derecho a la Vivienda en Mexico" (March 1994), prepared by Casa y Ciudad, Cenvi, Copevi and Fosovi.

59. Kitty Arambulo Wilson, Human Rights Officer, OHCHR, interview by author, Geneva, Switzerland, 9 June 2000.

60. Dandan interview.

61. Philippines, UN Doc. E/C.12/1995/18; Belgium, UN Doc. E/C.12/1994/20, quoted in Leckie, "The Committee on Economic, Social and Cultural Rights," 136–137.

62. Committee on Economic, Social and Cultural Rights, "Globalization and Economic, Social and Cultural Rights" (May 1998), reprinted in Economic Rights Committee, "Note on the Eighteenth Session" (27 April–15 May 1998), at www.unhchr.ch/html/menu2/6/EconomicRightsTreatynote.htm#note18th (accessed 16 July 2001).

63. Committee on Economic, Social and Cultural Rights, "Statement of the UN Economic Rights Treaty Committee to the Third Ministerial Conference of the World Trade Organization (Seattle, 30 November to 3 December 1999)," UN Doc. E/C.12/1999/9 (26 November 1999).

64. Dandan interview.

65. World Bank, *World Development Report 2000/2001: Attacking Poverty* (New York: Oxford University Press, 2001), 15.

66. Committee on Economic, Social and Cultural Rights, "Globalization and Economic, Social and Cultural Rights."

67. For example, see Sarah Anderson, ed., *Views from the South: The Effects of Globalization and the WTO on Third World Countries* (Oakland, Calif.: Institute for Food and Development Policy, 2000).

68. Arambulo Wilson interview.

69. Dandan interview.

70. Committee on Economic, Social and Cultural Rights, "The Incorporation of Economic, Social and Cultural Rights into the United Nations Development Assistance Framework (UNDAF) Process" (15 May 1998), at www.unhchr.ch/html/menu2/6/EconomicRightsTreatynote.htm#note18th (accessed 16 July 2001).

71. See United Nations, "Guidelines: Common Country Assessment (CCA)" (April 1999); United Nations, "Guidelines: United Nations Development Assistance Framework (UNDAF)" (April 1999).

72. UN High Commissioner for Human Rights, Research and Right to Development Branch, "Note on the United Nations Development Assistance Framework (UNDAF) Process (draft)" (May 2000).

73. United Nations, "Guidelines," 17–21.

74. Sylvie Saddier, Human Rights Officer, Research and Right to Development Branch, OHCHR, interview by author, Geneva, Switzerland, 8 June 2000.

75. These examples are from an internal OHCHR review of CCA and UNDAF country team documents.

76. Saddier interview.

77. UNDP–OHCHR, *Human Rights Strengthening–HURIST, Program Document.*

78. Saddier interview.

79. Stefanie Grant, Chief, Research and Right to Development Branch, OHCHR, interview by author, Geneva, Switzerland, 8 June 2000.

80. OHCHR, Fact Sheet no. 16 (Rev. 1), "The Committee on Economic, Social and Cultural Rights," 22, at www.unhchr.ch/html/menu6/2/fs16.htm (accessed 11 March 2001). For a comprehensive and thoughtful critique of the proposal for an individual complaint procedure for the Economic Rights Committee, see Kitty Arambulo, *Strengthening the Supervision of the International Covenant on Economic, Social and Cultural Rights: Theoretical and Procedural Aspects* (Antwerpen: Intersentia, 1999).

81. Vienna Declaration and Programme of Action, adopted by the UN World Conference on Human Rights, 25 June 1993, UN Doc. A/CONF.157/24; reprinted in 32 ILM 1661 (1993), see paragraph 75.

82. The Netherlands Institute of Human Rights published the proceedings of the Expert Meeting on the Adoption of an Optional Protocol to the Economic Rights Treaty. See Fons Coomans and Fried van Hoof, eds., *The Right to Complain about Economic, Social and Cultural Human Rights* (Utrecht: Netherlands Institute of Human Rights, 1995).

83. Commission on Human Rights, "Draft Optional Protocol to the International Covenant on Economic, Social and Cultural Rights," UN Doc. E/CN.4/1997/105 (18 December 1996): 4–5.

84. Arambulo Wilson interview; Dandan interview.

85. Erika de Wet, "Labor Standards in the Globalized Economy: The Inclusion of a Social Clause in the General Agreement on Tariff and Trade/World Trade Organization," *Human Rights Quarterly* 17, no. 3 (1995): 450.

86. de Wet, "Labor Standards," 453.

87. Population Council, "Female Garment Workers Study in Bangladesh," New York: Population Council (1998): 1–8.

88. Population Council, "Female Garment Workers."

89. For a useful and thorough analysis of these issues, see David M. Smolin, "Strategic Choices in the International Campaign against Child Labor," *Human Rights Quarterly* 22, no. 4 (2000): 942–987.

90. Dan Cunniah, "The Dangers of Complacency in the Face of a Global Social Crisis," *Social Development Review* 2, no. 2 (June 1998): 18.

91. Stephen Herzenberg, "In from the Margins: Morality, Economics, and International Labor Rights," in *Human Rights, Labor Rights and International Trade,* ed. Lance A. Compa and Stephen F. Diamond (Philadelphia: University of Pennsylvania Press, 1996), 100–101, 108.

92. Denis MacShane, "Human Rights and Labor Rights: A European Perspective," in *Human Rights, Labor Rights, and International Trade,* ed. Lance Compa and Stephen Diamond (Philadelphia: University of Pennsylvania Press, 1996), 52.

93. See "The Social Clause—No Panacea for Workers' Rights," in UNDP, *Human Development Report 2000,* 85.

Chapter 4

1. Antonio Augusto Cançado Trindade, "Human Rights and the Environment," in *Human Rights: New Dimensions and Challenges,* ed. Janusz Symonides (Paris: UN Educational, Scientific, and Cultural Organization, 1998), 118.

2. Craig S. Smith, "150 Nations Start Groundwork for Global Warming Policies," *New York Times,* 18 January 2001, 7(A).

3. Bill McKibben, "Too Hot to Handle," *New York Times,* 5 January 2001, 17(A).

4. Maarten Hajer and Frank Fischer, "Beyond Global Discourse: The Rediscovery of Culture in Environmental Politics," in *Living with Nature: Environmental Politics As Cultural Discourse,* ed. Maarten Hajer and Frank Fischer (New York: Oxford University Press, 1999), 1–2.

5. Kofi Annan, "We the Peoples: The Role of the United Nations in the 21st Century" (2000), at www.un.org/millennium/sg/ (accessed 19 June 2001).

6. Aaron Sachs, *Eco-Justice: Linking Human Rights and the Environment, World-Watch Paper 127* (Washington, D.C.: Worldwatch Institute, 1995).

7. Michael R. Anderson, "Human Rights Approaches to Environmental Protection: An Overview," in *Human Rights Approaches to Environmental Protection,* ed. Alan E. Boyle and Michael R. Anderson (New York.: Oxford University Press, 1996), 1–4.

8. The International Bill of Human Rights encompasses the Universal Declaration of Human Rights, the International Covenant on Civil and Political Rights (Political Rights Treaty), and the International Covenant on Economic, Social and Cultural Rights (Economic Rights Treaty).

9. African Charter on Human and Peoples' Rights, Banjul, 26 June 1981, entered into force 21 October 1986, OAU Doc. CAB/LEG/67/3 Rev. 5.

10. Robin Churchill, "Environmental Rights in Existing Human Rights Treaties," in *Human Rights Approaches to Environmental Protections,* ed. Alan E. Boyle and Michael R. Anderson (New York: Oxford University Press, 1966), 105–107.

11. Additional Protocol to the American Convention on Human Rights in the Area of Economic, Social and Cultural Rights, OAS Treaty Series no. 69, reprinted at 28 ILM 156 (1989), enacted at San Salvador in November 1988, at www.oas.org (accessed 19 June 2001).

12. Ratification information is available at the Inter-American Commission on Human Rights, website www.cidh.oas.org/B%E1sicos/basic6.htm (accessed 19 June 2001).

13. Churchill, "Environmental Rights," 99–100.

14. "Convention on the Rights of the Child," UN Doc. A/Res/44/49, at www.unhchr.ch/html/menu3/b/k2crc.htm (accessed 19 June 2001).

15. Antonio Augusto Cançado Trindade, "Human Rights and the Environment," in *Human Rights: New Dimensions and Challenges,* ed. Janusz Symonides (Paris: UN Educational, Scientific, and Cultural Organization, 1998).

16. Extracts of the constitutional provisions on environmental rights and duties are reproduced in Edith Brown Weiss, *In Fairness to Future Generations: International Law, Common Patrimony, and Intergenerational Equity* (Tokyo: United Nations University Press, 1989), 297–327. The constitution of Brazil is on 298.

17. "Stockholm Declaration of the United Nations Conference on the Human Environment," UN Doc. A/CONF.48/14 (16 June 1972), at www.unep.org/ (accessed 19 June 2001).

18. Charter of Economic Rights and Duties of States, adopted by the UN General Assembly, 12 December 1974, GA Res. 3281, UN GAOR, 29th sess., Supp. no. 31, at 50, UN Doc. A/9631 (1975); 14 ILM 251 (1975).

19. UN General Assembly Resolution on a World Charter for Nature, 37 UN GAOR (Supp. no. 51) 17 (28 October 1982).

20. UN General Assembly Resolution 44/228 of 1998.

21. "Agenda 21," UN Doc. A/CONF.151/26, at www.unep.org/ (accessed 19 June 2001).

22. "Vienna Declaration and Programme of Action," 32 ILM 1661 (1993) (see in particular point eleven), at www.unhchr.ch/huridocda/huridoca.nsf/(Symbol)/A.CONF.157.23.En?OpenDocume nt (accessed 19 June 2001).

23. Fatma Zohra Ksentini, "Human Rights and the Environment," Final Report of the Special Rapporteur, UN Doc. E/CH.4Sub.21994/9 (6 July 1994).

24. Draft Principles on Human Rights and the Environment, UN Commission on Human Rights, Sub-commission on Prevention of Discrimination and Protection of Minorities, Final Report of the Special Rapporteur, UN Doc. E/CN.4/Sub.2/1994/9 (6 July 1994).

25. Draft Principles on Human Rights and the Environment.

26. UN General Assembly Resolution 2997 on Institutional and Financial Arrangements for International Environmental Co-Operation, 27 UN GAOR (Supp. no. 30) 43 (15 December 1972).

27. Hilary French, *Vanishing Borders: Protecting the Planet in the Age of Globalization* (New York: Norton, 2000), 157–158.

28. David Hunter, James Salzman, and Durwood Zaelke, *International Environmental Law and Policy* (New York: Foundation, 1998), 395.

29. UN General Assembly Resolution 37/7 on a World Charter for Nature, 37 UN GAOR (Supp. no. 51) 17 (28 October 1982).

30. Declaration of Environmental Policies and Procedures Relating to Eco-

nomic Development, adopted by the African Development Bank, Arab Bank for Economic Development in Africa, Asian Development Bank, Caribbean Development Bank, Inter-American Development Bank, World Bank, Commission of European Communities, Organization of American States, UN Development Program, and UN Environment Program, 1 February 1980, 19 ILM 524 (1980).

31. Alexander Timoshenko and Mark Berman, "The United Nations Environment Programme and the United Nations Development Programme," in *Greening International Institutions*, ed. Jacob Werksman (London: Earthscan Publications, 1996), 40.

32. Philip Shabecoff, *A New Name for Peace: International Environmentalism, Sustainable Development, and Democracy* (Hanover, N.H.: University Press of New England, 1996), 47–49.

33. David L. Downie and Marc A. Levy, "The UN Environment Programme at a Turning Point: Options for Change," in *The Global Environment in the Twenty-First Century: Prospects for International Cooperation*, ed. Pamela S. Chasek (Tokyo: United Nations University Press, 2000), 358.

34. United Nations, "Review and Appraisal of the Implementation of Agenda 21: Contribution of the United Nations Environment Programme to the Special Session," UN Doc. A/S-19/5, section II B (1997), at un.org/00/ga/docs/S-19/plenary/As19-5.EN (accessed 19 June 2001).

35. UN Environment Program, "Implementation by UNEP of Agenda 21: Note by the Executive Director" (prepared for the 19th sess., Nairobi, 17 January–7 February 1997, Item 5 of provisional agenda, "Preparations for the 1997 Review and Appraisal of Agenda 21"), UN Doc. UNEP/GC.19/INF 17, quoted in Downie and Levy, "UN Environment Programme," 360.

36. Downie and Levy, "UN Environment Programme," 366.

37. Chris Mensah, "The United Nations Commission on Sustainable Development," in *Greening International Institutions*, ed. Jacob Werksman (London: Earthscan Publications, 1996), 21.

38. Resolution on Institutional Arrangement to Follow up the United Nations Conference on Environment and Development, UNGA Res. 47/191, GAOR, 47th sess., UN Doc. A/RES/47/191 (1993).

39. UN Department for Policy Coordination and Sustainable Development, "Terms of Reference: Commission on Sustainable Development" (1993), at www.un.org/dpcsd/dsd/csdback.thm (accessed 19 June 2001).

40. Pamela S. Chasek, "The UN Commission on Sustainable Development: The First Five Years," in *The Global Environment in the Twenty-First Century: Prospects for International Cooperation*, ed. Pamela S. Chasek (Tokyo: United Nations University Press, 2000), 383.

41. Mensah, "United Nations Commission," 24.

42. Hilary F. French, *Partnership for the Planet: An Environmental Agenda for the United Nations* (Washington, D.C.: Worldwatch Institute, 1995), 32–34.

43. French, *Vanishing Borders*, 161–162.

44. Chasek, "UN Commission," 384.

45. Chasek, "UN Commission," 385.

46. *UN Chronicle* 34, no. 2 (Summer 1997): 34.

47. Chasek, "UN Commission," 386.

48. *UN Chronicle* 34, no. 2 (Summer 1997): 34.

49. Helen Sjöberg, "The Global Environment Facility," in *Greening International Institutions*, ed. Jacob Werksman (London: Earthscan Publications, 1996), 149.

50. Hunter, Salzman, and Zaelke, *International Environmental Law*, 1485.

51. "Instrument for the Establishment of the Restructured Global Environment Facility" (1994), paragraphs 2 and 3, at www.gefweb.org/Documents/Instrument/instrument.html (accessed 19 June 2001), also quoted in Hunter, Salzman, and Zaelke, *International Environmental Law*, 1482.

52. French, *Vanishing Borders*, 153.

53. Sjöberg, "Global Environment Facility," 151.

54. Sjöberg, "Global Environment Facility," 157–158.

55. French, *Vanishing Borders*, 154–155.

56. See Zoe Young, "NGOs and the Global Environmental Facility: Friendly Foes?" *Environmental Politics* (Spring 1999).

57. Hunter, Salzman, and Zaelke, *International Environmental Law*, 1485.

58. Hunter, Salzman, and Zaelke, *International Environmental Law*, 1489.

59. See Paul Wapner, *Environmental Activism and World Civic Politics* (Albany: SUNY Press, 1996); Paul Wapner, "The Transnational Politics of Environmental NGOs: Governmental, Economic, and Social Activism," in *The Global Environment in the Twenty-First Century: Prospects for International Cooperation*, ed. Pamela S. Chasek (Tokyo: United Nations University Press, 2000), 87–108.

60. World Commission on Environment and Development, *Our Common Future* (Oxford: Oxford University Press, 1987), 43.

61. Andrew Dobson, *Justice and the Environment: Conceptions of Environmental Sustainability and Theories of Distributive Justice* (New York: Oxford University Press, 1998), 33.

62. Anthony D'Amato, "World Conferences and the Cheapening of International Norms," *St. Louis-Warsaw Transatlantic Law Journal* 1 (1995), reprinted in Anthony D'Amato and Kirsten Engle, eds., *International Environmental Law Anthology* (Cincinnati, Ohio: Anderson, 1996), 29.

63. Sharachandra Lélé, "Sustainable Development: A Critical Review," *World Development* 19, no. 6 (1991): 607–621, quoted in Dobson, *Justice and the Environment*, 33.

64. "Sustainable Development: A New Consensus," Final Report of the President's Council on Sustainable Development, quoted in Leslie Paul Thiele, *Environmentalism for a New Millennium* (New York: Oxford University Press, 1999), 53.

65. Herman Daly, "The Steady-State Economy: Toward a Political Economy of Biophysical Equilibrium and Moral Growth," in *Toward a Steady-State Economy* (San Francisco: Freeman, 1973), 167, quoted in Thiele, *Environmentalism for a New Millennium*, 55.

66. John Nichols, interview in *The Workbook* (Southwest Research and Information Center), (Spring 1992): 20–21, quoted in Thiele, *Environmentalism for a New Millennium*, 41–42.

67. Thiele, *Environmentalism for a New Millennium*, 58–59.

68. Edith Brown Weiss, *In Fairness to Future Generations: International Law, Common Patrimony, and Intergenerational Equity* (Tokyo: United Nations University Press, 1989), 2.

69. David Reed, ed., *Structural Adjustment, the Environment, and Sustainable Development* (London: Earthscan Publications, 1996), 32–37. Reed outlines the eco-

nomic, social, and environmental components to sustainable development on these pages.

70. In June 2001, for example, a *New York Times*–CBS News Poll showed that 57 percent of Americans were willing to pay higher prices for electricity and gasoline if it meant protecting the environment. See Richard L. Berke and Janet Elder, "Bush Loses Favor Despite Tax Cut and Overseas Trip," *New York Times*, 21 June 2001, 1(A).

71. Paul Hawken, Amory Lovins, and L. Hunter Lovins, *Natural Capitalism: Creating the Next Industrial Revolution* (New York: Little, Brown, 1999), 2–3.

72. Hawken, Lovins, and Lovins, *Natural Capitalism*, 4.

73. Hawken, Lovins, and Lovins, *Natural Capitalism*, 3.

74. Hawken, Lovins, and Lovins, *Natural Capitalism*, 4.

75. These proposals are outlined in great detail in Hawken, Lovins, and Lovins, *Natural Capitalism*. This exceptional book is a notable contribution to the development of workable solutions to our massive environmental problems.

76. Vandana Shiva, "Ecological Balance in an Era of Globalization," in *Principled World Politics: The Challenge of Normative International Relations*, ed. Paul Wapner and Lester Edwin J. Ruiz (Lanham, Md.: Rowman and Littlefield, 2000), 130, 137.

Chapter 5

1. See William F. Felice, *Taking Suffering Seriously: The Importance of Collective Human Rights* (Albany: SUNY Press, 1996).

2. International Convention on the Elimination of All Forms of Racial Discrimination (Minority Rights Treaty), adopted and open for signature and ratification by General Assembly resolution 2106 (XX) of 21 December 1965, and entered into force 4 January 1969, in accordance with article 19, at www.unhchr.ch/html/menu3/b/dicerd.htm (accessed 27 June 2001); also reprinted in Natan Lerner, *The U.N. Convention on the Elimination of All Forms of Racial Discrimination* (Alphen aan den Rijn, Netherlands: Sijthoff and Noordhoff, 1980), 217–230.

3. Rüdiger Wolfrum, ed., *United Nations: Law, Policies and Practice* (Dordrecht: Martinus Nijhoff, 1995), 1005–1006.

4. Natalie Angler, "Do Races Differ? Not Really, Genes Show," *New York Times*, 22 August 2000, 1(F).

5. Kevin Danaher, "Getting at Hunger's Roots: The Legacy of Colonialism and Racism," in *The Color of Hunger: Race and Hunger in National and International Perspective*, ed. David L. Shields (Lanham, Md.: Rowman and Littlefield, 1995), 89–91.

6. Philip Gourevitch, *We Wish to Inform You That Tomorrow We Will Be Killed with Our Families* (New York: Farrar, Straus, and Giroux, 1998), 47–48.

7. See Centre for Human Rights, *Report of the Seminar on the Political, Historical, Economic, Social and Cultural Factors Contributing to Racism, Racial Discrimination and Apartheid* (New York: United Nations, 1991), HR/PUB/91/3. "The Seminar affirms that racial discrimination means any distinction, exclusion, restriction or preference based on race, colour, descent, or national or ethnic origin which has the purpose or effect of nullifying or impairing the recognition, enjoyment or exer-

cise, on an equal footing, of human rights and fundamental freedoms in the political, economic, social, cultural or any other field of public life" (23).

8. James Gustave Speth, "The Plight of the Poor: The United States Must Increase Development Aid," *Foreign Affairs* 78, no. 3 (May–June 1999): 14.

9. World Bank, *World Development Report 2000/2001: Attacking Poverty* (New York: Oxford University Press, 2001), 3.

10. Christopher S. Wren, "U.N. Report Maps Hunger 'Hot Spots,'" *New York Times*, 9 January 2001, 8(A); see also Map of Global Hunger, 1997 (fig. 1.1), in *Hunger in a Global Economy* (Washington, D.C.: Bread for the World Institute, 1997), 11.

11. "Blacks Lead the Way in Income Growth," *St. Petersburg Times*, 10 October 1998, 1(E).

12. Sylvia Nasar with Kirsten B. Mitchell, "Booming Job Market Draws Young Black Men into Fold," *New York Times*, 23 May 1999, 1(1).

13. Fox Butterfield, "More Blacks in Their 20's Have Trouble with the Law," *New York Times*, 5 October 1995, 18(A).

14. Fox Butterfield, "Number of Inmates Reaches Record 1.8 Million," *New York Times*, 15 March 1999, 14(A).

15. Marc Miringoff and Marque-Luisa Miringoff, *The Social Health of the Nation: How America Is Really Doing* (New York: Oxford University Press, 1999), 66–71, 80–85.

16. "Report: Low Pay, Benefits Still Plague U.S. Hispanics," *St. Petersburg Times*, 5 July 2000, 3(A).

17. See Minority Rights Treaty, article 8.

18. Ratification information is available at www.unhchr.ch/pdf/report.pdf (accessed 4 March 2002).

19. Michael Banton, "Decision-Taking in the Committee on the Elimination of Racial Discrimination," in *The Future of UN Human Rights Treaty Monitoring*, ed. Philip Alston and James Crawford (Cambridge: Cambridge University Press, 2000), 60.

20. See Minority Rights Treaty, articles 1 and 5.

21. Cecilia Möller, Human Rights Officer, Committee on the Elimination of All Forms of Racial Discrimination, interview by author, Geneva, Switzerland, 6 June 2000.

22. Karl Josef Partsch, "The Committee on the Elimination of Racial Discrimination," in *The United Nations and Human Rights*, ed. Philip Alston (New York: Oxford University Press, 1992), 360.

23. See Drew Mahalic and Joan Gambee Mahalic, "The Limitation Provisions of the International Convention on the Elimination of All Forms of Racial Discrimination," *Human Rights Quarterly* 9 (1987): 82–83.

24. Minority Rights Treaty, article 2(2).

25. Theodor Meron, "The Meaning and Reach of the International Convention on the Elimination of All Forms of Racial Discrimination," *American Journal of International Law* 79 (1985): 287, emphasis added.

26. Meron, "Meaning and Reach," 288–289.

27. Ratification information is available at www.unhchr.ch/pdf/report.pdf (accessed 4 March 2002).

28. Möller interview.

29. Banton, "Decision-Taking," 57.

30. Committee on the Elimination of All Forms of Racial Discrimination (Minority Rights Committee), Communication no. 13/1998: Slovakia, CERD/C/57/D/13/1998 (1 November 2000).

31. Minority Rights Treaty, article 9. The Minority Rights Committee decided in 1990 that after the submission of an initial comprehensive report, states should submit further comprehensive reports every four years and brief updating reports in the intervening two-year periods.

32. Office of the High Commissioner for Human Rights (OHCHR), *Manual on Human Rights Reporting* (Geneva: United Nations, 1997), 267–304.

33. Möller interview; see also Banton, "Decision-Taking," 67.

34. Data on "late reports" is available at the UN High Commissioner for Human Rights website www.unhchr.ch/tbs/doc.nsf/newhvoverduebytreaty?OpenView (accessed 4 March 2002); see also OHCHR, "Recent Reporting History under the Principal International Human Rights Instruments As of 31 March 2000," UN Doc. HRI/GEN/4 (27 April 2000), 332.

35. It should be noted that the Minority Rights Committee is the oldest treaty body committee, which partially explains its large number of overdue states parties' reports in comparison with the other treaty body committees. The treaty body committee with the second most overdue reports is the Women's Rights Committee, with 257 late as of March 2002. See www.unhchr.ch/tbs/doc.nsf/newhvover duebytreaty?OpenView.

36. Möller interview.

37. See Stefanie Grant, "The United States and the International Human Rights Treaty System: For Export Only?" in *The Future of UN Human Rights Treaty Monitoring*, ed. Philip Alston and James Crawford (Cambridge: Cambridge University Press, 2000), 317–329.

38. United States, "Initial Report of the United States of America to the United Nations Committee on the Elimination of Racial Discrimination" (September 2000), 17–18, 76, at www1.umn.edu/humanrts/usdocs/cerdinitial.html (accessed 21 March 2001).

39. United States, "Initial Report," 66, 40–41.

40. "U.S. Reservations, Understandings and Declarations, International Convention on the Elimination of All Forms of Racial Discrimination," 140 Cong. Rec. 14326 (1994). U.S. adherence effective 20 November 1994. Available in Louis Henkin et al., *Human Rights: Documentary Supplement* (New York: Foundation, 2001), 192–193.

41. United States, "Initial Report," 75–76.

42. International Covenant on Economic, Social and Cultural Rights (Economic Rights Treaty), adopted at New York 16 December 1966, and entered into force 3 January 1976, UNGA Res. 2200 (XXI), 21 UN GAOR, Supp. (no. 16) 49, UN Doc. A/6316 (1967), see, in particular, article 11.

43. "Concluding Observations of the Committee on the Elimination of Racial Discrimination: United States of America," CERD/C/59/Misc.17/Rev. 3 (14 August 2001).

44. Minority Rights Committee, 50th sess., "Concluding Observations of the Committee on the Elimination of Racial Discrimination: Panama," CERD/C/304/Add. 32 (23 April 1997).

45. Food and Agriculture Organization, *Mapping Undernutrition—An Ongoing*

Process (Rome: Food and Agriculture Organization, 1996); see also Bread for the World Institute, *Hunger in the Global Economy* (Silver Springs, Md.: Bread for the World Institute, 1998), 100.

46. Committee on Economic, Social and Cultural Rights (Economic Rights Committee), "Concluding Observations: Report on the Technical Assistance Mission: Panama," E/C.12/1995/8, 12th sess. (20 June 1995).

47. Minority Rights Committee, "Report of the Committee on the Elimination of Racial Discrimination, Fifty-Fourth Session (1–19 March 1999) and Fifty-Fifth Session (2–27 August 1999)," A/54/18 (29 September 1999).

48. See Banton, "Decision-Taking," 71.

49. OHCHR, *Manual on Human Rights Reporting,* 294–295.

50. Interviews at the OHCHR, Geneva, Switzerland, June 2000; see also Philip Alston, "Final Report on Enhancing the Long-Term Effectiveness of the United Nations Human Rights Treaty System," UN Doc. E/CN.4/1997/74 (7 March 1997). Alston estimates that somewhere between seven and twenty-four years would be required to review the overdue state reports, if they were all to be submitted.

51. Commission on Human Rights Resolution 1995/92, paragraph 8(d).

52. Economic Rights Treaty, article 6.

53. OHCHR, *Manual on Human Rights Reporting,* 93.

54. OHCHR, *Manual on Human Rights Reporting,* 120.

55. Andrew Clapham coined the phrase "splendid isolation" to describe the separation of the treaty bodies from the rest of the UN system. See Andrew Clapham, "UN Human Rights Reporting Procedures: An NGO Perspective," in *The Future of UN Human Rights Treaty Monitoring,* ed. Philip Alston and James Crawford (Cambridge: Cambridge University Press, 2000), 175–198.

56. Philip Alston reports: "[M]embers of the Human Rights Committee, the Committee on the Elimination of Discrimination Against Women and the Committee on the Rights of the Child will receive US$3,000 per year (apart from their daily allowance) and others (members of the Committee on Economic, Social and Cultural Rights, the Committee on the Elimination of Racial Discrimination and the Committee Against Torture) will receive nothing (apart from the same allowances)." See Final Report of Philip Alston, UN Doc. E/CN.4/1997/74 (7 March 1997), para. 84.

57. Elizabeth Evatt, "Ensuring Effective Supervisory Procedures: The Need For Resources," in *The Future of UN Human Rights Treaty Monitoring,* ed. Philip Alston and James Crawford (Cambridge: Cambridge University Press, 2000), 471.

58. The *New York Times* reported that there was a movement among some states at the UN to abolish the OHCHR after Mary Robinson left office. See Barbara Crossette, "Kofi Annan: An Idealist Who Took the Heat, Shook up the U.N. and Keeps Top Post," *New York Times,* 28 June 2001, 8(A).

59. Preparatory Committee, World Conference against Racism, Racial Discrimination, Xenophobia and Related Intolerance, "Contribution of the Committee on Economic, Social and Cultural rights to the Preparatory Process for the World Conference Against Racism, Racial discrimination, Xenophobia and Related Intolerance," A/CONF.189/PC.1/14, 1st sess. (29 February 2000).

60. Santosh Mehrotra, "Social Development in High-Achieving Countries: Common Elements and Diversities," in *Development with a Human Face,* ed. Santosh Mehrotra and Richard Jolly (Oxford: Clarendon, 1997), 29, 32.

Chapter 6

1. John Stuart Mill, *Three Essays: On Liberty [1859], Representative Government [1861], and The Subjection of Women [1869]* (London: Oxford University Press, 1912), 443–444, 451–452.

2. See Karl Marx and Frederick Engels, *The German Ideology* (1931; reprint, New York: International, 1970), 51.

3. Philip Gourevitch, *We Wish to Inform You That Tomorrow We Will Be Killed with Our Families* (New York: Farrar, Straus, and Giroux, 1998), 181.

4. Beijing Declaration, adopted by the Fourth World Conference on Women 15 September 1995, UN Docs.A/CONF.177/20 (17 October 1995) and A/CONF.177/20/Add. 1 (27 October 1995).

5. International Covenant on Economic, Social and Cultural Rights (Economic Rights Treaty), concluded at New York 16 December 1966, and entered into force 3 January 1976, 993 UNTS 3.

6. Hilary Charlesworth, "Human Rights As Men's Rights," in *Women's Rights, Human Rights: International Feminist Perspectives*, ed. Julia Peters and Andrea Wolper (New York: Routledge, 1995), 108.

7. Barbara Stark, "The 'Other' Half of the International Bill of Rights As a Postmodern Feminist Text," in *Reconceiving Reality: Women and International Law*, ed. Dorinda Dallmeyer (Washington, D.C.: American Society of International Law, 1993), 20–21, 27, 33.

8. For example, see Jessica Stern, "Women in the Labour World: What about the Commitment?" in *Social Watch 1999*, ed. Roberto Bissio (Montevideo, Uruguay: Instituto Del Tercer Mundo, 1999), 72–76.

9. R. J. Barry Jones coined the term "structural constructivism" to call our attention to both "structures" and "social construction." See R. J. Barry Jones, "Globalization and Change in the International Political Economy," *International Affairs* 75, no. 2 (1999): 361.

10. Stark, "'Other' Half," 20–21.

11. Economic Rights Treaty, article 2.2.

12. Economic Rights Treaty, article 3.

13. Economic Rights Treaty, article 10.2.

14. Paul Hunt, *Reclaiming Social Rights: International and Comparative Perspectives* (Aldershot, Hants: Dartmouth, 1996), 88.

15. Stark, "'Other' Half," 27.

16. Stark notes that there are countless examples of states relieving women of some burdens. For example, "Sweden assures benefits for disabled children; Norway has established an ombudsman (*sic*) for children 'to deal with complaints of child abuse, physical conditions of children, child care, and schools'; and Belarus provides subsidies for children's clothing." See Stark, "'Other' Half," 31.

17. Carole Pateman, "Feminist Critiques of the Public/Private Dichotomy," in *Public and Private in Social Life*, ed. S. Benn and G. Gaus (London: Croom Helm, 1983), 281.

18. Hunt, *Reclaiming Social Rights*, 87.

19. Ratification information is available at www.unhchr.ch/pdf/report.pdf (accessed 7 March 2002).

20. International Convention on the Elimination of All Forms of Discrimina-

tion against Women (Women's Rights Treaty), concluded at New York 18 December 1979, and entered into force 3 September 1981, 1249 UNTS 13.

21. Women's Rights Treaty, article 1.

22. Women's Rights Treaty, article 4.1.

23. Women's Rights Treaty, article 4.2.

24. Women's Rights Treaty, article 11.

25. Women's Rights Treaty.

26. Hilary Charlesworth, Christine Chinkin, and Shelley Wright, "Feminist Approaches to International Law," *American Journal of International Law* 85 (1991): 631–632.

27. Charlesworth, Chinkin, and Wright, "Feminist Approaches," 632.

28. Charlesworth, Chinkin, and Wright, "Feminist Approaches," 634.

29. Mara R. Bustelo, "The Committee on the Elimination of Discrimination against Women at the Crossroads," in *The Future of UN Human Rights Treaty Monitoring*, ed. Philip Alston and James Crawford (Cambridge: Cambridge University Press, 2000), 82.

30. Bustelo, "Committee," 82.

31. The one male member, Johan Nordenfelt of Sweden, served on the Women's Rights Treaty Committee from 1982 to 1984. Since 1984, the Women's Rights Treaty has been all female. See Bustelo, "Committee," 80.

32. Roberta Jacobson, "The Committee on the Elimination of Discrimination against Women," in *The United Nations and Human Rights*, ed. Philip Alston (New York: Oxford University Press, 1992), 459.

33. Charlesworth, Chinkin, and Wright, "Feminist Approaches," 624.

34. Data on "late reports" is available at the UN High Commissioner for Human Rights website www.unhchr.ch/tbs/doc.nsf/newhvoverduebytreaty?OpenView (accessed 7 March 2002).

35. Bustelo, "Committee," 85.

36. "Initial Report of Guatemala Submitted to the Women's Rights Treaty Committee," Women's Rights Treaty/C/Gua/1–2 (2 April 1991), reprinted in Henry J. Steiner and Philip Alston, eds., *International Human Rights in Context: Law, Politics, Morals* (New York: Oxford University Press, 1996), 888–891.

37. Ratification information is available at www.unhchr.ch/pdf/report.pdf (accessed 7 March 2002).

38. The text of the Optional Protocol to Women's Rights Treaty is available at www.unhchr.ch/html/menu3/b/optWomen'sRightsTreaty.htm (accessed 30 June 2001).

39. United Nations, "Compilation of General Comments and General Recommendations Adopted by Human Rights Treaty Bodies," HRI/GEN/1/Rev. 4 (7 February 2000), 154–201.

40. "Compilation of General Comments and General Recommendations," 156.

41. "Compilation of General Comments and General Recommendations," 160–161.

42. "Compilation of General Comments and General Recommendations," 164.

43. "Compilation of General Comments and General Recommendations," 165.

44. "Compilation of General Comments and General Recommendations," 166.

45. "Compilation of General Comments and General Recommendations," 194–201.

46. "Compilation of General Comments and General Recommendations," 168.

47. Andrew Clapham, *Human Rights in the Private Sphere* (Oxford: Clarendon, 1993), 100.

48. Upendra Baxi, "Voices of Suffering, Fragmented Universality, and the Future of Human Rights," in *The Future of International Human Rights*, ed. Burns H. Weston and Stephen P. Marks (Ardsley, N.Y.: Transnational, 1999), 123; Walter Kaufmann, *The Portable Nietzsche* (New York: Viking Penguin, 1959), 160–161.

49. Women's Environment and Development Organization (WEDO), *Mapping Progress* (New York: Women's Environment and Development Organization, 1998), 13.

50. WEDO, *Mapping Progress*, 13.

51. WEDO, *Mapping Progress*, 13.

52. WEDO, *Mapping Progress*, 67–68.

53. Nalini Visvanathan, "Introduction to Part 1," in *The Women, Gender and Development Reader*, ed. N. Visvanathan et al. (London: Zed, 1997), 20.

54. Ester Boserup, *Women's Role in Economic Development* (New York: St. Martin's, 1970).

55. Rosi Braidotti et al., *Women, the Environment and Sustainable Development* (London: Zed, 1994), 80.

56. Visvanathan, "Introduction," 18–19.

57. Anne Marie Goetz, "Introduction: Getting Institutions Right for Women in Development," in *Getting Institutions Right for Women in Development*, ed. Anne Marie Goetz (London: Zed, 1997), 5.

58. Cynthia Enloe, *Bananas, Beaches and Bases: Making Feminist Sense of International Politics* (Berkeley: University of California Press, 1990), 159–160.

59. R. Pearson, A. Whitehead, and K. Young, "Introduction: The Continuing Subordination of Women in the Development Process," in *Of Marriage and the Market: Women's Subordination Internationally and Its Lessons*, ed. K. Young, C. Wolkowitz, and R. McCullagh (London: Routledge and Kegan Paul, 1984), x.

60. Ruth Pearson and Cecile Jackson, "Introduction: Interrogating Development," in *Feminist Visions of Development*, ed. C. Jackson and R. Pearson (New York: Routledge, 1998), 5.

61. Rounaq Jahan, *The Elusive Agenda: Mainstreaming Women in Development* (London: Zed, 1995), 21.

62. Goetz, "Introduction," 3–4.

63. Braidotti et al., *Women*, 82.

64. Sally Baden and Anne Marie Goetz, "Who Needs [Sex] When You Can Have [Gender]?" in *Feminist Visions of Development*, ed. C. Jackson and R. Pearson (New York: Routledge, 1998), 24.

65. Baden and Goetz, "Who Needs [Sex]," 21.

66. Braidotti et al., *Women*, 117–118.

67. Jahan, *Elusive Agenda*, 78–79.

68. R. Braidotti et al., "Women, the Environment and Sustainable Development," in *The Women, Gender and Development Reader*, ed. N. Visvanathan et al. (London: Zed, 1997), 57–58.

69. Maria Mies, *Patriarchy and Accumulation on a World Scale* (London: Zed, 1986), 16–17, 55.

70. Vandana Shiva, "Women in Nature," in *Staying Alive* (London: Zed, 1989),

quoted in N. Visvanathan et al., eds, *The Women, Gender and Development Reader* (London: Zed, 1997), 63.

71. Miriam Abramovay and Gail Lerner, "Introduction: Gender and Sustainable Development in Latin America and the Caribbean," in *Gender and Sustainable Development, a New Paradigm: Reflecting on Experience in Latin America and the Caribbean,* ed. Ana Maria Brasileiro (New York: UN Development Fund for Women, 1996), 11–12; see also Margaret Snyder, *Transforming Development: Women, Poverty and Politics* (London: Intermediate Technology Publications, 1995).

72. Braidotti et al., *Women,* 162–163.

73. Bina Agarwal, "The Gender and Environment Debate: Lessons from India," *Feminist Studies* 18, no.1 (1992).

74. Women's Rights Treaty, article 2.

75. Declaration on the Right to Development, adopted by the UN General Assembly 4 December 1986, GA Res. 41/128 (Annex), UN GAOR, 41st sess., Supp. no. 53, at 186, UN Doc. A/41/53 (1987).

76. Universal Declaration of Human Rights, adopted by the UN General Assembly 10 December 1948, Resolution 217 A, UNGAOR, 3rd sess., pt. 1, Resolutions, at 71, UN Doc. A/810 (1948).

77. Women's Rights Treaty, article 5.

78. International Convention on the Elimination of All Forms of Racial Discrimination (Minority Rights Treaty), adopted and open for signature and ratification by General Assembly resolution 2106 (XX) of 21 December 1965, and entered into force 4 January 1969, in accordance with article 19.

79. Women's Rights Treaty, article 4.1.

80. Declaration on the Right to Development, article 2.3.

81. "Rio de Janeiro Declaration on Environment and Development," UN Doc. A/CONF.151/26 (13 June 1992).

82. "Stockholm Declaration of the United Nations Conference on the Human Environment," UN Doc. A/CONF.48/14 (16 June 1972), at www.unep.org/ (accessed 19 June 2001).

83. World Charter for Nature, adopted by the UN General Assembly, 28 October 1982, GA Res. 37/7 (Annex), UN GAOR, 37th sess., Supp. no. 51, at 17, UN Doc. A/37/51.

84. Caroline O. N. Moser, "Gender Planning in the Third World: Meeting Practical and Strategic Needs," in *Gender and International Relations,* ed. Rebecca Grant and Kathleen Newland (Bloomington: Indiana University Press, 1991), 83–88.

85. Maxine Molyneux, "Mobilization without Emancipation? Women's Interests, State and Revolution in Nicaragua," *Feminist Studies* 11, no. 2 (1985), quoted in Moser, "Gender Planning," 90.

86. Moser, "Gender Planning," 90–91.

87. Martha C. Nussbaum, *Sex and Social Justice* (New York: Oxford University Press, 1999), 34.

88. Amartya Sen, *Development As Freedom* (New York: Knopf, 1999), 109.

89. Martha C. Nussbaum, *Women and Human Development: The Capabilities Approach* (Cambridge: Cambridge University Press, 2000), 4.

90. Nussbaum, *Women and Human Development,* 75.

91. Nussbaum, *Women and Human Development,* 113–114.

92. Nussbaum too often presents the capabilities approach as an alternative to

human rights. She painstakingly details how this approach is supposedly superior to a human rights focus. It does not carry the "baggage" of "rights" language, which is understood in many different ways and is often seen as privileging Western culture. Furthermore, people differ about both the basis of a rights claim (e.g., rationality, artifacts of law, or mere life) and whether rights are held by individuals or groups. Her solution is to propose that the best way of thinking about rights is to see them as "combined capabilities." Yet, in the end, she agrees that we still need the languages of rights "despite its unsatisfactory features." She acknowledges the power of a human rights claim to a certain type of treatment. See Nussbaum, *Women and Human Development*, 100. I found this discussion confusing and unhelpful.

93. Hilary Charlesworth, "What Are 'Women's International Human Rights?'" in *Human Rights of Women: National and International Perspectives*, ed. Rebecca J. Cook (Philadelphia: University of Pennsylvania Press, 1994), 71.

Chapter 7

1. Jean-Paul Sartre, preface to *The Wretched of the Earth* by Frantz Fanon (New York: Grove, 1963), 22.

2. The International Bill of Human Rights encompasses the Universal Declaration of Human Rights, the International Covenant on Civil and Political Rights, and the International Covenant on Economic, Social and Cultural Rights.

3. Boutros Boutros-Ghali, *An Agenda for Development* (New York: United Nations Publication, 1995), 20.

4. Jeff Gerth and Tim Weiner, "Arms Makers See Bonanza by Selling NATO Expansion," *New York Times*, 29 June 1997, 1(1).

5. David B. Guralnik, ed., *Webster's New World Dictionary of the American Language* (New York: World, 1972), 901.

6. George W. Bush, State of the Union Address, 29 January 2002, at www.whitehouse.gov/news/releases/2002/01/20020129-11.html (accessed 22 March 2002).

7. James Dao, "Bush Sees Big Rise in Military Budget for Next 5 Years," *New York Times*, 2 February 2002, 1(A); Thom Shanker and James Dao, "Rumsfeld to Seek $33 Billion Rise for Military, and Critics See Too Much and Too Little," *New York Times*, 23 June 2001, 10(A); "The Military Spending Crunch," *New York Times*, 2 July 2001, 14(A).

8. Tim Weiner, "Clinton As a Military Leader: Tough On-the-Job Training," *New York Times*, 28 October 1996, 1(A).

9. Michael Ignatieff, "The New American Way of War," *New York Review of Books*, 20 July 2000, 42.

10. The political justification for the U.S. defense posture is an expansive conception of national security. The Pentagon argued in the 1990s for the ability to fight the equivalent of two gulf wars simultaneously on different sides of the globe. War planners assumed that the United States would get no help from allies and that the war must be won in a matter of weeks. The Bush administration appears to be scuttling this strategy while maintaining a global posture. A classified Pentagon strategy document, completed in July 2001, orders "the armed forces to 'win

decisively' in a single major conflict, defend American territory against new threats, and, at the same time, conduct a number of holding actions elsewhere around the globe." See Tom Shanker, "Military Scuttles Strategy Requiring '2-War' Capability," *New York Times*, 13 July 2001, 1(A). The gruesome terrorism of 11 September 2001 is pushing the Pentagon to develop a new strategic doctrine.

For alternative approaches to national security, see Michael H. Shuman and Hal Harvey, *Security without War: A Post–Cold War Foreign Policy* (Boulder, Colo.: Westview, 1993); Michael Klare, *Rogue States and Nuclear Outlaws: America's Search for a New Foreign Policy* (New York: Hill and Wang, 1995).

11. See David P. Calleo, *Beyond American Hegemony: The Future of the Western Alliance* (New York: Basic, 1987), 109–126; Paul Kennedy, *The Rise and Fall of the Great Powers* (New York: Random House, 1987), 514–535.

12. Ruth Leger Sivard, *World Military and Social Expenditures*, 16th ed. (Washington, D.C.: World Priorities, 1996), 48–53; Ruth Leger Sivard, *World Military and Social Expenditures*, 14th ed. (Washington, D.C.: World Priorities, 1991), 54–56.

13. Ron Smith, "Military Expenditure and Investment in OECD Countries, 1954–1973," *Journal of Comparative Economics* 4 (1980): 19–32; see also Karen Rasler and William Thompson, "Defense Burdens, Capital Formation, and Economic Growth," *Journal of Conflict Resolution* 32, no. 1 (1988): 61–86.

14. William K. Tabb, *The Amoral Elephant: Globalization and the Struggle for Social Justice in the Twenty-First Century* (New York: Monthly Review, 2001), 54–55.

15. Tabb, *Amoral Elephant*, 77.

16. Michael O'Hanlon, "What Price for Military Readiness?" *New York Times*, 27 June 2001.

17. World Bank, *World Development Report 2000/2001: Attacking Poverty* (New York: Oxford University Press, 2001), 306–307.

18. Carl Conetta, "Toward a Smaller, More Efficient, and More Relevant US Military," PDA Briefing Memo 17 (October 2000), at www.comw.org/pda/0010bm17.html (accessed 7 April 2001).

19. Center for Defense Information, *The Defense Monitor* 28, no. 7 (1999): 5.

20. Project on Defense Alternatives, "The Paradoxes of Post–Cold War US Defense Policy: An Agenda for the 2001 Quadrennial Defense Review," Briefing Memo 18 (5 February 2001), at www.comw.org/pda/0102bmemo18.html (accessed 7 April 2001).

21. See Lloyd J. Dumas, "Finding the Future: The Role of Economic Conversion in Shaping the Twenty-First Century," in *The Socio-Economics of Conversion from War to Peace*, ed. Lloyd J. Dumas (Armonk, N.Y.: Sharpe, 1995).

22. Adam Smith, *The Wealth of Nations* (New York: Modern Library, 1937), 315.

23. See William F. Felice, *Taking Suffering Seriously: The Importance of Collective Human Rights* (Albany: SUNY Press, 1996), 117–120.

24. Jason DeParle, "Report, Delayed Months, Says Lowest Income Group Grew," *New York Times*, 12 May 1992, 15(A).

25. "Children in Poverty: 1 Million More in 80's," *New York Times*, 8 July 1992, 20(A).

26. Jason DeParle, "Census Report Sees Incomes in Decline and More Poverty," *New York Times*, 7 October 1994, 1(A).

27. Alan B. Krueger, "The Truth about Wages," *New York Times*, 31 July 1997, 23(A).

28. Marc Miringoff and Marque-Luisa Miringoff, *The Social Health of the Nation: How America Is Really Doing* (New York: Oxford University Press, 1999), 80.

29. Miringoff and Miringoff, *Social Health of the Nation*, 74–75.

30. Miringoff and Miringoff, *Social Health of the Nation*, 86.

31. Miringoff and Miringoff, *Social Health of the Nation*, 92.

32. Miringoff and Miringoff, *Social Health of the Nation*, 98.

33. Miringoff and Miringoff, *Social Health of the Nation*, 104.

34. "Millions Still Going Hungry in the U.S., Report Finds," *New York Times*, 10 September 2000, 26(1).

35. Robert W. DeGrasse Jr., *Military Expansion, Economic Decline* (New York: Council on Economic Priorities, 1983), 55–73.

36. Steve Chan, "The Impact of Defense Spending on Economic Performance: A Survey of Evidence and Problems," *Orbis* (Summer 1985): 413–414.

37. Alex Mintz and Randolph T. Stevenson, "Defense Expenditures, Economic Growth, and the 'Peace Dividend,'" *Journal of Conflict Resolution* 39 no. 2 (1995): 283–305.

38. Dumas, "Finding the Future," 7.

39. Todd Sandler and Keith Hartley, *The Economics of Defense* (Cambridge: Cambridge University Press, 1995), 220.

40. DeGrasse, *Military Expansion*, 29.

41. DeGrasse, *Military Expansion*, 23–36.

42. Congressional Budget Office, *The Economic Effects of Reduced Defense Spending* (Washington, D.C.: Congressional Budget Office, 1992), 9.

43. Alex Mintz and Chi Huang, "Guns and Butter: The Indirect Link," *American Journal of Political Science* 35, no 3 (1991): 752; see also Alex Mintz and Chi Huang, "Defense Expenditures, Economic Growth, and the 'Peace Dividend,'" *American Political Science Review* 84, no. 4 (1990): 1283–1293.

44. John Isaacs and Dan Koslofsky, "Trim Pentagon Fat," *Bulletin of the Atomic Scientists* 57, no. 1 (January–February 2001): 26.

45. Isaacs and Koslofsky, "Trim Pentagon Fat," 26.

46. William A. Owens and Stanley A. Weiss, "An Indefensible Military Budget," *New York Times*, 7 February 2002, 23(A).

47. UN Development Program (UNDP), *Human Development Report 1994* (New York: Oxford University Press, 1994), 34, 47–51.

48. World Bank, *World Development Report 2000/2001*, 284–285, 306–307.

49. UNDP, *Human Development Report 1994*, 50.

50. UNDP, *Human Development Report 1994*, 50.

51. World Bank, *World Development Report 2000/2001*, 50.

52. The statistics on Costa Rica and Latin American and the Caribbean are from UNDP, *Human Development Report 2000* (New York: Oxford University Press, 2000), 169–171.

53. Leonardo Garnier et al., "Cost Rica: Social Development and Heterodox Adjustment," in *Development with a Human Face: Experiences in Social Achievement and Economic Growth*, ed. Santosh Mehrotra and Richard Jolly (New York: Oxford University Press, 1997), 372.

54. World Bank, *World Development Report 2000/2001*, 306.

55. Maria Stern, *Security Policy in Transition* (Stockholm: Padriger, 1991), 26–28; Robert Elias and Jennifer Turpin, "Introduction: Thinking about Peace," in *Rethink-*

ing Peace, ed. Robert Elias and Jennifer Turpin (Boulder, Colo.: Rienner, 1994), 4; Johan Galtung, "Violence, Peace and Peace Research," *Journal of Peace Research* 6, no. 3 (1969): 167–191.

56. Elias and Turpin, "Thinking about Peace," 4–5.

57. UNDP, *Human Development Report 1994,* 24–25.

58. Norberto Bobbio, *The Age of Rights* (Cambridge, Mass.: Polity, 1996), 53.

59. Steven Lee Myers, "U.S. Lifts a Ban on Weapon Sales to Latin America," *New York Times,* 2 August 1997, 1(1).

60. On 30 January 2002, the government of Chile announced that it would buy ten F-16 fighter jets from the United States for $660 million. This transaction represented the first time in two decades that Washington had approved the transfer of sophisticated weapons to a Latin American country. Brazil, Peru, Bolivia, and Argentina will feel pressure to respond in kind. See Christopher Marquis, "In Unusual Deal, Chile Will Buy Advanced U.S. Fighter Jets," *New York Times,* 31 January 2002, 8(A).

61. Philip Shenon, "U.S. Increases Its Lead in World Market for Weapons," *New York Times,* 16 August 1997, 3(1).

62. Steven Lee Myers, "Global Arms Sales Swell to $30 Billion," *New York Times,* 21 August 2000, 9(A).

63. William D. Hartung, "Stop Arming the World," *Bulletin of the Atomic Scientists* 57, no. 1 (January–February 2001): 35.

64. See Domenick Bertelli, "Military Contractor Conversion in the United States," in *The Socio-Economics of Conversion from War to Peace,* ed. Lloyd J. Dumas (Armonk, N.Y.: Sharpe, 1995).

65. William Kaufmann and John Steinbruner, *Decisions for Defense: Prospects for a New Order* (Washington, D.C.: Brookings Institution, 1991), 70.

66. Kaufmann and Steinbruner, *Decisions for Defense,* 70–74.

67. Michael O'Hanlon, *Defense Planning for the Late 1990's: Beyond the Desert Storm Framework* (Washington, D.C.: Brookings Institution, 1995).

68. Randall Forsberg, "Defense Cuts and Cooperative Security in the Post–Cold War World," *Boston Review* 17, nos. 3–4 (May–July 1992).

69. Business Leaders for Sensible Priorities, "Does the Pentagon Need Another $10,000,000,000?" *New York Times,* 24 March 1999, 21(A).

70. See J. Lynch, ed., *Economic Adjustment and Conversion of Defense Industries* (London: Westview, 1987); Alejandro E. Nadal, "Military R&D: The Economic Implications of Disarmament and Conversion," *Defense and Peace Economics* 5, no. 2, (1994): 131–151; United Nations, *Economic Aspects of Disarmament: Disarmament As an Investment Process* (New York: United Nations Publications, 1993); Anthony Voss, *Converting the Defense Industry* (Oxford: Oxford Research Group, 1992).

71. See Bertell Ollman, introduction to *The United States Constitution,* ed. Bertell Ollman and Jonathan Birnbaum (New York: New York University Press, 1990), 6.

72. See Boutros Boutros-Ghali, *An Agenda for Peace 1995* (New York: United Nations Publications, 1995); Richard Falk, *On Humane Governance: Toward a New Global Politics* (University Park: Pennsylvania State University Press, 1995), 207–240; Saul H. Mendlovitz and Burns H. Weston, eds., "Symposium: Preferred Futures for the United Nations," *Transnational Law and Contemporary Problems* 4, no. 2 (Fall 1994).

Chapter 8

1. See Maurice Williams, "Beyond Development Cooperation: Toward a New Era of Global and Human Security" (opening statement to the international conference Beyond Development Co-Operation: Toward a New Era of Global and Human Security, Ottawa, Canada, 15–16 October 1993).

2. World Bank, *World Development Report 2000/2001: Attacking Poverty* (New York: Oxford University Press, 2001), 3.

3. UN Development Program (UNDP), *Human Development Report 2000* (New York: Oxford University Press, 2000), 8.

4. Mahbub ul Haq, *Reflections on Human Development* (New York: Oxford University Press, 1995), 187.

5. Haq, *Reflections on Human Development*, 91, 186–199.

6. William F. Felice, *Taking Suffering Seriously: The Importance of Collective Human Rights* (Albany: SUNY Press, 1996), 85–86; see also UNDP, *Human Development Report 1994* (New York: Oxford University Press, 1994), 7, 50, 77.

7. UNDP, *Human Development Report 2000*, 9; see also UNDP, UNESCO, UNFPA, UNICEF, WHO, and the World Bank, *Implementing the 20/20 Initiative: Achieving Universal Access to Basic Social Services* (New York: UNDP et al., 1998).

8. UNDP, *Human Development Report 2000*, 9.

9. UNDP, *Human Development Report 2000*, 9.

10. UNDP, *Human Development Report 2000*, 120.

11. See Haq, *Reflections on Human Development*, 197–198.

12. Inge Kaul and John Langmore, "Potential Uses of the Revenue from a Tobin Tax," in *The Tobin Tax: Coping with Financial Volatility*, ed. Mahbub ul Haq, Inge Kaul, and Isabelle Grunberg (New York: Oxford University Press, 1996), 263.

13. James Tobin, prologue to *The Tobin Tax: Coping with Financial Volatility*, ed. Mahbub ul Haq, Inge Kaul, and Isabelle Grunberg (New York: Oxford University Press, 1996), x.

14. UNDP, *Human Development Report 1994*, 9, 59, 70; see also Felice, *Taking Suffering Seriously*, 86–87.

15. Tobin, prologue, xvii.

16. Inge Kaul and John Langmore, "Potential Uses of the Revenue from a Tobin Tax," in *The Tobin Tax: Coping with Financial Volatility*, ed. Mahbub ul Haq, Inge Kaul, and Isabelle Grunberg (New York: Oxford University Press, 1996), 267.

17. Tobin, prologue, xii.

18. For an outstanding summary and evaluation of the draft Optional Protocol to the Economic Rights Treaty, see Kitty Arambulo, *Strengthening the Supervision of the International Covenant on Economic, Social and Cultural Rights* (Antwerpen: Intersentia, 1999).

19. Ved P. Nanda, "Environment," in *United Nations Legal Order*, vol. 2, ed. Oscar Schachter and Christopher C. Joyner (Cambridge: Cambridge University Press, 1995), 667.

20. Daniel C. Esty, *Greening the GATT: Trade, Environment, and the Future* (Washington, D.C.: Institute for International Economics, 1994), 230. Esty named his proposed environmental IGO the Global Environmental Organization. To avoid confusion, I have kept the name WEO throughout the book.

21. Michael W. Doyle and Rachel I. Massey, "Intergovernmental Organiza-

tions and the Environment: Looking towards the Future," in *The Global Environment in the Twenty-First Century: Prospects for International Cooperation*, ed. Pamela S. Chasek (Tokyo: United Nations University Press, 2000), 421–422.

22. Alexandre Kiss, "An Introductory Note on a Human Right to Environment," in *Environmental Change and International Law: New Challenges and Dimensions*, ed. Edith Brown Weiss (Tokyo: United Nations University Press, 1992), 203.

23. Hilary French, *Vanishing Borders* (New York: Norton, 2000), 159–160.

24. P. M. Haas, R. O. Keohane, and M. A. Levy, eds., *Institutions for the Earth: Sources of Effective International Environmental Protection* (Cambridge: MIT Press, 1993).

25. Esty, *Greening the GATT*, 80–81.

26. "Rio de Janeiro Declaration on Environment and Development," UN Doc. A/CONF.151/26 (13 June 1992), at www.unep.org/Documents/Default.asp?DocumentID=78&ArticleID=1163 (accessed 23 March 2002).

27. Quoted in Leslie Paul Thiele, *Environmentalism for a New Millennium: The Challenge of Coevolution* (New York: Oxford University Press, 1999), 84.

28. Kyoto Protocol to the UN Framework Convention on Climate Change, at unfccc.int/resource/protintr.html (accessed 23 March 2002).

29. Francisco Orrego Vicuña, "State Responsibility, Liability, and Remedial Measures under International Law: New Criteria for Environmental Protection," in *Environmental Change and International Law: New Challenges and Dimensions*, ed. Edith Brown Weiss (Tokyo: United Nations University Press, 1992), 151.

30. Orrego Vicuña, "State Responsibility," 132–133.

31. Lester R. Brown, "Challenges of the New Century," in *State of the World 2000* (New York: Norton, 2000), 8.

32. Roberto Bissio, ed., *Social Watch 1999* (Montevideo: Instituto Del Tercer Mundo, 1999), 125.

33. Santosh Mehrotra, "Health and Education Policies in High-Achieving Countries: Some Lessons," in *Development with a Human Face*, ed. Santosh Mehrotra and Richard Jolly (New York: Oxford University Press, 1997), 64–65.

34. Bissio, *Social Watch 1999*, 118.

35. UN International Children's Emergency Fund (UNICEF), *The State of the World's Children 1999* (New York: UN International Children's Emergency Fund, 1999), 80.

36. Bissio, *Social Watch 1999*, 178, 210.

37. UNDP, *Human Development Report 2000*, 33.

38. UNICEF, *State of the World's Children 1999*, 81.

39. UNDP, *Human Development Report 2000*, 153.

40. UN Development Fund for Women, *Progress of the World's Women 2000* (New York: UN Development Fund for Women, 2000), 110–111.

41. Naomi Neft and Ann E. Levine, *Where Women Stand: An International Report on the Status of Women in 140 Countries, 1997–1998* (New York: Random House, 1997), 5.

42. Women's Rights Committee, General Recommendation no. 24 (20th sess., 1999), in United Nations, "Compilation of General Comments and General Recommendations Adopted by Human Rights Treaty Bodies," HRI/GEN/1/Rev. 4 (7 February 2000), 194–201.

43. UNDP, *Human Development Report 2000*, 96.

44. Neft and Levine, *Where Women Stand*, 29–30.

45. Neft and Levine, *Where Women Stand*, 3.

46. World Bank, *World Development Report 2000/2001*, 119.

47. World Bank, *World Development Report 2000/2001*, 119.

48. World Bank, *World Development Report 2000/2001*, 119.

49. Michael Renner, "Budgeting for Disarmament: The Costs of War and Peace," *Worldwatch Paper 122* (November 1994): 44.

50. CWC ratification record can be found at projects.sipri.se/cbw/docs/cw—cwc—rat.html (accessed 15 February 2001).

51. Derek Boothby, "Arms Control and Disarmament," in *A Global Agenda: Issues before the 55th General Assembly of the United Nations*, ed. John Tessitore and Susan Woolfson (Lanham, Md.: Rowman and Littlefield, 2000), 86.

52. "Early Success Is Reported for Global Treaty Banning Land Mines," *New York Times*, 7 September 2000, 3(A).

53. Boothby, "Arms Control," 77. Details of the international monitoring system are available at pws.ctbto.org/ (accessed 9 October 2001).

54. See also William J. Broad, "Useful Legacy of Nuclear Treaty: Global Earphones," *New York Times*, 19 June 2001, 1(F).

55. UNDP, *Human Development Report 1994*, 59.

56. UNDP, *Human Development Report 1994*, 9.

57. UNDP, *Human Development Report 1994*, 59.

58. Leslie Kaufman and David Gonzalez, "Labor Progress Clashes with Global Reality," *New York Times*, 24 April 2001, 1(A).

59. Kaufman and Gonzalez, "Labor Progress Clashes with Global Reality," 1(A).

60. Due to aggressive growth and acquisitions, the GAP is expected to lose money in 2002. This financial fallout, however, is the result of the accumulation of $2 billion debt from ill-conceived expansion. Even in the midst of restructuring, the GAP is obligated under international law to pay workers a living wage. See Leslie Kaufman, "GAP: Scrambling to Regain Its Cool," *New York Times*, 24 February 2002, 1(3).

61. My thanks to the publisher's anonymous reviewer for calling to my attention Roosevelt's use of the blue eagle to promote the New Deal.

62. Union of International Organizations, *Yearbook of International Organizations* (Munich: Sauer Verlag, 2000–2001), appendix 3, table 1.

63. Margaret Keck and Kathryn Sikkink, *Activists beyond Borders: Advocacy Networks in International Politics* (Ithaca, N.Y.: Cornell University Press, 1998), ix.

Index

About the Author

Eckerd College students from William Felice's class "Geneva and International Cooperation" lift him in front of the United Nations in Geneva, Switzerland. From left to right: Erik Boothe, Shin Tanaka, Andy Gibbs, Johannes Mayr, Patrick Gray, Nevin Marshall, Anthony Hesselius, and Kathleen Deegan.

William F. Felice is associate professor of political science and head of the International Relations and Global Affairs discipline at Eckerd College. In 1999, he was the recipient of both the Robert A. Staub Distinguished Teacher of the Year Award at Eckerd College and the Outstanding Teacher in Political Science Award from the American Political Science Association and Pi Sigma Alpha, the National Political Science Honor Society. His courses focus on human rights and international law, ethics and international relations, and international political economy. His classes on international organization include "Global Studies at the United Nations" in New York City and "Geneva and International Cooperation" in Geneva, Switzerland.

Felice is the author of *Taking Suffering Seriously: The Importance of Collective Human Rights* (1996) and numerous articles on the theory and practice of human rights. He has published articles in *International Affairs, Human Rights Quarterly, Ethics and International Affairs, Social Justice,* and other journals. He is a trustee on the board of the Carnegie Council on Ethics and International Affairs. He was also the past president of the International Ethics Section of the International Studies Association. He received his Ph.D. from the Department of Politics at New York University.